UNIFIED ACTION HANDBOOK SERIES

This *Handbook for Military Participation in the Interagency Management System for Reconstruction and Stabilization* is Book One in a set of five handbooks developed to assist the joint force commander design, plan, and execute a whole-of-government approach. Included with the series is an overview J7/J9 Pamphlet, *Executive Summary of the Unified Action Handbook Series*, that describes the handbooks, suggests how they should be used, and identifies the significant interrelationships among them. The following is a short summary of each handbook:

Book One: *Military Participation in the Interagency Management System for Reconstruction and Stabilization*

The handbook outlines joint force roles and responsibilities in the Interagency Management System (IMS) and existing interagency coordination authorities and mechanisms. It aligns with the *USG Planning Framework for Reconstruction, Stabilization, and Conflict Transformation.* It will also align with the *IMS Guide* under development at the Department of States' Office of the Coordinator for Reconstruction and Stabilization.

Book Two: *Military Support to Essential Services and Critical Infrastructure*

This handbook defines services essential to sustain human life during stability operations (water, sanitation, transportation, medical, etc.), the infrastructure needed to deliver such services, and potential joint force responsibilities.

Book Three: *Military Support to Governance, Elections, and Media*

The last comprehensive guide to military governance was written in 1943. Combatant commanders have directed joint forces to rebuild media, support election preparations, and provide advisors to embryonic executive ministries and legislative committees in recent and current operations. This handbook provides pre-doctrinal guidance for joint force support to good governance, political competition, and support to media.

Book Four: *Military Support to Economic Stabilization*

This handbook outlines joint force support to economic development. It addresses conducting a comprehensive economic assessment, employment and business generation, trade, agriculture, financial sector development and regulation, and legal transformation.

Book Five: *Military Support to Rule of Law and Security Sector Reform*

This handbook defines the "Rule of Law;" explains the interrelationship between rule of law, governance, and security; and provides a template to analyze the rule of law foundation essential to successful stability operations.

NOTICE TO USERS

All approved and current Joint Warfighting Center (JWFC) Pamphlets, Handbooks, and White Papers are posted on the Joint Doctrine, Education, and Training Electronic Information System (JDEIS) Web page at https://jdeis.js.mil/jdeis/jel/template.jsp?title=jwfcpam&filename =jwfc_pam.htm. If a JWFC product is not posted there; it is either in development or rescinded.

PREFACE

1. Scope

This *Handbook for Military Participation in the Interagency Management System for Reconstruction and Stabilization* provides fundamental guidance and information for joint force participation in the Interagency Management System (IMS) in support of United States Government (USG) reconstruction and stabilization operations.

2. Purpose

This handbook is intended to be used as a guide to help explain the roles and responsibilities of military participation within the IMS to better integrate all elements of national capacity in response to an overseas contingency or in support of military engagement, security cooperation, and deterrence activities. **Its primary purpose is to better prepare military planners and implementers for interaction, coordination, and communication with IMS participants through the identification of key interagency relationships and standardization of basic processes**. It also is designed as a companion document to the *IMS Guide* and the *Practitioner's Guide of the USG Planning Framework for Reconstruction, Stabilization, and Conflict Transformation*. Both of these documents will be produced by the Department of State Office of the Coordinator for Reconstruction and Stabilization (S/CRS).

3. Background and Content

a. Since the close of the Cold War, the United States military has been involved in a series of regional conflicts. These engagements have covered the range of military operations from military engagement, security cooperation, and deterrence activities to major operations that include stability operations. The importance of interagency coordination to plan and execute these operations has become increasingly clear as the success of these engagements is determined by a whole-of-government approach utilizing the full set of capabilities resident within the interagency community. In response to the need for better interagency coordination for conflict transformation reconstruction and stabilization operations, the Department of State created the Office of the Coordinator for Reconstruction and Stabilization (S/CRS) in June 2004. Thereafter, S/CRS created the IMS for Reconstruction and Stabilization, which the National Security Council subsequently approved applicable to participating agencies within the executive branch of the United States Government.

b. The IMS is designed to organize and support Washington DC, joint force headquarters, and field-level implementation during a stabilization and reconstruction operation. The IMS serves to integrate planning and coordinate operations, ensuring harmonization of USG planning and operations within the context of a whole-of-government response. Most other nations involved in reconstruction and stabilization operations will work within the context of the US whole-of-government approach individually and collectively. Several nations have developed compatible whole-of-government approaches in parallel with US efforts and embrace the mutual benefits to engaging cooperatively across national and organizational boundaries.

c. This handbook identifies and describes the relationships between military and non-military participants within the IMS. It describes how the military interacts and coordinates with the different levels of the IMS, specifically the Country Reconstruction and Stabilization Group (CRSG) – and its Secretariat, Integration Planning Cell (IPC), Advance Civilian Team (ACT), and Field Advance Civilian Team (FACT) when applicable. **Certain information in the handbook is considered pre-decisional and may not necessarily reflect final agency action as of the date of printing.**

4. Development

a. JP 1-02, *Department of Defense Dictionary of Military and Associated Terms*, 31 October 2009, defines unified action as, "The synchronization, coordination, and/or integration of the activities of governmental and nongovernmental entities with military operations to achieve unity of effort." To this end, United States Joint Forces Command (USJFCOM) embarked on a multi-year "Unified Action" project to carry forward the principles of unified action through concept development and experimentation. This project focused on two lines of operations (LOOs) to achieve its objectives. The first line included limited objective experiments contributing to the implementation of the DOD work plan to support National Security Presidential Directive 44 (NSPD-44). The second LOO included spiral events to produce a series of handbooks and overview (see inside of the front cover). The products of both LOOs were developed and validated through a rigorous process of experimentation that was conducted with military and civilian partners across the United States Government.

b. This handbook was developed in close coordination with, and used significant input from, both civilian and military subject matter experts. The authors also regularly vetted the content with these experts to assure currency and accuracy of both theory and practice. As a result, it represents the current state of best practices regarding the IMS.

c. An important issue which arose during the drafting of this handbook is the widespread use of jargon and acronyms that may not translate particularly well between various agencies within the US Government. Insofar as possible, the authors have attempted to improve the readability of this handbook by using common terms in plain English. Additionally, "steady state[1]" is utilized by the US Department of State to describe the full range of engagement with host nations in a non-crisis environment. This handbook also includes a glossary of terms commonly used within the interagency community that may not be familiar to military planners.

5. Application

a. **This handbook is not approved joint doctrine and not directive in nature.** Military personnel participating in support of USG reconstruction and stabilization operations should utilize this handbook in conjunction with existing joint doctrine, to assist in planning, execution, and assessment of those operations with their interagency counterparts. It also should be utilize by military planners and implementers to assist in de-conflicting efforts and to empower more effective communication between interagency participants concerning the military's roles and responsibilities within the IMS. The information herein can help the joint community develop stability operations doctrine, mature IMS concepts for possible transition into joint doctrine, and further the effectiveness of military support to reconstruction and stabilization operations

    b. This handbook should be treated as a guide and not as a template. It is important to understand the dynamic nature of interagency coordination and not use it as a step-by-step "how-to" manual. **Commanders should consider the potential benefits and risks of using this information in actual operations**

6. Distribution and Contact Information

    a. Distribution of this handbook to US Government Agencies and their Contractors is authorized. Other requests for this document shall be submitted to USJFCOM, Joint Concept Development and Experimentation, Attn: Maj Arnold Baldoza, 115 Lake View Parkway, Suffolk, VA 23435-2697; or by phone to Maj Arnold Baldoza n at 757-203-3698.

    b. Comments and suggestions on this important topic are welcomed. The USJFCOM JWFC points of contact are Lt Col Jeffrey Martin, 757-203-6871, jeffrey martin@jfcom mil; and Mr. Chuck Shaver, 757-203-6062, charles.shaver.ctr@jfcom.mil.

DAN W. DAVENPORT
Rear Admiral, U.S. Navy
Director, Joint Concept Development
& Experimentation, J9

STEPHEN R. LAYFIELD
Major General, U.S. Army
Director, J7/Joint Warfighting Center

Intentionally Blank

TABLE OF CONTENTS

CHAPTER V
DEPARTMENT OF DEFENSE PARTICIPATION
IN THE COUNTRY RECONSTRUCTION AND STABILIZATION
GROUP AND SECRETARIAT

CHAPTER VI
INTEGRATION PLANNING CELL PARTICIPATION IN THE
GEOGRAPHIC COMBATANT COMMAND

CHAPTER VII
MILITARY PARTICIPATION IN THE ADVANCE CIVILIAN TEAM

CHAPTER VIII
MILITARY PARTICIPATION IN THE FIELD ADVANCE CIVILIAN TEAM

CHAPTER IX
PRE-INTERAGENCY MANAGEMENT SYSTEM RECONSTRUCTION AND STABILIZATION OPERATIONS PREPARATION AND PLANNING

CHAPTER X
JOINT FORCE COMMANDER RECONSTRUCTION AND STABILIZATION PLANNING AND IMPLEMENTATION UTILIZING THE INTERAGENCY MANAGEMENT SYSTEM

APPENDIX

GLOSSARY

FIGURES

CHAPTER I
INTRODUCTION

1. Unified Action

a. US operations in both Afghanistan and Iraq have highlighted the need for effective interagency coordination mechanisms. Additionally, the US Government (USG) National Security Strategy recognizes that failing states can become breeding grounds for transnational terrorism, proliferation of weapons of mass destruction, trafficking in humans and narcotics, organized crime and other threats. From that strategic guidance, USG Departments and Agencies determine how they will support the USG as a whole to achieve national security objectives.

b. This shift in strategy and the need to respond rapidly and flexibly to dynamic environments requires adaptation of our national security architecture to create and implement a new approach to the organization and use of all instruments of national power to achieve strategic success. Central to this new approach is the need for unified action to ensure the activities and resources of diverse participants across the USG are coordinated and integrated and work in cooperation with a variety of critical non-USG actors to achieve the desired strategic affect.

c. Unified action is the synchronization, coordination, and/or integration of the activities of governmental and nongovernmental entities with military operations to achieve unity of effort. In this context military commanders can conduct either single Service or joint operations to support the overall operation and achieve unity of effort with USG civilian agencies, Allies, coalition partners, multinational organizations, intergovernmental organizations (IGOs), nongovernmental organizations (NGOs), and when applicable and specifically authorized, the private sector.

d. An important element of unified action is the recognition that unity of command within the military instrument of national power is vitally important and supports the national strategic direction through the close coordination with the other instruments of our national power. Joint Publication 1, *Doctrine for the Armed Forces of the United States*, states unity of command in the Armed Forces of the United States starts with national strategic direction. For US military operations, unity of command is accomplished by establishing a joint force and Joint Force Commander (JFC), assigning a mission, or objective(s) to the designated JFC, establishing command relationships, assigning and/ or attaching appropriate forces to the joint force, and empowering the JFC with sufficient authority over the forces to accomplish the assigned mission.

e. Attaining unity of effort through unity of command for a multinational operation may not be politically feasible, but it should be the goal. Establishment of a Multinational Force under the guidance of a Multinational Force Commander (MNFC) can help achieve this goal. Though each case is unique, rarely, if ever, will nations relinquish command of their forces directly to an MNFC. At least two distinct chains of command will result: a national chain of command for each participating nation and a multinational chain of command. Organizational structures created below the MNFC level (e.g. Commander,

Joint Task Force (JTF) or Coalitions Forces Land Component Command) are better suited to meet objectives, political realities and constraints of each participating nation. When operating in a multinational environment, US Commanders and their staffs should strive to achieve unity of effort with their partners to the maximum extent possible that is consistent with their policies and authorities.

2. Summary and Evolution of US Government Policy Regarding Reconstruction and Stabilization

a. Public Law 110-417, hereafter called National Defense Authorization Act (NDAA) 2009 in this handbook, states, "If the President determines that it is in the national security interests of the United States for United States civilian agencies or non-Federal employees to assist in reconstructing and stabilizing a country or region that is at risk of, in, or is in transition from, conflict or civil strife, the President may …furnish assistance to such country or region for reconstruction or stabilization …." NDAA 2009 does not negate or replace NSPD-44, which was promulgated by the Bush Administration in December 2005, rather it codifies the institutions, policies, procedures, and responsibilities originally set up in NSPD-44.

b. In 2005 the Department of Defense (DOD) promulgated DOD Directive (DODD) 3000.05. This directive recognized that increasing stability operations capabilities within DOD are essential to conducting major operations and advancing US national security interests in the 21st century. To address these challenges, DODD 3000.05 directed DOD to ensure that stability operations are "given priority comparable to [major] combat operations." It also directed military commanders to plan for and execute stability operations in coordination and cooperation with non-military instruments of national power. DODD 3000.05 was designed to complement and support the President's objectives by making DOD a better partner in responding to reconstruction and stabilization (R&S) operations within the interagency process. In 2009 DOD Instruction (DODI) 3000.05, was signed reissuing DODD 3000.05 as DODI 3000.05. The new Instruction affirms the guidance in the Directive and updates policy and assigns responsibilities for the identification and development of DOD capabilities to support stability operations.

c. The Department of State (DOS) has developed the IMS for R&S from the guidance established within NSPD-44. Success for the IMS will rest upon many sets of unified actions (e.g., unity of effort and unity of purpose without unity of command). In this venue commanders at all levels, the Chairman of the Joint Chiefs of Staff, and the Secretary of Defense should ensure unified action is practiced and planned for according to the guidance received from their chain of command in coordination with other authorities.

d. NSPD-44 recognized the need for improvement in coordination, planning, and implementation for R&S efforts for foreign states and regions at risk of, in, or in transition from conflict or civil strife. This directive assigned the Secretary of State as the lead to coordinate and integrate USG efforts involving all US Departments and Agencies with relevant capabilities to plan, prepare, and conduct R&S activities. It also directed Secretary of State and Secretary of Defense to integrate stability and reconstruction contingency plans and activities and harmonize efforts with US Military plans and operations when relevant and appropriate.

e. NDAA 2009 reaffirms NSPD-44 and DODI 3000.05 and establishes in law the guidance that directs the civilian component of the USG to develop the capacity to plan, prepare and conduct civilian aspects of stability and reconstruction operations. The DOS has a clear mandate as the lead agency to coordinate and integrate USG efforts under this process. The DOD has and continues to provide its expertise in assisting the DOS with the development of mechanisms to implement NDAA 2009. The key elements that emerge can be summarized as follows:

(1) The USG has significant stake in reconstructing and stabilizing countries or regions to help establish a sustainable path toward peaceful societies, democracies, and market economies.

(2) The USG goal is to enable governments abroad to exercise sovereignty over their territories to prevent them from being used as a base of operations for extremists, terrorists, organized crime, or other groups that pose a threat to US foreign policy, security, or economic interests.

(3) Towards this end, State and Defense will integrate R&S contingency plans and R&S activities and military operations when relevant and appropriate and endeavor to harmonize efforts with US Military plans and operations.

f. Bothe NDAA 2009 and DODI 3000.05 recognize that stability operations are a core US military mission that the DOD shall be prepared to conduct and support and be given priority comparable to combat operations. DOD shall be prepared to perform all tasks necessary to establish or maintain order when civilians cannot do so and integrate civilian and military efforts to enable successful stability operations. Civil-military teams are a critical USG stability operations tool, development of which the DOD will continue to support. Assistance and advice shall be provided to and sought from the DOS and other US Departments and Agencies in the development of DOD stability operations capabilities.

g. While NDAA 2009 and DODI 3000.05 focus primarily on coordinating efforts within the USG, the US will likely participate in the context of a coalition or alliance. USG guidance is not intended to limit US involvement in coordinating coalition and alliance strategy, policy or actions; nor will it ever suggest relinquishing US sovereignty to a coalition or alliance. Rather, it suggests the importance of developing a consistent approach within the USG while coordinating with multinational counterparts to accomplish the overall mission.

3. Evolving State and Defense Department Policy

a. The policies associated with addressing fragile states (stability operations, peacekeeping, reconstruction and stabilization) in both the DOD and the civilian agencies, particularly the DOS and the US Agency for International Development (USAID) have been undergoing a process of change since the late 1990s. Indeed, these policies have never been in a state of evolution as they are currently undergoing. Nevertheless, the US military and the civilian agencies, especially the DOS, have a long history of policies designed to address fragile states. Participating in R&S operations is not a new phenomenon for DOD. As far back as 1815 the military was engaged in operations intended to stabilize diplomatic relations between the USG and governments along the Barbary Coast in the Mediterranean Sea. Later, from 1889 to 1914 the military, especially the US Marine Corps, stepped in to influence and, in some cases, run governments in the Caribbean nations of Cuba, Panama, Nicaragua, Mexico, and Haiti. The most significant foreign interventions by far that involved both the military and the civilian agencies was the post World War II period of rebuilding, especially Germany and Japan. The military played significant roles in both European and Pacific theaters. Military officers served as governors of cities and municipalities in Germany and US General Douglas McArthur played a significant role developing the post war Japanese constitution.[2]

b. With the onset of the Cold War, the US allowed its capabilities to engage in R&S operations to atrophy. The military was focused on maintaining its readiness to fight the Soviet threat and any mission that did not complement that war objective was seen as contrary to the overall readiness of the force. Accelerated by the experience in Korea which demonstrated to many that constabulary and occupation functions weakened the military and Vietnam which deepened the perceived division of responsibilities for war and peace between military and civilian agencies, this atrophy in government capabilities was accompanied by an increase in IGO, and NGO capabilities. The remarkable successes of the Japanese and German reconstruction efforts, and the Marshall Plan were not institutionalized or repeated in the 45 years between the fall of Berlin and the fall of the Berlin Wall.

c. The 1990s through present day has ushered in an era of change and a clear recognition that the old way of doing business does not work. US interventions in Somalia, Haiti, Bosnia, Afghanistan, and Iraq were not the successes expected. In each of these interventions the military was able to achieve its desired objectives and quickly defeat the opposing military capabilities within days or weeks. However, the subsequent post-conflict period was another story altogether. Armed violence, political squabbling, and criminal economic predations quickly reversed the initial successes achieved by the military. It has become readily apparent that the comparative advantage the US enjoys in traditional military capabilities are not matched by capabilities to provide economic, social, justice and good governance systems where they are weak or absent in a failed state. Also, it has become apparent that defense policy and planning capabilities, along with military operational capabilities will have to integrate to a much greater degree with civilian capabilities in order to successfully turn failed states around and create viable and sustainable national entities.

d. Presidential Decision Directive 56 (PDD-56), *Managing Complex Contingency Operations*,[3] promulgated by the Clinton Administration in the late 1990s, was the first clear and significant step taken to address the need for bringing all the instruments of national power together to address a failing state situation. This directive specifically addressed the need for both the military and civilian agencies to collaborate in planning and executing collaborative whole-of-government and military operations. The PDD was applied only a few times with limited success. It acknowledged the post-Cold War environment where the security environment was no longer balanced by two super powers, but was instead based on the potential for frequent and wide ranging smaller conflicts involving states and trans/sub-national actors. This included non-traditional actors such as warlords, religious leaders and even transnational non-state leaders. PDD-56 made the US national authority aware of the limitations that faced the government. The lessons learned from applying PDD-56 and from military led expeditions in Iraq and Afghanistan led to strong internal reassessments throughout the government from which emerged: NSPD-44, *Management of Interagency Efforts Concerning Reconstruction and Stabilization*, the DODD 3000.05, *Military Support For Stability, Security, Transition, And Reconstruction (SSTR) Operations*, and most recently, *NDAA 2009* and DOD Instruction (DODI) 3000.05, *Stability Operations*.

e. The decade of the 1990's also ushered in an awareness that regional security concerns in the US national interest emanate from failed or failing states. Made readily apparent is the comparative advantage the US possesses in conventional combat operations has not been matched by capacities to provide governance, economic, social well-being and justice systems in the vacuums created by the collapse or defeat of governments. Military forces are encouraged to broaden their knowledge base and actions beyond Cold War core competencies to encompass abilities that cover the full range of operations, including whole-of-government and military, in increasingly complex operational environments that require relevant, multi-source civilian capabilities. This lesson the military and civilian agencies are beginning to fully appreciate.

f. Defense policy, planning, and operational capabilities must be integrated to a greater degree with civilian capabilities to achieve national goals. For the military, modern capabilities of precision fires and information flows across the operational environment both compress the physical dimensions of the operational environment and give tactical actions strategic importance. It is possible to experience pre-conflict, close-combat, and post-conflict conditions within a very small area in a very short time where simultaneous actions are required across this spectrum and across the civil-military organizational divide. This "three-block war" compression demands unprecedented mental and physical agility and the ability to apply all instruments of national power in very discrete packages to achieve tactical, operational, and strategic goals. Today, actions by soldiers and civilians can cover all these sequences and categories in the span of a single day.

g. The evolution of a whole-of-government approach to address the challenges of the world today and into tomorrow continues. Civilian agencies are making the hard changes necessary to establish planning and integration capabilities. They are also establishing deployable capabilities never before considered. A Civilian Response Corps (CRC) comprising a stand-by reserve "force" of competent civilians is being developed and trained for future operations they will be called upon to conduct.

h. The military is also evolving in light of the interconnected political, military, economic, social, information, and infrastructure [PMESII] challenges that lay ahead. Today stability operations have the same level of priority as more traditional war-fighting objectives and more than ever the military is training with civilians, deploying with civilians and learning the culture of civilian agencies. The military is evolving its capability to understand and implement non-traditional missions including rule of law, governance, infrastructure rebuilding and economic stabilization. Today you are just as likely to find a "diplomat" in body armor alongside his or her military counterparts offering guidance and advice and a military officer sitting down with a group of village elders offering suggestions on rebuilding the capacities of the local government to provide essential services.

4. Essentials for Effective Military Participation

a. Essentials for effective military participation in interagency management start with the national strategic direction as well as the factors that contribute to the decision activating the IMS in response to an emerging crisis. This unity of command within the military enables unified actions that support the IMS and the overall objectives it seeks to achieve through unity of effort.

b. Important essential elements for effective participation within the IMS include authorities, roles, responsibilities, knowledge of the system, its participants, existing DOD interface and participation within interagency structures, and manpower and resource requirements. Clearly defined national strategic direction with measureable objectives and attainable outcomes are essential.

c. In multinational operations, an overarching strategy will be developed which sets the strategic direction. The European Union, North Atlantic Treaty Organization (NATO), and France have developed processes for creating a multinational strategy which have included substantial DOS and DOD input. These processes and the lexicon used in them are compatible with the IMS. Furthermore, setting measurable objectives and attainable outcomes have also been the focus of the international development community. Commonality in developing strategy and evaluation criteria within the multinational diplomatic, defense and development communities will help establish a clear direction and unity of effort in future operations.

(1) **Requirements**. A military requirement is an established need justifying the timely allocation of resources to achieve a capability to accomplish approved military objectives, missions, or tasks. Military requirements for effective participation in interagency management will be defined through the objectives and outcomes indicated in development of national strategic direction, to include:

(a) A realistic plan that provides for sufficient manpower and resources capable of enabling effective participation within an agreed timeframe.

(b) Maintaining adequate knowledge of interagency mechanisms and processes, participants, existing structures, capacity and capabilities, and limitations.

(c) Establishment of clearly defined authorities, roles, and responsibilities enabling unity of effort amongst the participants.

(2) **Principles**. Key principles for effective military participation within the IMS include:

(a) **Unity of command** starts with a national strategic direction, and is an important piece of the military instrument of national power.

(b) **Integration**, the IMS is designed to successfully integrate all of our instruments of national power – diplomatic, economic, informational, and military – to achieve our national strategic objectives.

(c) **Unity of effort**, defined as coordination and cooperation toward common objectives, even if the participants are not necessarily part of the same command or organization - the product of successful unified action.

5. Purpose

a. The purpose of unified action is to synchronize, coordinate and integrate activities to achieve unity of effort. Military planners and operators should not approach R&S operations as being solely a military responsibility. Instead they should recognize that the most effective way to meet their goals is to coordinate and if possible partner with non-military participants that likely are already engaged in such functions.

b. The Interagency Management System (IMS) is designed for highly complex crises and operations, which are national or security priorities, involve widespread instability, are likely to require military operations, and where multiple US agencies will be engaged in the policy and programmatic response. It is not intended to respond to the political and humanitarian crises that are regularly and effectively handled through the current Washington D.C. and Embassy based systems. The IMS, therefore, is likely to be activated when a crisis in a foreign nation or region is of sufficient importance that it directly impacts on US national interests or is likely to do so. Analyses of likely scenarios have identified a range of causes of crisis, and while not all can be identified, some common themes have emerged. States that fail or fall into crisis usually do so for reasons of weak governance, failing economies or economic policies, a collapse of the rule of law, internal social, cultural or religious strife or a military that is either corrupt, inept, abusive or a combination of all of these things. Collectively these represent "root causes of crisis." These sectors are addressed by various government and non-government sources. These source documents are likely to be used by planners and implementers participating in the system. Thus they may inform or even complement the overarching *USG Planning Framework for Reconstruction, Stabilization, and Conflict Transformation* and its response mechanisms through the IMS.

Intentionally Blank

CHAPTER II
INTERAGENCY MANAGEMENT SYSTEM FOR RECONSTRUCTION AND STABILIZATION

1. Introduction

This chapter will inform military personnel involved in an R&S operation about the IMS. While much of this chapter is covered in other publications, it is provided to ensure that military personnel have a context from which to develop their understanding of the essential role they play in the broader whole-of-government effort.

2. Description of the Interagency Management System

a. A major element of the effort to coordinate USG R&S operations has been the creation of the IMS, which was approved by the Deputies' Committee of the NSC in March 2007. Responding to the direction of the National Security Strategy, NSPD-44, and most recently NDAA 2009, the IMS establishes a means to successfully integrate the instruments of national power and leverage the capabilities of all participants to achieve national strategic objectives. When a significant crisis occurs or begins to emerge, the Secretary of State, the Secretary of Defense and/or the appropriate NSC director may decide to activate the IMS based on a decision by the Principals' or Deputies' Committees and implemented at the direction of the NSC. The IMS is designed to assist Washington, D.C. policymakers, Chiefs of Mission (COMs), and military commanders to manage complex R&S engagements by ensuring coordination among all USG stakeholders at the strategic, operational, and tactical/field levels. The lessons learned from Iraq, Afghanistan, Bosnia, and Kosovo demonstrate that the US must employ an approach in these types of engagements that draws upon the full range of diplomatic, development, defense, intelligence, and economic resources available to the USG. This system, through three-levels of planning and operations, creates a framework to unify effort among all USG stakeholders. Many of our multinational partners and the European Union (EU) have similar mechanisms, which should help unify overall coalition/alliance R&S efforts as well. The IMS is intended to facilitate and support:

(1) Integrated planning processes for unified USG strategic and implementation plans, including funding requests;

(2) Joint interagency field deployments; and,

(3) A joint civil-military operations capability such as shared communications and information management.

b. The IMS functions at three levels (which is somewhat distinct from the military's strategic, operational, and tactical levels of definition):

(1) A Country Reconstruction & Stabilization Group (CRSG) at the strategic/policy level with a dedicated support staff or Secretariat located principally in Washington D.C.,

(2) An Integration Planning Cell (IPC) that supports the GCC, and

(3) An Advance Civilian Team (ACT) which supports Whole-of-government structures and processes at the Embassy and, if appropriate, be augmented by Field Advance Civilian Teams (FACTs) at the tactical field level.

c. These structures are flexible in size and composition to meet the particular requirements of the situation and integrate personnel from all participating agencies. Each team is designed to support and augment, not replace, existing structures in Washington, at the Geographic Combatant Command (GCC), and in the field. International or coalition partners may also be represented.

d. The IMS is a response management mechanism. It does not preclude interagency scenario-based, prevention or contingency planning, which may occur independently. The system will draw upon such plans when they exist.

e. Military participation within the IMS will come in many forms and at all levels. Participation within the IMS will depend largely upon the nature and scale of the operation, as dictated by policy and strategic objectives. In some cases there will not be a requirement for military forces; in other cases, the military may be the predominate element with participation by the Office of the Secretary of Defense (OSD), Joint Staff (JS), Services, GCCs, functional commands, and JTFs, their Major Subordinate Commands (MSCs), and other forces. Each element will have direct interface or membership in a corresponding structural element within the IMS. For example:

(1) OSD and the JS will represent DOD on the Country Reconstruction and Stabilization Group (CRSG). The applicable GCC could be asked to provide expertise by OSD and the JS, in accordance with DOD policies, but the GCC will not fill a representational role.

(2) The IPC will reside at and integrate into a GCC to assist in harmonizing civilian and military planning.

(3) The JTF and ACT will, at a minimum, have direct interface and communication and perhaps co-locate certain elements as the ACT plans for and coordinates R&S related tasks. The JTF may provide further logistics, transportation, and security to support the activities of the ACT and may be requested to provide personnel and units that have high value civil-military capabilities such as Engineers, Civil Affairs, and Psychological Operations.

(4) If FACT(s) are established, they will be located in provinces or outlying areas and are may operate relatively autonomously or be dependent on MSC(s) for support and sustainment. Either way, MSC(s) are likely to be called upon to coordinate and collaborate with FACT(s).

3. Country Reconstruction and Stabilization Group

a. The CRSG is the central Washington, DC coordinating body for the USG effort. The CRSG is comprised of two components: an augmented Interagency Policy Committee established for the specific country response, and an interagency planning, operations, and coordination staff; CRSG Secretariat. The Interagency Policy Committee is jointly chaired by a regional Assistant Secretary of State, the Coordinator for Reconstruction and Stabilization and a regional National Security Council (NSC) Director. Representatives from the OSD and the JS and the affected GCC (when circumstances warrant, and are in compliance with DOD policy) can be involved with policy development and strategic level planning by providing technical planning expertise to members of the CRSG and provide input into a decision to establishing the IMS.

b. With the decision to activate the IMS, a new situation-specific Interagency Policy Committee will usually be established as the CRSG. However, it may be appropriate to designate an existing Interagency Policy Committee to take on these expanded functions. This designation signals a change in status for the country and requires an assessment of current USG activities and plans, and additional staff to support an increased workload. Establishing a CRSG must take into account any international or political sensitivity surrounding prospective interventions and steps must be taken to minimize any potential negative implications of public knowledge of the effort. In exceptional cases, the planning and resource mobilization procedures envisioned in this handbook may be conducted under an Interagency Policy Committee to avoid the higher profile that might result from establishing a formal CRSG.

c. The CRSG may prepare the USG R&S Strategic Plan, including a common USG strategic goal, a concept of operations, the major essential tasks, including the Major Mission Elements (MMEs) the USG must undertake (including with international and host nation (HN) partners), and resource requirements to achieve stability. It can build on earlier interagency contingency planning. The CRSG prepares and forwards recommendations for decision to the NSC Deputies' and/or Principals' Committee.

d. The CRSG also facilitates preparation and integration of country-level planning, operations support, information management, international/coalition partnership development, and resource mobilization, as well as reach-back, monitoring and reporting functions.

4. Integration Planning Cell

a. An IPC, which should not be confused with the Interagency Policy Committee, is a team of interagency planners and regional and sectoral experts who will be deployed to a GCC Headquarters (HQ) or to the equivalent multinational HQ. The team leader for the IPC is considered to be at peer level and will have direct access to the supported geographic combatant commander (CCDR). The IPC supports civil-military communication and harmonizes civilian and military planning to achieve unity of effort for R&S implementation activities. The IPC is not designed to create a USG R&S operations or implementation plan.

b. The CRSG will establish and deploy an IPC in response to an emerging crisis potentially requiring military intervention or support, a DOD request for assistance with R&S planning or a request from an equivalent multinational HQ. The IPC will be established in conjunction with the development of a US R&S Strategic Plan. The affected GCC will have a key role in advising strategic and implementation plan development – specifically those with possible military tasks. The GCC be responsible for providing the right force, manpower and equipment, to structure a JTF, to achieve its assigned tasks under an overarching strategy within the IMS. The GCC will also host and help align the IPC with its relevant staff elements, to facilitate harmonization of civilian and military R&S efforts.

5. Advance Civilian Team

a. The CRSG may recommend (with the Chief of Mission's concurrence) that the Secretary of State deploy an ACT to support country-level whole-of-government structures and processes at the Embassy. The ACT is comprised of personnel who deploy to provide additional capacity to existing and/or newly created structures and processes in an R&S environment and who operate under the guidance and authority of the chief of mission (COM). Country-level whole-of-government structures and processes are the integrated systems at the country-level which provide the COM and JTF commander with capacity to integrate the activities of all allocated assets in time, space, and purpose in order to achieve unity of effort and unity of action. These integrated structures and processes do not exist apart from the COM and JTF commander, include both new and existing structures, processes, and personnel, and originate from within the embassy and the JTF, if present. ACT personnel provide capabilities and capacities to support, and if necessary assist in building, these integrated structures and processes.

b. The ACT is both strategic and operational in nature, assisting the COM to direct R&S planning and operations, and provides reach-back to parent, Washington, DC agencies for support. ACT(s) provide core R&S implementation planning and operations expertise to the COM and military commanders. The ACT joins existing Embassy personnel (if present) to provide specific R&S functions in order to support the COM in executing the USG Country Plan.

c. The ACT operates under COM authority. The ACT can operate with or without US military involvement. In situations when the military is involved, the ACT will assist in integrating JTF and Embassy R&S operations in support of both the COM and the JFC. In all circumstances, US civilian field operations are conducted under COM authority, and the COM bears ultimate responsibility for the execution of the Country Plan. In the absence of an existing USG diplomatic presence, the ACT leader may be designated as the President's Special Representative or Special Envoy, act as the COM, and will oversee the establishment of a more permanent USG presence.

d. If a decision is made to establish and deploy a JTF, its participation within the IMS will require interface with many different components such as the ACT, FACT, COM, and the US Country Team. For unity of effort, ACT(s) integrate and coordinate the execution of the Country Plan with existing USG civilian and military plans and operations. Success or failure of a US R&S operation in the field largely will depend on ensuring the COM and the JTF Commander having a shared operational picture, an agreed plan and vision for its execution, and a shared process for raising and making decisions.

6. Field Advance Civilian Team

a. If necessary, the ACT can deploy a number of FACT(s). FACT(s) are usually deployed outside of the ACT to establish a US presence, provide direct information about conditions on the ground and support R&S operations conducted at a provincial and local level. They are flexible, scalable teams responsible for a range of operations in governance, security, rule of law, infrastructure and economic stabilization to provide the COM with maximum capacity to implement R&S programs. As required, they may coordinate the field execution of projects that involve not only USG resources, but also foreign governments, UN, other IGOs, NGOs, or HN activities. While remaining under COM authority, FACT(s) may integrate with US or foreign military forces to maintain unity of effort. In this regard, FACT(s) build upon the lessons learned from Provincial Reconstruction Teams (PRTs) established for the conflicts in Afghanistan and Iraq.

b. A MSC or elements thereof such as Brigade Combat Teams/Regimental Combat Teams (BCT/RCT), within a JTF, will interact with many ACT/FACT implementers, who plan, coordinate and execute projects. The primary interface at this level will be the FACT. FACT(s) are equipped and trained to perform in hostile or uncertain operating environments in coordination with the US military or multinational forces. Functional units, elements or selected personnel within a MSC with inherent civil-military capabilities may be tasked to support, be attached or detailed (in the case of individuals) to a FACT to provide assistance and expertise. Arrangements concerning direction, guidance, and sustainment should be established through an MOA prior to any unit tasks or personnel moves between military and civilian elements.

7. Key Proponents and Participants

Key participants and proponents in unified action within the context of complex operations conducted since the close of the Cold War have included the majority of the departments and agencies of the Executive Branch. Participants have included multi-national and coalition contingents, IGOs, NGOs, and the private sector. Increasingly individual States have provided manpower and resources through their National Guard Bureaus.

8. Key Interagency Proponents and Participants

As approved by Deputies' Committee, the IMS is the process for how the USG will organize when responding to an R&S intervention. The proponent for the IMS is the DOS. The NSC, DOD, and USAID serve as the other key proponents for the IMS. Participants in the process are all agencies and departments of the USG that will have a role in an approved R&S operation. These include, but are not limited to: the Departments of Justice, Commerce, Homeland Security, Agriculture, Treasury, and Health and Human Services.

9. Civilian Response Corps

a. Despite their roles and responsibilities in the IMS, USG civilian agencies may not have the manpower necessary to support pre-crisis training or extra personnel available to be dedicated to IMS specific duties. Civilian agencies in many cases are staffed "one deep", meaning an individual with particular expertise needed during an R&S operation will be holding down responsibilities in his or her agency on a daily basis that will be left unfilled if that individual is "deployed" to fulfill duties specific to the R&S operation. In recognition of this reality, the DOS has been authorized to establish and sustain a pool of professionals to provide assistance in support of an R&S operation. This section is not intended to offer a detailed description of the CRC. It is designed to provide military personnel involved in an R&S operation an understanding and appreciation of the civilian counterparts they will encounter at the different levels of the IMS. The civilians that the military may encounter during a R&S operation could likely be a mix of CRC personnel but also USAID or State personnel posted in-country serving in the Embassy or USAID mission (if there is USG presence already). If they do encounter CRC members they can expect a common level of training on whole-of-government planning and operations, whereas other civilians posted in-country may not have this training.

b. The CRC is a group of civilian federal employees and, eventually, volunteers from the private sector and state and local governments, who will be trained and equipped to deploy rapidly to countries in crisis or emerging from conflict to provide R&S assistance. The CRC is comprised of diplomats, development specialists, public health officials, law enforcement and corrections officers, engineers, economists, lawyers, public administrators, agronomists and others – offering the full range of skills needed to help fragile states restore stability and the rule of law, and achieve economic recovery and sustainable growth as quickly as possible. The President has empowered the Secretary of State to coordinate and lead integrated USG efforts to prepare, plan for, and conduct stabilization and reconstruction activities, and to coordinate with the Secretary of Defense to harmonize civilian and military activities. Because no single government entity has all of the relevant expertise, the CRC is a partnership of eight departments and agencies: the DOS, USAID, Department of Agriculture, Department of Commerce, Department of Health and Human Services, Department of Homeland Security, Department of Justice, and Department of the Treasury.

c. The CRC consists of three components, an Active Component, a Standby Component and a Reserve Component. The DOS and USAID are major contributors that have dedicated personnel, whose daily work is centered on IMS planning and preparation, including training. These staffs are small and while military personnel may encounter these personnel during R&S operations they will be the exception rather than the rule. Most civilians involved in R&S operations under an established IMS will come from one of the three components of the CRC.

d. Active component officers are full-time employees of their departments or agencies whose specific job is to train for, prepare, and staff R&S operations for conflict transformation. They may spend 50-60% of the year in overseas conflict areas, deployed on average for 90 days at a time. They provide "first responder" expeditionary capabilities in civil-military environments and operate in whole-of-government structures such as the IMS or ad hoc response teams. They focus on critical initial interagency functions such as assessment, planning, management; and administrative, logistical, and resource mobilization in order to stand-up or increase the capabilities of USG systems and structures for implementation of R&S operations. When not deployed these personnel participate in exercises, train for R&S operations, conduct training and contribute to lessons learned, best practices, development of standards and standard operating procedures (SOPs).

e. The Standby Component is comprised of officers that are full-time employees of their departments/ agencies who may or may not have current positions related to R&S

sector areas. However, they have specialized subject matter expertise useful in R&S operations, and have committed and secured permission from their office to be available for call-up in the event of an R&S operation, have been pre-screened and trained, and have committed to be available to leave their home office within 30 days of call-up.

f. The initial period of operational support for Standby officers will be for 90 days. Standby officers can be asked to extend for an additional 90 days and most should expect to do so. Standby Component members attend orientation training in the first year and additional training in following years. When activated, they serve as employees of their home departments/agencies assigned to US-based planning, assessment, exercises or overseas deployment, under the supervision of a designated individual within a whole-of-government response structure. They provide critical reinforcement and follow-up for the Active Component, as well as pertinent skills and expertise. Deployments will be on average for a 90 day period.

g. The final component of the CRC is the Reserve Component. Officers designated to the Reserve Component are US citizens who have committed to be available within 45-60 days of call-up to serve as temporary USG employees in support of inherently governmental functions. They provide a pool of qualified, pre-trained, and ready civilian professionals with specialized expertise and skills not readily found within the USG—such as municipal administration, policing, and local governance—that are critical for R&S operations.

h. CRC Reserve officers are vital to efforts to bring "normalcy" to countries going through R&S engagement by filling capabilities career USG employees simply cannot match in expertise or in number. Reserve Component officers are expected to serve a minimum of three months when deployed but are likely to be asked to extend for up to one year. Although Reserve Component officers can be utilized at all levels of the IMS, they will mostly be assigned to positions in the ACT or FACT(s). Congress has yet to authorize resources for the development of the Reserve Component of the CRC and remains in the conceptual phase.

10. Other Partners and Contributors

The military will find other non-military and nongovernmental actors very much involved in a range of activities that relate to R&S operations. In many, if not most cases, these actors will be essential participants, yet once again they are not the "normal" or expected partners of the past. In any crisis state or region there are IGOs and NGOs that were present before the crisis loomed, are present during the crisis, and will be present long after the US military has left. These IGOs and NGOs bring resources, skills, and experience that can benefit whole-of-government planning and implementation efforts. The willingness of these organizations to work with the military will vary depending on their mission. Those in humanitarian assistance may refuse to talk with the military for fear of compromising their neutrality, a prerequisite for their mission. However, others in humanitarian assistance may request the assistance of the military for its logistic and transportation capabilities. Some organizations cannot be co-opted and, in fact, attempts to do so can be counter-productive. The military must develop the processes and procedures to work with all these organizations or at least attempt to de-conflict geographically with those who need to maintain neutrality. Working or collaborating with those willing to do so can serve the commander well since these organizations usually understand the local situation very well and can help determine what the root causes of crisis are and how to address them.

CHAPTER III
MILITARY PARTICIPATION

1. Introduction

a. A significant way to improve interagency coordination is to develop a common understanding for authorities of agencies participating in the IMS, and the existing controls that will guide R&S activities in the affected country or region. It is essential that clearcut, mutually understood principles, authorities, and control relationships are established during the course of any planning process, prior to the deployment of implementing personnel into an operational area. This chapter describes a series of principles, authorities, and control and coordination measures by which the IMS is established to ensure successful interagency cooperation. These mechanisms will be refined by planners, implementers, and leaders during the establishment and operation of the IMS to ensure unity of effort during R&S operations.

b. Effective execution of interagency R&S operations begins by establishing unity of effort through the designation of a leader with the requisite authority to accomplish assigned tasks using an uncomplicated chain of leadership. The COM is the primary USG official tasked with implementing the USG Strategic Plan for R&S. However; the President may designate a special envoy or senior official for such purposes. The authorities granted to the COM and the JFC are statutory and must be taken into account during the establishment and operation of the IMS. The IMS does not obviate these authorities. It is essential for the COM and JFC to ensure that subordinate leaders and staff understand their authority to act as well as their role in decision making and relationships with others. The assignment of responsibilities and the delegation of authorities both foster initiative and ensure unified action. The authorities and control mechanisms contained in the IMS are summarized in this chapter. Appendix A: *Authorities for Military Participation in Stabilization and Reconstruction Operations*, provides further detail of authorities governing command and control relationships, acquisitions, and interagency coordination involving military participation in the IMS.

c. Interagency staff in the CRSG, IPC/GCC, and ACT/JTF must understand that their primary roles are to provide sufficient, relevant information to enhance their leadership's situational awareness critical to decision-making and to execute the decisions of their leaders by focusing the appropriate capabilities within their organizations to achieve the leader's intent. Therefore, leaders must give staff the authority to make routine decisions while conducting operations consistent with the objectives in the USG Strategic Plan for R&S.

2. Authorities for Military Participation in the Interagency Management System

a. Authorities for military participation in the IMS are addressed in US Code, Acts of Congress, Directives – both Presidential and DOD, DOD Instructions, doctrine, and regulations. The *US Government Planning Framework for Reconstruction, Stabilization and Conflict Transformation*, further describes the IMS, its participants and authorities, and how the system enables the planning framework.

b. The principles of unity of effort are essential to IMS R&S operations. For example, an ACT serves under COM authority. All ACT members, including detailed military members, are under COM control. Another example of an established relationship between the COM and DOD is the Defense Attaché. The Defense Attaché and all the military personnel detailed to that office are integral members of the country team and serve under the authority of the COM. If the COM decides to make his or her senior military attaché the principal liaison with the JTF commander, that attaché continues to work for the COM, in effect serving as the COM's representative.

3. Control Authorities

a. The military refers to control in the context of an authority that may be less than full command exercised by a commander over part of the activities of subordinate or other organizations. Examples of control are Operational Control (OPCON), Tactical Control (TACON) and Administrative Control. Current military definitions for OPCON, TACON, and Administrative Control do not account for or incorporate the addition of the interagency perspective, which will be brought to the forefront if the IMS is established.

b. When necessary, the DOS, in coordination with the DOD will develop MOA(s) with a GCC to ensure effective and timely attachment of an IPC to its HQ. The IPC reports to the CRSG and maintains a coordinating relationship with the COM. When deployed, members of the IPC will fall under the security rules of the host GCC HQ based on the terms stipulated in a MOA, but will otherwise fall under the authority of the CRSG or the relevant COM if the GCC is located outside of CONUS. Implied in this is the close coordination and de-confliction of security rules established by the Regional Security Officer (RSO), COM, and the GCC inside the country of deployment. These should be clearly stated and understood by all parties who operate under an arrangement utilizing an MOA.

c. An underlying principle of the IMS is that the COM retains authority and control over all USG activities in country not under the GCC. The COM may be accredited to more than one country. The COM interacts daily with DOS strategic-level planners and decision makers and provides recommendations and considerations for crisis action planning directly to the GCC Commander and/or JTF Commander. While forces in the field under a GCC Commander are exempt from the COM's statutory authority, the COM confers with the CCDR regularly to coordinate US military activities with the foreign policy direction being taken by the USG toward the host country. The COM's political role is important to the success of military operations. Each COM has a formal agreement with the GCC Commander as to which DOD personnel fall under the force protection responsibility of each.

d. The USG Planning Framework reinforces the importance of the COM in the early development of policy and strategic planning for the USG response to an IMS triggering event. While IMS teams may deploy to the location of the military to maximize unity of effort and assist with planning and implementation of tasks, this does not mean they fall under the control of a military commander. Instead they will either report to a higher element in the IMS or, when deployed, the COM. This is also true when US civilian and military HQ are co-located. The IPC, for example, will report to the CRSG and has a coordinating relationship with the relevant COM. If deployed to a foreign country with the GCC, the IPC will fall under COM authority.

e. Similar to the IPC, the ACT when deployed serves under the COM authority. If FACT(s) are established, they too will remain under the COM authority. FACT(s) may integrate with US military forces when appropriate to maintain unity of effort. This implies the development of Memorandum of Agreement (MOA)(s) outlining the requirements, responsibilities, duties and authorities of each party to the signed document. At a minimum the JFC (and relevant MSC), COM, ACT/FACT leaders, and RSO plus the appropriate legal advisors should be consulted when constructing these documents.

f. Personnel drawn from the US military should be fully trained and qualified to perform the functions necessary to support an ACT or FACT. Members of the US Military may find themselves in the unique position of being part of an IMS body under the control of the COM while being a member of a military force deployed into theater under the control of a GCC. In these instances careful consideration should be made to determine what functions will be performed by these personnel to maintain the authorities of both the COM and GCC.

g. According to the IMS (R&S) paper approved by the NSC Deputies Committee (DC) in March 2007, "ACT HQ and FACT members are under the operational control of the ACT/FACT leader, though they remain in contact with their parent agencies and may still be rated or evaluated by their parent agencies, with input from the ACT/FACT Leader. Alternately, if agreed in advance, ACT/FACT members may be rated directly by the ACT/FACT leadership and reviewed by their parent agency." Furthermore, "the ACT, as directed by the COM, exercises operational control over interagency personnel assigned or attached to it. Operational control in no way denies or alters any officer's right and duty to remain in communication with his/her parent agency, to exchange information and recommendations with that agency, and to appeal to more senior parent agency representatives when necessary." These guidelines coupled with COM authority for all USG activities in country not under the control of the GCC exemplify the need for clearly articulated arrangements utilizing MOAs between the GCC and COM before military personnel are detailed to an ACT or FACT.

h. It is important to note that there may be US military forces and USG civilian agency organizations already deployed and operating in the affected country prior to the establishment of the IMS. If these elements are conducting operations related to the implementation of stabilization and reconstruction plans, the COM may authorize the ACT or FACT(s) upon arrival to synchronize the operations of these elements in support of the Country Plan. For the military this will require additional coordination measures to be implemented between the ACT/FACT(s) and military units with inherent civil-military capabilities during on-going operations. These units will already be engaged providing stabilization and reconstruction activity support to military commanders from the JTF level down to battalion and below level. Because of this it will be important to incorporate the input of commanders for the synchronization of operations concerning military units who impact the implementation of stabilization and reconstruction plans.

4. Resource Authorities

a. Under the IMS, USG executive agencies and their programs will retain their established legal authorities and responsibilities concerning the use of appropriated funds and implementation of programs. DOD funds and programs that are existing or created to execute the Country Plan will be managed by DOD appointed officers or designated representatives assigned to support or detailed to the ACT HQ or FACT(s).

b. Within the ACT/FACT area of responsibility, control of DOD resources and programs will be maintained by the DOD or by one of its designated subordinate agencies. Designated DOD (or subordinate agency) program officers or representatives may conduct their activities centrally from the JTF/MSC or can choose to decentralize and delegate program implementation and funding authorities to their designated representatives on the ACT/FACT(s) while maintaining the necessary level of oversight as required.

c. The options surrounding the use of DOD resources will be dependent upon, existing policy, R&S program requirements and an overall assessment of the situation on the ground. Funds to support any option selected will be obligated by appointed contracting officers, per policy and law. Responsibility for implementing programs will be maintained by the agency that funds the program. For example, a FACT team leader could not tell a FACT member with certifying authority to certify a voucher for payment that is not legally proper under the appropriation or funds involved. Similarly, the FACT team leader could not have authority to direct a fund certifier to authorize the obligation of funds. However, FACT team leaders may participate in determinations of spending priorities, to include approval or coordination of requirements in accordance with the Country Plan.

5. Resource Planning

a. Planning resource requirements for military participation within the IMS should start as early as possible after the USG policy guidance and a decision to involve military forces have been established. Representatives from OSD and Joint Staff serving on the CRSG SPT will assist in the planning and development of the USG policy guidance, strategy and MME development to determine the need for military participation and resources. The OSD and JS representatives will utilize established DOD procedures, when communicating with elements inside DOD, for policy guidance and approval of plans. Once an approved policy and strategy is adopted the Joint Staff will produce a PLANORD that will address the military related objectives and resources outlined in the MME(s). The JS will distribute the PLANORD utilizing established procedures to the affected GCC participating in the response effort.

b. The PLANORD will serve as the initial notification to the GCC of the forces available for utilization under the response. The affected GCC will then be able to conduct planning for force development utilizing the policy guidance, strategy, and objectives it receives from the Joint Staff. GCC requests for forces should incorporate whole-of-government planning objectives while utilizing established processes and mechanisms for submission through established channels.

c. The IPC may not be established and deployed to the GCC to inform initial planning, therefore the GCC should be prepared to make adjustments and/or modifications to its planning when the IPC arrives and is integrated into the GCC. Insights and recommendations gained from the IPC members may help inform the development of resource requirements to accomplish the objectives assigned to the military.

d. Resource requirements should align to assigned tasks to accomplish designated objectives as illustrated in the USG Strategic Plan Overview Template utilized by the IMS. Structures within the IMS may require selected military personnel based on specialty (MOS), level of experience, and subject matter expertise (e.g. a military reservist's civilian employment) to be detailed. In these instances Economy Act Orders and written agreements such as MOUs need to be constructed between the affected military command and the receiving organization gaining these personnel. Requests for support may extend to certain types of military units whose core mission generally involves civil military operations (CMO). Security, logistic, sustainment, and support to interagency implementation teams may be accomplished by DOD upon reimbursement by the DOS under an Economy Act order.

e. Planning resource requirements supporting military participation within the IMS needs to start early in the whole-of-government planning process. This will already be underway in the affected GCC and will have to be aligned to the objectives and tasks assigned to the military under in the strategic plan devised by the CRSG. It will be important for the military to understand what other resources implementation partners within the IMS are bringing with them to leverage resources, reduce duplication, and increase unity of effort.

f. Resource planners should be prepared to support requests for contingency funding related to the implementation of R&S related programs and projects much like the use of Commander's Emergency Response Program (CERP) funds in Iraq and Afghanistan. This type of resource planning should be coordinated with the ACT/FACT elements of the IMS as well as the COM, relevant country team members and appropriate host country officials. It is important to note that this type of expanded and coordinated resource planning should not interfere with established legal authorities concerning department or agency programs and their allocated funds. The military may be requested to resource training and equipping programs of a HN's security forces. These activities need to be planned and coordinated with the implementing bodies of the IMS as well as the COM, and other executive and legislative bodies as dictated by laws and regulations. The goal of the training and equipping programs should build host country capacity to hasten transition to the appropriate host country officials.

g. As with any military deployment information on resources available within the affected country will be of value to military planners. How the military employs the use of another country's resources will be dependent upon how the military enters a country, whether by invitation or through the application of force. Some resource considerations for the military will be land or facility use and their restrictions as well as life support related resources such as water, and power generation. Additionally, the military may require the use of ports, rail, and roads to deliver critical sustainment resources.

6. Responsibilities and Coordination Processes

a. NDAA 2009 states, "The Secretary of State and the Coordinator for Reconstruction and Stabilization are also charged with coordination with the DOD on R&S responses, and integrating planning and implementing procedures." In June 2008, the DC of the NSC approved the *United States Principles for Planning for Reconstruction, Stabilization, and Conflict Transformation*. This framework provides a whole-of-government process for planning for stabilization, reconstruction and conflict transformation.

b. The CRSG, on behalf of NSC Principals' and Deputies' Committees, will coordinate interagency crisis response and provide recommendations on strategic guidance to Deputies' and Principals' Committees on all policy and resource issues related to the specific country or crisis. This includes recommendations on lead roles between all elements of the interagency.

c. The IPC leadership will keep the host GCC HQ leadership apprised of communications with the CRSG. The IPC and DOD representatives on the CRSG will keep the CRSG informed of military planning and operations so that the planning process can take into account the military operations and their potential effects. The IPC will also coordinate with the ACT through the CRSG and COM. Coordination between the IPC and CRSG does not obviate the defense policy guidance and plan approval process codified in law and implementing through internal DOD procedures.

d. The IPC may require frequent coordination with and guidance from key implementing agencies. Ideally, such communication should be channeled through the CRSG to implementing agencies in order to facilitate the development of timely, field-informed recommendations for program development, and supplemental budget requests. Recommendations should be based on an understanding of the host GCC HQ plans and field-identified R&S conditions and requirements. If necessary, disputes among interagency partners within the IPC or between the IPC and the host GCC HQ can be referred to the CRSG for resolution.

e. ACT(s) support the COM in coordinating and integrating the execution of the Country Plan with existing USG civilian and military operations. Where gaps in existing civilian operations are identified, ACT personnel can initiate or manage a response that includes whole-of-government structures and processes. ACT(s) provide core R&S implementation planning and operations expertise to COM(s) and military commanders. They also may extend the USG's civilian presence via FACT(s) reporting to the ACT. ACT(s) will work to ensure that US efforts focus on supporting both USG and host country goals and interests. As required, FACT(s) may coordinate the field execution of projects that involve USG resources. They may also coordinate with UN, other IGOs, NGOs or host country entities to execute projects.

f. The ACT/FACT areas of responsibility should mirror those of the military forces deployed, so that each area of responsibility has a dual US civilian and military leadership structure, starting at the COM-CJTF level and working to the lowest tactical level feasible/ necessary. However, having common areas of responsibilities (or areas of operations as defined by the military) may not be possible. In the earlier phases of military involvement, especially in armed conflict, the priority may be to capture and hold key terrain. In these cases the geographic objectives and key terrain that form the boundaries of a military area of operation may not align with political boundaries utilized by civilian professionals operating within the IMS.

g. To maximize coordination and effectiveness, the National Security Counsel Deputies' Committee approved IMS paper recommended that at each level of the IMS military and civilian HQ be co-located. This will be influenced by the level of military involvement, the phase and timing of operations, and the security situation. The feasibility of co-locating HQ for planning and conducting stabilization and reconstruction activities will be influenced by other factors such as the need for USG civilian professionals to be in close proximity to HN government officials and their offices and the location allocated for a military HQ.

h. In some instances other factors will intervene making it necessary for the military and civilian HQ to be separate. Decisions should be made concerning liaison capabilities needed and what interagency "slice" elements of both civilian and military HQ should co-locate within each other's HQ. Separate HQ will also require careful planning and implementation for communications, transportation, security, and sustainment capabilities that could otherwise be leveraged when both HQ are co-located.

i. As the situation dictates and stabilization and reconstruction activities are transitioned to civilian professionals then a realignment of military areas of operations to civilian areas of responsibility should be considered to unify the actions of and maximize the capabilities resident in both civilian and military organizations to achieve unity of effort.

j. ACT/FACT and military coordination with the host country is of great importance to stabilization and reconstruction activities. The primary objective in any R&S operation is to identify and work to reduce drivers of conflict and instability and build host country government capacity sufficient to put the country on a path towards sustainable peace. Although specific ACT and FACT operations could range from direct governance to advisory missions to reporting and program-implementation functions, all civil military operations should be conducted with a view towards creating local host government capabilities to sustain stable and functional governance.

7. Joint Force Command Coordination with IMS Civil Military Teams

a. Integrated civilian and military efforts are key to successful stability operations. Civil military teams are a critical USG stability operations tool. Participation in such teams will be open to representatives from other US departments and agencies, foreign governments and security forces, IGOs, NGOs, and members of the Private Sector with relevant skills and expertise. Relevant to the IMS is the responsibility for the Under Secretary of Defense for Policy, USD(P), to develop a process to facilitate information sharing for stability operations among the DOD Components, and relevant US Departments and Agencies, which is a core function of the IMS. The Chairman of the Joint Chiefs of Staff supports the USD(P) and appropriate US departments and agencies through participation in USG and multinational stability operations planning processes. Commander's of GCC(s) will engage relevant US departments and agencies, foreign governments and security forces, IGOs, NGOs, and members of the Private Sector in stability operations planning, training, and exercising, as appropriate, in coordination with the Chairman of the Joint Chiefs of Staff and the USD(P).

b. GCC coordination with the IPC will initially focus on reception and integration of the team into the appropriate elements of the GCC planning staff. The IPC will require space in which to conduct their activities and access to communication networks to maintain contact and information sharing with their home agencies, the CRSG, the COM (and the Embassy), while allowing for the sharing of information between them and the GCC. It is likely that procedures for clearance and access to GCC staff and for facilities and plans stored at the GCC will have to be developed so that the IPC can provide the maximum benefit to the GCC to facilitate integration into the IMS.

c. The JTF Commander participating in the IMS will coordinate with many different actors and entities – some of whom may not be operating under the system. These other elements may include the host country (public and private sector) and its military, coalition militaries, and NGOs. Within the IMS, the JFC will have reoccurring coordination and interaction with members representing the ACT and the FACT (if deployed). Coordination with the IPC will occur through the GCC via existing procedures and also through the ACT. Coordination with the CRSG will likely occur through guidance and direction received from OSD, JS, and the GCC utilizing existing procedures. It will be important for the JTF Commander and staff to know and understand the mission and purpose of each IMS body so coordination requirements can be better supported.

d. JTF coordination with the ACT/FACT implementing bodies in the IMS will come in many forms and increase or decrease depending on the scale of the operation, the level of military involvement, phase and timing, and if civilian and military HQ are co-located or in separate locations. It will also be dependent upon the level of civilian involvement due to restrictions such as department or agency capacity shortfalls or a determination by the COM, RSO or military commander that security is inadequate for USG civilians to perform the tasks necessary to accomplish R&S objectives.

e. Coordination requirements the military should consider are not limited to security and clearance requirements, force protection, transportation, communications, and other life support functions, such as housing, workspace facilities, fuel, power generation, food, water, medical. During an R&S crisis, imbedded in the JTF Commander's OPLAN, will be numerous tasks and actions designed to support not just the JTF Commander but to support the larger whole-of-government R&S Strategic Plan. Military commanders and leaders must clearly understand the specified tasks imbedded in the JTF plan as well as have an understanding of the implied tasks that military personnel will most likely be called upon to perform in support of deployed civilians and in support of the R&S Strategic Plan. In addition to the JTF Commander's OPLAN, military leaders must also clearly understand the USG Policy and the USG Strategic Plan.

f. Important IMS related activities for the JTF Commander to prepare for are the development of the Country Plan, coordinated through the ACT, and the field execution of (R&S) projects that involving USG resources, coordinated through the FACTs. If the JTF Commander has contingency funds available to apply to stabilization and reconstruction activities the project nomination and approval process should incorporate the recommendations of the appropriate civilian personnel in country. This may include co-located USG civilian team members, Embassy personnel, and/or FACT leadership to established processes where extant. This process should, in most cases, incorporate the viewpoint and recommendations of the relevant and legitimate host country officials. Coordination with the ACT, FACT, and host country should be a reoccurring step within the R&S project life cycle processes. The goal of the whole-of-government approach utilizing the IMS is to create a common operational picture (COP) enabling coordinated planning and implementation for programs and projects.

8. Supported/Supporting Roles

a. Generally, the US military serves in a supporting role during whole-of-government planning and implementation of stabilization and reconstruction activities within the construct of the USG Planning Framework. While the primary effort for planning and conducting these activities are best suited for civilian professionals, the interagency community has recognized that in some instances it may not be possible for civilian professionals to engage in conducting R&S activities when order has yet to be established. In these situations the military may be called upon to perform R&S tasks necessary to establish and maintain order allowing for transition to the civilian professionals. These supported and supporting roles are codified in NDAA 2009.

b. At each level of the IMS the military generally serves in a supporting role and may detail personnel with the requisite experience upon request or when determined by DOD to the organizational structures resident within the system. However, there may be some instances where the military may find itself in the supported role. An example could be the DOD being designated to lead an Objective Team– one that is predominately security related utilizing a preponderance of military resources. In this instance the DOD would be responsible for coordinating the development of sub-objectives as well as executing the majority of tasks to achieve the overall objectives in the MME. Likewise, the DOD may be called upon to provide its expertise and support to another department or agency leading another MME or Objective. Supporting and supported roles do not affect legal authorities concerning department or agency specific programs and funding.

c. Military personnel, especially commanders and leaders, recognize the authority of the military chain of command as it flows from the President down to the JTF commander. They need to also understand the supporting role the military will often assume during an R&S crisis where the COM or a senior civilian official has overall responsibility. Command authority will always reside in the duly appointed military commanders.

9. Coordination and Integration with Existing Interagency Structures

a. Although elements of the recently established CRC are permanently standing bodies (i.e., the Active and Standby Corps), there is not a permanently established IMS. This will require the CRSG, IPC, and ACT/FACT(s) to coordinate or integrate with existing interagency structures resident within GCCs, JTFs or falling under COM authority. These existing interagency structures bring with them regional knowledge and subject matter expertise of the affected country or region. They will likely have pre-existing regional and country level contacts with IGOs, NGOs, COMs, Country Teams, and HN officials. It will be important for military participants in the IMS to leverage this knowledge and apply it to their planning processes. The following are examples of existing interagency organizations, although not all may be considered a standing organization.

b. The Joint Interagency Coordination Group (JIACG) is an interagency staff group that establishes regular, timely, and collaborative working relationships between civilian and military operational planners, it is composed of USG civilian and military experts detailed to the CCDR. The JIACG is tailored to meet the requirements of a supported JFC, and provides the capability to coordinate with USG civilian agencies and departments. The JIACG has been refined and in many cases renamed at the Combatant Commands where they were established. This standing interagency staff element will likely have direct interface with an IPC in the event the IMS is established. Due to their expertise, members of the JIACG will be consulted and expected to offer advice to the IPC and some members may participate on the IPC. However, first and foremost they remain members of the JIACG and detailed to the GCC with daily and established consultative and advisory responsibilities that will continue during the crisis.

c. The Joint Interagency Task Force (JIATF) is an interagency organization under a single military director that coordinates specific operations (i.e., counterdrug, counter terrorism, IW) at the operational and tactical level. The JIATF concept has been expanded at Combatant Commands that previously established JIACGs as well as exported down to JTFs operating within the AOR of a GCC. Further development of this concept will increase the need for coordination or integration of its activities with implementing bodies of the IMS.

d. The Joint Civil Military Operations Task Force (JCMOTF) is a JTF composed of Civil-Military Operations (CMO) units from more than one Service. They are established as required to provide support to the JFC in humanitarian or nation assistance operations, theater campaigns, or civil military operations concurrent with or subsequent to regional conflict. It can organize military interaction among many governmental and nongovernmental humanitarian agencies and NGOs within the theater. The JCMOTF is not a standing interagency organization instead it can coordinate or facilitate interaction between various participants within USG civilian agencies. It focuses on providing the JFC with certain CMO capabilities subsequent to, during, and after a regional conflict. This organization may find itself coordinating and interfacing with the IPC, ACT and FACTs while planning for or conducting stabilization and reconstruction related activities.

e. A Civil Military Operation Center (CMOC) is an ad hoc organization, normally established by the GCC or subordinate JFC, to assist in the coordination of activities of engaged military forces, and USG civilian agencies, NGOs, and IGOs. There is no established structure, and its size and composition are situation dependent. CMOC(s) may include representatives from the USG interagency community. They are normally established to assist military commanders in the coordination of CMO related activities. The CMOC is not a standing organization. Due to its role, facilitating implementation of stability and reconstruction related tasks, may find itself interacting with ACT or FACT field elements and in some cases the COM or designated country team members. Because CMOC(s) have been used in the past to manage the interaction of military organizations in the field with NGO(s), and local host country entities, a JTF may establish a CMOC from the outset and prior to USG civilian agency presence on the ground. Once the ACT is established and operational, the JTF commander and ACT leader should determine the subsequent relationship between a CMOC and the ACT.

f. The PRT builds on the foundations of the Joint Civil Military Operations Task Force (JCMOTF) and Joint Interagency Task Force (JIATF), providing a unique interagency approach to stability operations. A PRT is an interim Civil-Military Operations (CMO) organization that is able to help stabilize the operational environment in an unstable or insecure province or locality through its combined diplomatic, military, informational, and economic capabilities. Generally, PRT(s) help create conditions for development and improvements in governance capacity in areas where traditional development NGOs and IGOs are inhibited from full operation, whether the area is considered stable or unstable. It combines representatives from DOD, DOS, USAID, Department of Agriculture (in Afghanistan) and other interagency partners into a cohesive unit capable of independently conducting operations to enhance the legitimacy and the effectiveness of a host country government. PRT(s) are currently operating only in Iraq and Afghanistan. The FACT structure within the IMS closely resembles the mission and purpose of a PRT and incorporates the best practices of Whole-of-Government R&S operations. In future operations, which require the activation of the IMS, it is expected that the FACT will replace the PRT to avoid duplication of effort and ensure the implementation of stabilization and reconstruction activities remain coordinated within the established structures of the IMS.

g. The Joint Contingency Acquisition and Support Office (JCASO) is a relatively new organization. JCASO provides the necessary contingency acquisition management capability and capacity required when a JFC is challenged with extensive contractor support in complex operations involving multiple components, coalition forces and governmental agencies. A key component is the ability to ensure expeditionary support in a rapidly deployable manner. Accordingly, the JCASO will have a minimum of two scalable Joint Operational Contract Support Teams (JOCSTs). These teams would be most appropriately deployed in the initial phases of a declared contingency. The JCASO will support the JOCST to ensure it is fully mission capable to meet its operational requirements, to include reach-back capability.

10. Coordination with non-US Government Structures

a. Stabilization and reconstruction operations are conducted in the context of larger multinational operations where the primary or secondary focus of planning is in a multinational HQ. A multinational operation can be conducted by a coalition formed for a particular purpose, an alliance based on a treaty (e.g. NATO), or under the umbrella of an international or regional organization such as the United Nations (UN), or African Union, or a combination of all three. Many non-US militaries operate under regimental systems and do not have structures analogous to the GCC. They perform operational level planning at the HQ level.

b. Each multinational operation is different. Differences can be highlighted due to doctrine, language and culture, organizational structures and planning processes. Despite these differences, NATO doctrine has become the military standard for many operations. In Afghanistan NATO has cleared its doctrine for use by NATO and non-NATO members. Another consideration is that multinational bodies will either develop a collective strategic plan or adopt the plan of the predominant nation, which is often the United States. Most nations will not have likely approved nor participated in the development of the USG Strategic Plan for R&S and are under no obligation to implement it. Therefore, diplomacy will play a vital role ensuring smooth coordination and cooperation. Understanding the potential political sensitivities of working in the multilateral context will be a challenge at both the strategic and operational levels.

c. Information sharing can be a challenge. Where relationships exist (i.e., NATO), information sharing is easier. Others, such as the UN, have no way of securing classified material. Those organizations, who we do not have formal sharing arrangements with, will arguably be the most difficult. Coalition information sharing will be determined largely by bilateral agreements already negotiated between individual countries, which can easily become difficult to manage in a multinational environment. Coalition staffs must also be aware of how to handle controlled unclassified information, which can result in legal pitfalls when not executed properly. Some countries are required by their national laws to release ALL unclassified information into the public domain, regardless of its "FOUO" markings. As a result US forces may over-classify information or not share at all. Both of these options make collaborating with other nations in R&S operations more difficult.

d. Fortunately many partner countries and organizations are currently in the process of developing their own approaches to "whole-of-government" or integrated mission planning. Most appear to be compatible with our own.

e. UN Coalition Force - The UN does its military planning within the Department of Peacekeeping Operations, Office of Military Affairs, Military Planning Service. The UN does not accept gratis personnel, which means the UN does not allow member countries to detail personnel "at no charge to the UN" to work, even temporarily, in UN offices. Should the USG or CRSG decide that personnel are necessary to work with counterparts in the UN on plans or other aspects of an operation, these personnel would be assigned to the US Mission to the UN, receive UN badges, and then could spend time working with their UN counterparts. This requires close coordination and assistance from the Bureau for International Organizations of the DOS and the US Mission to the UN, particularly the military advisor. Traditionally, military planners have worked with UN military planners in this way. Inserting civilian planners is untested. The UN has established integrated operational teams (IOT), which takes subject matter experts from various disciplines to plan from a "whole-of-UN" perspective. It will take further consideration to determine the most appropriate relationship. The UN also has an "integrated mission" concept, which is currently being employed and brings together various organs of the UN that may be operating in-country. This is a new model, which is still evolving as lessons are learned in the field, but represents the same integration trend that characterizes the USG efforts to develop the IMS. When operating in-country, USG whole-of-government planners should coordinate to the extent possible the USG R&S plans and actions with those of major international actors, like the UN.

f. NATO Force - To integrate into NATO planning efforts would require close coordination with the US Ambassador to NATO. At NATO, initial planning is conducted in the Allied Command Operations HQ, and initially approved by nations through their Military Representatives in the NATO Military Committee prior to engagements with the North Atlantic Council, and is where integration would be most appropriate.

g. African Union (AU) Coalition - Personnel can be assigned to work in Addis Ababa, Ethiopia, although there it can also be difficult to provide personnel gratis to the AU. The AU conducts its military planning within its conflict management division. This planning is conducted in either the early warning and post–conflict reconstruction section or the operations section within the conflict management division. The nature of the intervention would determine the best place for cooperation. Similarly, close cooperation would be established with USAU.

h. Regional military coalitions (i.e., The Economic Community Of West African States - ECOWAS) are recent innovations and there are no precedents for how the USG will engage and coordinate with them. ECOWAS, the Economic Community of West African States, is a leading contender for a future cooperative effort. It is still developing its planning and execution capabilities so diplomacy and flexibility will be necessary if and when the USG decides to cooperate with ECOWAS or another regional coalition. It is unlikely, in the near term, that prior exercising or training will occur to establish familiarity with these organizations.

Intentionally Blank

CHAPTER IV
MILITARY CONTRIBUTION TO ORGANIZATION OF THE INTERAGENCY MANAGEMENT SYSTEM

1. Department of Defense Participation within the Core Staff

a. The standing up of the IMS will occur at the Washington DC strategic level once a decision is made to activate the system based on input from the necessary participants as laid out in the triggering guidance. The organization will be dependent upon many factors to include the nature of the crisis the USG is facing, the USG policy and strategy objectives for a response, determination of the scale of effort required, the actors involved, the affected region and country or countries, manpower and resources available as well as the level of commitment from coalition partners and the international community to the response effort. The greater the commitment from our coalition partners and the international community may, in fact, decrease the resource requirements to be provided by the USG.

b. The DOD contribution to the organization of the IMS will, for the most part, come from the OSD and Joint Staff up to and including the Secretary of Defense. Input from the affected GCC, when necessary, may be requested to inform the DOD contribution to planning and development occurring within OSD/JS participation on the CRSG. Requested inputs from the GCC will utilize the appropriate and established DOD communications channels to the JS and the OSD. It is important to note that the IMS may not require the participation of the military. In this case the DOD contribution to organization of the IMS may not extend beyond the initial phase of planning and preparation in the decision making process to establish the system.

c. According to the IMS triggering guidance in the case of imminent crises with R&S or conflict implications, senior officials (DC, PC, direct request from the Secretary of State or Secretary of Defense) can trigger whole-of-government planning. A decision of the R&S Interagency Policy Committee can also trigger whole-of-government planning, with the concurrence of the State Regional Assistant Secretary and COM. Recommendations could also come from any member of the R&S Interagency Policy Committee, State or USAID regional or functional bureaus, a country or regional Interagency Policy Committee, or other Interagency Policy Committee member.

d. The decision to trigger whole-of-government planning is not the same as triggering the activation of the IMS. The threshold for triggering the establishment of the IMS is much higher than what triggers whole-of-government planning, although many of the participants in both processes may be the same and some of the initial steps may be similar.

e. Some examples of criteria for triggering any level of whole-of-government planning for a crisis response in countries/regions of policy importance could include, but is not limited to:

(1) Significant actual or potential (near-term) US military involvement;

(2) Events with significant potential to undermine regional stability and development progress, (e.g., a coup, economic collapse, severe environmental damage or degradation);

(3) Actual or imminent state failure, particularly where the host government is unwilling or unable to respond;

(4) Excessive mortality rates;

(5) Large-scale displacement of people;

(6) Recommendation of COM(s) in affected country(ies) or the appropriate Regional Assistant Secretary;

(7) Rapid increase in USG-funded civilian programs operating in an R&S environment;

(8) Activation of USG agencies' crisis assessment, planning, or response teams (such as a Disaster Assistance Response Team);

(9) Embassy drawdown or evacuation in an R&S environment and/or significant threat to US citizens and US facilities;

(10) International or allies' crisis response, such as the formation of a UN peacekeeping operation; and/or,

(11) Determination of an impending or actual genocide, ethnic cleansing, or massive and grave violations of human rights.

f. It is the Secretary of State who may decide to establish the IMS based on the decision by the Principals' or Deputies' Committees and implemented at the direction of the NSC. The DOD will have representation on the DC, PC and/or Interagency Policy Committees to provide its input and position with regards to a decision to establish the IMS or whole-of-government planning. If the IMS is established these same representatives may be involved in the initial policy planning and strategy development within an R&S Interagency Policy Committee that is crisis specific, which forms the basis or core of the structure for the CRSG element of the IMS.

g. The staffing of the CRSG will include Co-chairs at the appropriate DOS Regional A/S and/or Special Envoy, S/CRS Coordinator, and NSC Director. All agencies with involvement in programs or policy relating to the crisis should be represented on the CRSG at the Assistant Secretary-level including DOD, USAID, the DOS, Department of Justice, and other agencies as appropriate. Agency representatives to the CRSG must be able to speak authoritatively on behalf of their agencies or bring issues for decision to their leadership. The representatives from the DOD essentially become members of the CRSG core staff and may occupy positions on the CRSG itself, its Secretariat, and/or the SPT.

h. The Secretariat is jointly managed by a Policy Director (DOS Regional Bureau) and a Chief Operations Officer (S/CRS). Interagency staff for the Secretariat may include agency planners, sectoral and resource experts including the DOS's Director of Foreign Assistance and DS staff, DOD, USAID, Department of Justice, and other agencies as necessary given the situation.

i. The SPT, within the CRSG Secretariat, will become the center of gravity for policy planning and strategy development. It will develop policy options and recommendations for approval at the CRSG, DC, PC, or NSC levels depending on the political and strategic importance as well as the complexity of the situation. After approved policy guidance is established further strategy planning, development and refinement will proceed and inform DOD planning processes from the strategic to operational levels and ultimately the execution of plans at the tactical levels while ensuring alignment to guidance as a participating member of the IMS.

j. Strategy development at the multinational level will be challenging and will require a very deliberate effort to coordinate efforts and de-conflict. Multinational partners, particularly the UN, the EU and the AU, have no requirement to consider USG planning and, indeed, when the US is not the lead country, US planners will be pressed to adapt their planning to that of the multination organization with the lead. Even when the USG is the lead nation it must always recognize that other entities plan differently and may not understand US processes, especially military planning processes. There are efforts ongoing to find more common ground between partners in crisis response collaboration. The EU and France developed a multinational interagency strategic planning guide very similar to the S/CRS strategic planning process. The UK and Canada have both created and stood-up crisis response organizations very similar to S/CRS. All of these efforts are intended to specifically facilitate a collaborative effort among the multinational community while respecting national sovereignty. Gaining buy-in and perspective by working with the international community and sharing the risk usually make this dual-track endeavor well worth the effort.

k. For the US Military this means recognizing that by the time the USG has joined or entered a multinational response to a regional or state crisis a significant amount of US and international policy planning and strategy development has likely been accomplished. The US Military will normally not lead the USG engagement concerning high level policy and strategy development with the international community. Instead it will inform this process and present recommendations through its participation and representation on the CRSG, DC, or PC levels of the NSC depending on the importance and complexity of the situation. Military planners, as well as civilian ones, will need to be flexible and innovative in efforts to align USG planning efforts with those of the other multinational players. It is very likely, for example, to find the USG, the UK and Germany to each have robust levels of planning completed that must then be adjusted to accommodate UN plans that are neither as well along nor as detailed.

2. Potential Department of Defense Support Requirements

a. The support requirements for DOD participation within the core staff will be dependent on the situation, level of involvement, and scale of the anticipated response effort. These requirements will generally support the activities taking place at the strategic level in Washington DC and will focus on the military component of participation within the IMS. If the establishment of the IMS requires a large commitment of DOD manpower and resources the effort to support these activities will be much more intensive.

b. Support requirements could include, but are not limited to; facilities and workspace specifically set-aside and capable of supporting interagency planning and collaboration efforts, lodging and transportation, temporary hire (under contract) of subject matter experts and temporary transfer of government civilian and military personnel with skill sets and requisite experience to contribute to interagency planning efforts under the IMS. An updated roster or a listing of occupational specialties relevant to interagency planning under the IMS (R&S) should be maintained to quickly identify these individuals. It is recommended that DOD personnel identified to support whole-of-government planning and the establishment of the IMS be "fenced off" from other activities to fully focus on their contribution to the organization of the IMS and the specific crisis that led to the establishment of the IMS.

c. Interagency personnel will need to be cleared with the appropriate access to facilities and information systems in order to conduct planning and collaborative efforts as required under the IMS. Information systems supporting the planning and collaborative efforts of interagency personnel must be capable of reaching back to the sending or home agency for these personnel so they can provide an immediate and effective contribution to the planning effort. Information management is another capability where robust capacity in this area will need to be available to interagency personnel. GCC(s) will likely be asked to provide dedicated information management personnel, when appropriate, to assist interagency teams. In interagency forums, the interagency community has accepted and incorporated the term Knowledge Management in lieu of the joint forces' accepted and defined doctrinal term - Information Management.

3. Department of Defense Manpower and Resource Requirements

a. Relevant offices and staff elements designated to respond to the crisis from the JS and the OSD will make up the bulk of the contribution from the DOD upon the initial organization of the IMS. Representatives from these elements will participate in the initial policy planning and strategy development contributing to whole-of-government planning under the IMS.

b. Under the IMS, additional planning capabilities may be required from the DOD at the OSD/Joint Staff level than their current capacity may be able to handle due to their current force structure and manning. Specifically, the JS will need to be prepared to absorb additional planners from the affected GCC and/or other sources to assist in the whole-of-government planning efforts to support an R&S mission.

c. The manning requirements should remain flexible and scalable to address the needs of the situation or crisis confronting the USG that initiated whole-of-government planning and the decision to activate the IMS. These requirements could utilize existing structures, like Interagency Policy Committees, requiring no additional personnel or in the case of a major event bring together many of the relevant staff elements in the OSD/

JS to support whole-of-government strategic planning and policy development and the initial establishment and organization of the IMS.

d. Due to current planning capacities at the OSD/JS levels a decision may be necessary to involve planners from the affected GCC to cover the capacity gap and inform DOD contribution to the strategy development of the R&S Strategic Plan. These planners may be geographically dispersed from the OSD/JS in Washington DC. The OSD/JS should officially represent concerns raised by the affected GCC to the other interagency elements participating in the IMS.

e. In addition to relevant staff and personnel from the OSD and the JS, certain DOD personnel with functional skill sets and background experience useful for the DOD contribution to whole-of-government planning contributing to the response to the crisis at hand may be called upon to assist. These personnel may be drawn from combatant commands (both functional and geographic) and the Services. Examples of personnel or staff elements with functional areas relevant to activities surrounding the establishment of the IMS may include engineers, military police, medical, civil affairs, psychological operations, information operations, public affairs, staff judge advocate, finance/comptroller, contracting, and subject matter experts who may be under contract. The amount of personnel drawn from these various functional backgrounds will vary based upon the requirements facing the OSD and the Joint Staff as it pertains to their participation on the CRSG and its SPT.

f. Additional resource requirements for DOD contributing to the organization of the IMS are expected to be minimal at the beginning stages of whole-of-government planning before the activation of the IMS. In many of these cases the personnel contributing to the organization of the IMS will utilize resources already resident within their own organizations. There may be additional resources required for these personnel to effectively communicate and collaborate with other interagency actors involved in the organization of the IMS. This could come in the form of additional facility requirements for planning and collaboration purposes or the need for information management systems to be interoperable and interface with other agency systems to enable whole-of-government planning.

g. Additional resources may be required for personnel in the way of travel, transportation, lodging, and other life support requirements if they are not assigned to the OSD/JS and/or reside in the Washington DC area. This could be the case if GCC personnel are required to be present to assist the planning effort on-going at the OSD/JS. This could also be the case where an advance party to include a planning element from the DOD is sent forward to assist in the base-line assessment of an affected country or region to support the whole-of-government planning effort. It is also likely that additional resources may be required when the USG R&S effort is part of a larger international effort and DOD resources are to be located at an international or multinational HQ such as NATO, the AU, or the UN.

h. Resource requirements for DOD functional elements are likely to be similar to those described in the DOD specific elements. As many of the identified functional personnel may not be from the OSD or the JS it is likely that additional resources may be required in the way of travel, transportation, lodging, and other life support requirements. This could also be the case in the instance where an advance party to include functional elements or personnel from the DOD is sent forward to assist in the base-line assessment of an affected country or region to support the whole-of-government planning effort – in some cases prior to the establishment of the IMS.

4. Joint Force Commander Communications within the Interagency Management System

For additional detail regarding JFC Communications within the IMS see Appendix F, "Communications."

CHAPTER V
DEPARTMENT OF DEFENSE PARTICIPATION IN THE COUNTRY RECONSTRUCTION AND STABILIZATION GROUP AND SECRETARIAT

1. Introduction

a. The CRSG is made up of two components: an augmented Interagency Policy Committee-level entity established for a specific crisis response, and a dedicated interagency planning, operations, and coordination staff called the CRSG Secretariat. The CRSG's purpose, on behalf of Principals' Committee (PC) and Deputies' Committee (DC) of the NSC, is to unify the USG's response to a R&S crisis. The CRSG achieves this through whole-of-government strategic-level planning and operations utilizing the IMS for R&S. This system enables effective decision-making through the standardization of processes resulting in improved information management, mobilization of resources, and interagency coordination.

b. For planning purposes when the USG decides to establish a CRSG to address a crisis in a foreign country the following assumptions can be made:

(1) The crisis requires a reconstruction and/or stabilization response that is in the national interest to pursue.

(2) There is a security vacuum that requires the USG and the DOD specifically, to plan for the execution of a stabilization operation.

(3) The CCDR responsible for the country in crisis will task organize a JTF, to assume lead for the military components of the R&S Country Plan.

(4) The CRSG will develop and execute a whole-of-government R&S Strategic Plan.

(5) The CRSG consists of representatives of all the participating agencies and departments involved in the R&S effort. The DOD representation includes those that have authority to speak for the CCDR.

c. DOD participation within the CRSG and its Secretariat will occur at the strategic level involving designated representatives from the OSD and the Joint Staff (JS). CRSG representation will be at the Assistant Secretary-level. Those who serve on the Secretariat and act in a capacity representing their Assistant Secretary will be sufficiently senior and both knowledgeable about the area and/or situation and capable of reaching back into the DOD for expertise and advice as needed. Representatives of the Geographic Combatant Command (GCC) will also participate. The level of GCC participation will be determined by both OSD and JS based on the requirements of the CRSG for the planned USG response and recommendations from the GCC.

d. The role of DOD representatives from both OSD and the JS are critical to ensure the military understands the non-military objectives and informs the non-military components of the CRSG about military capabilities and limitations. Regardless of actual representation on the CRSG or its Secretariat, the affected GCC will have an important role in advising the OSD and JS representatives about possible operational level courses of action and planning options that relate to and affect their contribution to the development of policy options, strategic plans, and MMEs – specifically those with possible military tasks.

2. Structure

a. CRSG Leadership - The CRSG is co-chaired by the appropriate Regional Assistant Secretary of State (A/S), a regional Director from the NSC, and the Coordinator for Reconstruction and Stabilization, with representation, at the Assistant Secretary-level, by all Agencies and Departments of the USG who will contribute resources or expertise to the crisis, including DOD.

b. DOD A/S level representatives to the CRSG may find it necessary to delegate their authority to a lower level representative who can focus solely on the affected country where the R&S response utilizing the USG Planning Framework and the IMS will be implemented. However, DOD representatives on the CRSG must be able to speak with authority on behalf of the department or bring issues for decision to their leadership.

c. CRSG Secretariat - The CRSG Secretariat members will be drawn from across the interagency representing departments and agencies participating within the IMS (R&S). The Secretariat is managed by a Policy Director from the relevant DOS Regional Bureau and a Chief Operations Officer from the Office of the Coordinator for Reconstruction and Stabilization (S/CRS). The Secretariat will have a "Core Staff" dedicated full time to the work of the CRSG as well as "Agency Staff" who fulfill certain CRSG functions as part of their overall department or agency responsibilities.

(1) Core Staff bring the expertise, context and contacts of their specific agencies but fill whole-of-government functions, report to and are reviewed by the CRSG Secretariat Leadership, and have no authority or responsibility to represent their specific department or agency's viewpoint.

(2) Agency Staff represent their agencies, providing specific expertise, ability to reach-back to other agency personnel and offices, and the ability to represent and influence efforts of their sending agency. Such personnel can be full or part-time.

d. DOD contributions to the Secretariat will include both Core Staff as well as Agency Staff. DOD personnel assigned to the Secretariat will include regional experts, strategic and operational planners, as well as sectoral and resource management experts. It will also include DOD civilian and military personnel who have been identified to be detailed to the ACT or FACT prior to their deployment.

e. The CRSG Secretariat may include individual cells focused on planning, operations, partnership, strategic communication, and resource mobilization to carry out its functions. The Secretariat includes the SPT, which is responsible for completing the USG Strategic Plan for R&S, and the planning integration team, which is responsible for supporting country-level planning led by the ACT. Secretariat members from the DOD will participate in all or some of these cells or teams depending on the subject matter as it relates to the DOD portfolio in the R&S plan. The SPT and the larger CRSG Secretariat also have the following planning responsibilities:

(1) Communicating the USG Strategic Plan to users in Washington, Combatant Commands, and the Field and ensuring clarity on the goals and objectives that guide all activities;

(2) Ensuring that agency implementation plans and the Country Plan support (and are necessary and sufficient to achieve) the USG Strategic Plan for R&S;

(3) Revising the USG Strategic Plan for R&S, as necessary, to respond to changing conditions, policy guidance, and new knowledge about assumptions;

(4) Providing necessary guidance and requirements to logistical planning and deployment management cell of the CRSG;

(5) Establishing MME Teams;

(6) Maintaining feedback loops between Washington and the field across the interagency;

(7) Ensuring Washington-level coordination between agencies, including keeping agencies informed about the activities of other participants;

(8) Identifying gaps in information, programs, and resources and requirements for decisions or corresponding actions by the CRSG; and

(9) Establishing and tracking strategic-level metrics, assumptions and other trend indicators.

3. Functions

a. Functions performed by the CRSG include policy and planning guidance preparation, coordination to achieve unity of effort across the interagency, monitoring the COP, mobilizing resources, and proposing further implementation of elements of the IMS.

b. The CRSG's core function is to enable effective decision-making at the lowest possible level, to channel any disputes with agreed options for higher decision, and to provide policy and planning guidance to the USG. The CRSG decides upon, and will rise to the Deputies' and Principals' Committees for decision as necessary, all policy and resource issues related to the specific crisis. This includes recommendations on changes to pre-existing policies and resources in response to the emerging crisis, and critical decisions for planning and executing the response including lead roles among the departments and agencies of the USG. The CRSG is responsible for developing, mobilizing resources for, monitoring, and revising a crisis-specific USG R&S Strategic Plan.

c. Functions performed by the CRSG Secretariat which support the CRSG include leading whole-of-government planning at the strategic level and supporting country-level planning, maintaining the COP, developing and maintaining partnerships, coordinating and informing strategic communication, mobilizing resources, and performing reach-back for the IPC and the ACT. Secretariat members from the DOD can be expected to contribute to or support all or some of these functions depending on the subject matter area of interest as it relates to the DOD portfolio within the R&S plan.

d. The Secretariat functions as the CRSG staff and provides day to day, strategic, and operational guidance for US whole-of-government planning and implementation activities within an affected country or region. The Secretariat is drawn from the USG interagency community as necessary to provide expertise in strategic assessment and planning, operations support, information management, resource mobilization, and strategic monitoring, as well as field team support and partner coordination. It will funnel requests for guidance, assistance, and support to the appropriate source and manage the process to get timely results. This central node works in the other direction as well: through standardized requests for information and reporting, the Secretariat manages the "Washington process" to avoid duplication or undue reporting burdens on implementers in the field. It works as a team to pull together the best possible whole-of-government response, within the context of, but not constrained by individual agency prerogatives.

e. Most importantly, the CRSG has overall responsibility for the development of the USG R&S Strategic Plan. To develop this plan, the CRSG executes an integrated planning process which ensures that the range of diplomatic, development, security, economic, trade, public affairs and strategic communication strategies, congressional consultations, and resource decisions are integrated and managed as part of overall engagement efforts.

f. The CRSG does not direct field operations. The COM retains control of all USG activities in country that are not under the authority of the GCC. The CRSG does not have a direct role in military operational planning conducted at the GCC(s). However, DOD representatives on the CRSG will provide relevant input from GCC planning into the development of the USG Strategic Plans. In addition, JS representatives on the CRSG will translate relevant portions of USG strategic planning into military operational planning through the existing Joint Operational Planning Process (JOPP). At the GCC, the IPC will harmonize its planning guidance with the JOPP and represent civilian implementation plans, resources, and expertise.

g. The JS is the appropriate US military organization to be an MME process lead and to ensure that MME(s) are supported by GCC planning and execution as necessary. Elements of the JS should be prepared to lead and support integrated strategic planning as described in the Practitioner's Guide of the *USG Planning Framework for Reconstruction, Stabilization, and Conflict Transformation* due to the different types of military plans over which they have cognizance.

h. DOD representatives at this level will forward department concerns to the CRSG for dispute resolution regarding proposed recommendations for R&S policy and planning – especially those that affect DOD authorities, policies, and resources. It is important that a unified position concerning the dispute be established inside the DOD to allow

DOD representatives on the CRSG to speak for the entire department. The CRSG should make every effort to resolve interagency disputes before raising them to the NSC DC for decision. The NSC co-chair of the CRSG plays an important role ensuring the CRSG anticipates the needs of higher-level decision makers, thus allowing policy recommendations to flow upward.

4. Operations Support

a. At the Washington-level there will be a need for the mobilization of logistics capabilities to support the functions of the CRSG, IPC, and the ACT. This support includes the following:

(1) Security

(2) Infrastructure (Room, board, water, sanitation)

(3) Transportation (Armored vehicles, transport systems)

(4) Administrative support (including Washington-based interpreter contracts)

(5) Communications

b. The military role in operations support will be vital and essential more than in any other area of planning and execution. Most of the support provided to an R&S operation at the beginning will come from the GCC – by designated military assets or through the use of contracts. The military will likely continue to provide support throughout the operation. It will be critical that the military contribution to the CRSG have the authority and capacity to plan and coordinate this support. It is essential that these support personnel understand the IMS and have a good familiarity with the functions and responsibilities of civilian agencies, particularly the DOS and USAID. It is also essential that the military representatives to the CRSG include personnel who fully understand the authorities and procedures for applying DOD funding and how to apportion funds.

c. There are three main phases of Washington-based Operations support:

(1) **Phase I – Planning Engagement**. The US R&S Strategic Plan and its Country Plan will include a logistics and security plan which will be developed with expertise from the Resource Mobilization team in the Secretariat with significant reach-back into all relevant agencies, particularly DOD. The logistics and security (force protection) plan will lay out the requirements, constraints, assumptions, timelines, current capacity in country, and current logistical footprint of the USG in country.

(2) **Phase 2 – Mobilization and Negotiation**. If the US already has representation and resources in country, the Secretariat and CRSG will work closely with the COM to support re-allocation for the new mission. This may include changes to SOPs, notifications to Congress, and a range of contractual and management shifts to be performed by agencies possessing those resources or assets, but coordinated by the Secretariat. Mobilization of resources and assets located elsewhere for "new" use in the country in

crisis will require identification of current supply-chain expected delivery timelines, decisions to re-divert assets to the crisis area, negotiations of warehousing space, air/sea/land transport, MOA(s) for sharing assets which are supported, coordinated, and monitored by the Secretariat but performed by the relevant agencies. The Secretariat, in coordinating this process, must be able to quickly push up to the CRSG information on critical bottlenecks or disputes so that they can be resolved with expediency. Most US embassies in countries where an R&S operation is likely to occur are not large and have very limited resources and assets. The assumption going in is that these resources, especially personnel, will require significant augmentation in all respects. Military planners should assume that all mission assets and logistics would have to be delivered to the US Mission AOR.

(3) **Phase 3 – Support and Sustainment**. The Secretariat will provide backstop to the "supported" management units outside of Washington. As the Secretariat works to design the scope and composition of the IPC and ACT in collaboration with the GCC and COM respectively, it will also obtain approval from the DC or PC to support these deployed elements with resources, mobilizing personnel, financial, logistical, and contractor resources in support of the plan, identifying legal constraints, and proposing legislative and budget recommendations to overcome limitations. The Secretariat will provide operations support by managing information and collection and implementation of best practices.

5. Geographic Combatant Command Relationship to the Country Reconstruction and Stabilization Group and Secretariat

a. The GCC does not have a direct or subordinate military chain of command relationship to the CRSG or its Secretariat. GCC relationships to the CRSG are established through the Joint Staff and the OSD representatives on the CRSG.

(1) According to 10 USC 164 and JP 1, a military chain of command is an uninterrupted flow of authority that extends from the President of the United States, to the Secretary of Defense, to the GCC, to subordinate military commanders, and finally to assigned or attached military forces. As such, channels of communication, direction, and other requests to and from the GCC will utilize existing channels established in US Code and military doctrine.

(2) If the circumstances warrant, a GCC (or a subordinate JFC) may be tasked to take guidance and direction from a COM. While not assigned to a COM, a GCC or subordinate JFC may take guidance and direction from a COM through Memorandum of Agreement (MOA) or other official document delineating the directive relationship between the COM and JFC.

b. Under the IMS, OSD and JS participants on the CRSG Secretariat's SPT will assume roles and perform planning functions that are not part of the JOPP and not defined in the Joint Operation Planning and Execution System (JOPES). It is imperative that the JS participants on the CRSG Secretariat's SPT have the capability to conduct rapid operational mission analysis to determine scope, scale and duration of the military's role in supporting a proposed USG course of action and development of MMEs, including the role of leading an MME. To do this the GCC may be tasked to provide an operation planning team (OPT) to support the JS planning contribution.

c. In addition to coordination with interagency elements assigned to the GCC (e.g., JIACG), IPC members deployed to the GCC will perform liaison functions with the CRSG Secretariat's SPT to assist in harmonizing the civilian and military planning processes and operations. This creates a potential new channel of communication between the GCC and the CRSG. Careful consideration must be taken into account to not interrupt the authorities that extend from the President of the United States to the GCC through the Secretary of Defense. The leadership of the IPC must keep the GCC leadership apprised of communications with the CRSG. Coordination between the IPC and CRSG does not obviate the defense policy guidance and plan approval process as established by law and through DOD procedures. The IPC leadership will have frequent communications with and seek guidance from both the COM and CRSG regarding:

(1) the strategic plan and its integration with the military operational plan;

(2) identifying and addressing gaps and deficiencies between the civilian and military plans;

(3) identifying impacts of planned military operations on future R&S efforts;

(4) and recommending processes and criteria to ensure smooth transition from military to civilian lead (what the military refers to as Phase V planning), when appropriate, by function and region as the environment is stabilized.

6. Geographic Combatant Command Relationships to other Departments and Agencies through the Country Reconstruction and Stabilization Group

The GCC relationship to the CRSG will be established through representatives from the OSD and the JS while reinforcing the integrity of authorities established between the JFC and the Secretary of Defense. Its relationship to other agencies and departments represented on the CRSG will be indirect and established through and coordinated with DOD representatives on the CRSG, preferably formalized at the CRSG level – although, informal, working-level action officer relationships may be established through its Secretariat. In addition, the IPC may facilitate the GCC relationship to other departments and agencies represented on the CRSG through proper coordination involving the DOD representatives on the CRSG.

Intentionally Blank

CHAPTER VI
INTEGRATION PLANNING CELL PARTICIPATION IN THE
GEOGRAPHIC COMBATANT COMMAND

1. Introduction

a. The IPC is an interagency team that brings operation-specific capabilities to a geographic combatant command or an equivalent multinational HQ. It is a scalable, tailored, civilian-led interagency R&S team that embeds into the combatant command planning staff. The IPC is established by, and reports to, the CRSG through the Washington-based whole-of-government planning process. Its purpose is to support civilian-military communication and harmonize civilian and military planning in order to achieve unity of effort. The size and composition of the IPC will change over the course of the planning for and execution of the R&S operation. The IPC is not designed to create a USG civilian R&S operations/tactical plan; that responsibility resides with the COM and the AMEMB. An IPC associated with a combatant command should not be confused with the strategic level Interagency Policy Committee. The same acronym, IPC, may be used for both. The context will help determine which IPC is being referenced. However, in this handbook the acronym "IPC" is used to refer to the "Integration Planning Cell". The "Interagency Policy Committee" is herein always spelled out.

b. An IPC may be established in response to:

(1) an emerging crisis potentially requiring military intervention or support,

(2) a DOD request for assistance with operational-level R&S planning, or

(3) a request from an equivalent multinational military HQ (i.e., UN Peacekeeping force, EU, AU or NATO).

c. R&S operations that do not involve significant military engagement normally do not require the establishment of an IPC. Harmonization of civilian and military planning is not limited to the establishment of an IPC or to crises. Working relationships between civilian and military planners should be developed on an on-going basis.

d. The IPC reports to the CRSG, it does not "work" for the GCC. This is an important distinction. For a specified mission, IPC members serve as a bridge between civilian agency staff in Washington and the field to the combatant command. They fill the civilian agency gap at the military operational level and ensure planning and decisions by civilian agency participants in Washington and the field are represented in and informed by planning and decision-making at the military operational HQ. However, unlike the combatant command in the military chain of command, the IPC has neither oversight nor control over USG field operations.

e. The size and composition of the IPC will be determined by the CRSG based upon operation-specific requirements from the GCC. While the final decision regarding where best to embed an incoming IPC rests with the GCC, this relationship will be discussed within the CRSG and is expected to facilitate direct involvement with the J3, J5 and existing interagency coordination or advising entities. Any combatant command to which an IPC is deployed will be responsible to provide necessary resources to include: work space, communications, and computers that are compatible with their operating systems. Deploying and operating an IPC at a multinational HQ will require special considerations for information sharing, staff skill-set, political sensitivities, and organizational structure and culture.

2. Capabilities

a. The IPC is a scalable, tailored, civilian-led interagency team that advises the combatant command planning staff. Each IPC will vary in structure based on the mission and available civilian resources. The composition of the IPC team enables it to provide expertise in R&S functional issues, the region/country, functional sectors, USG agencies and bureaus and their ongoing planning, and metrics, conflict assessment, planning processes of civilian agencies and knowledge of the whole-of-government process laid out in the *USG Planning Framework for Reconstruction, Stabilization, and Conflict Transformation.*

b. It is this operation-specific set of capabilities that distinguishes the IPC from other pre-existing interagency elements of the Combatant Command, such as a Joint Interagency Coordination Group (JIACG) or other interagency staff element. It is important to recognize the IPC is unique and distinct from these entities which will continue to execute their essential functions in support of the GCC(s) overall regional and steady-state missions.

c. IPC members have the capability to reach back into the expertise of the home Departments/Agencies and to obtain real-time information on corresponding civilian Department/Agency planning, which normally occurs both at civilian HQ and field locations. This enables the IPC to support the combatant command in integrating the evolving civilian components of the USG R&S Strategic Plan, Interagency Country Level Plan, and Department/Agency implementation plans with the military plan for operations. The goal is to create one unified USG plan with clearly assigned tasks.

d. IPC members should fully understand the strategic planning process, the approved USG R&S Strategic Plan, and resources available to implement it. This allows the IPC to provide insight on policy guidance and assumptions. In cases where the strategic planning process is still underway, the deployed IPC will consult with the combatant command to identify potential policy issues and, as appropriate, make recommendations to the CRSG. IPC members, whenever possible, should have a solid working knowledge of the military and the military planning process and system. This working knowledge will immeasurably aid in the smooth integration of civilian and military developed plans.

3. Leadership and Structure

The IPC will be led by a senior level civilian with significant crisis response experience who is a peer of and has direct access to the GCC. The team leader is responsible for setting priorities and communicating with the CRSG and COM. If a deputy is required

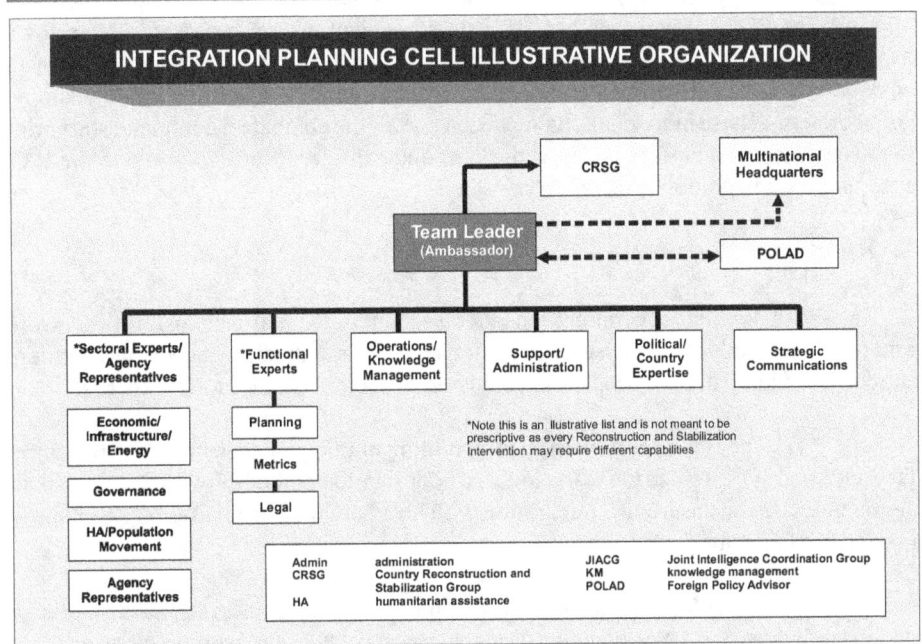

Figure VI-1. Integration Planning Cell Illustrative Organization

based on the size of the mission, he/she will also be a senior civilian, though not necessarily a peer ranked officer to the GCC. Although not required, it is likely that the team leader and the deputy will come from different agencies. For example, the team leader might come from the DOS and the deputy may come from the USAID. Below the leadership there will be leads for sections including, but not limited to: internal operations and information management; planning; support for administrative needs; political/country expertise, and strategic communication. Each IPC also has scalable capabilities, which include sectoral experts and agency representatives. The figure below provides an illustrative example.

4. Combatant Command Relationship to the Integration Planning Cell

a. The IPC will work closely with many individuals and offices within the combatant command to ensure coordination and unity of purpose including the CCDR, the J-Codes, the numerous non-standing boards, centers, and cells established for crisis planning, the joint interagency coordination group (JIACG) or its equivalent, and the political advisor (POLAD) or foreign policy advisor (FPA), as in the case of USAFRICOM, and the senior development advisor. The IPC will also need to have relationships with relevant functional elements at the combatant command which may or may not be located in 'J-Codes.' These may include: intelligence, logistics, policy/strategy, plans, resourcing (especially contracting), effects, engineering, medical, and civil affairs. Since not every combatant command is the same, the entry points for the IPC may vary. The JIACG, the POLAD or another section with interagency responsibilities (such as the J-3, J-5 or J-9), may facilitate the integration of the IPC into the combatant command.

b. The POLAD and the JIACG, or its equivalent do not necessarily have R&S expertise. However, the IPC will probably consider inviting the POLAD, senior development advisor, and JIACG representation to participate in its meetings to facilitate planning collaboration. These individuals, having been part of the combatant command staff prior to the emergence of any crisis, know the staff and can serve a bridging role to the IPC, speeding the integration process.

5. Roles and Responsibilities

a. Each IPC has a combination of roles, functions, and responsibilities. Core functions include: IPC leadership, operations and information management, planning, support for administrative needs, and provision of sectoral and regional expertise.

(1) The **IPC operations and information management element** will prioritize, facilitate, and synchronize the workflow and coordination of the IPC with the combatant command staff and ensure IPC integration with host networks, databases and systems to maximize information flow.

(2) The **IPC plans element** will comprise the USG planners that have a thorough understanding of the USG Planning Framework and DOD (as well as other agency) planning tools. IPC members supporting ongoing combatant command planning and operations may include personnel skilled in current operations and others skilled in transition or future operations.

(3) The **administrative support element** manages administrative functions for the team to include coordination of travel, billeting, meals, transportation, office space, supplies, and communications.

(4) **Sectoral and regional expert(s)** provide expert functional knowledge and skills based on requirements for the operation as determined by the CRSG. These skills may include but are not limited to: country, economic, IDP/migration, infrastructure, legal/rule of law, policy, strategic communication, and or security advisor.

6. Relationship to Combatant Command Staff

a. The IPC has a hierarchical/subordinate relationship with the CRSG. This means that the IPC receives its guidance directly from and reports back to the CRSG. The IPC leadership will keep the combatant command leadership apprised of communications with the CRSG. Coordination between the IPC and CRSG does not supersede the defense policy guidance and plan approval process as established by DOD procedures. The IPC and OSD/Joint Staff representatives on the CRSG will keep the CRSG informed of military planning and operations so that the planning process can take into account the military operations and their potential effects. The IPC may complement the GCC's intentions and/or concerns to the CRSG as they are brought to the CRSG via military channels (the JCS or OSD reps). Additionally, IPC leadership in consultation with the GCC will determine which information and policy guidance requests to or from the combatant command have sufficient importance or interagency implications (to include consideration of consistency with the existing plan) needing referral to the CRSG for decision. Finally, if necessary, disputes among interagency partners within the IPC or between the IPC and the combatant command will be referred to the CRSG if unresolved at lower levels.

b. The JIACG, POLAD or other sections with interagency responsibilities, may facilitate the integration of the IPC into the combatant command. The POLAD is normally an ambassador assigned as the GCC's senior political advisor. The JIACG (or its equivalent) is an advisory group at the combatant command, which will normally have one or two DOS officers, as well as a USAID officer, among others. The POLAD and the JIACG are steady-state entities within the combatant command. They do not necessarily have R&S expertise. However, the IPC should consider inviting both the POLAD, senior development advisor, and JIACG representation to participate in its meetings to facilitate planning collaboration.

c. The POLAD will have a role in the mission of the IPC however; their primary role remains the same - advising and helping the GCC remain focused on regional issues. Much like the POLAD, the JIACG members are regional generalists and have as their primary mission the responsibility of assisting the GCC and his staff and maintain a more regional focus. Not all combatant commands will have JIACG(s), but they should have some form of an interagency staff element. Another primary combatant command staff contact is the J-5. Their duties may vary from combatant command to combatant command; however, they normally will include long-term planning and military-to-military contacts/relationships. Regular contact among the IPC, POLAD, JIACG and J-5 is necessary to coordinate efforts and ensure that no process or task is overlooked. The division of labor should be addressed early on once an IPC arrives at the combatant command.

7. Combatant Command Planning in Conjunction with the Integration Planning Cell

a. The IPC is not a planning body. Nevertheless, it has a planning role advising and ensuring that military plans and the R&S plan are de-conflicted. It is likely that when the IPC arrives at a combatant command to assist in harmonizing the USG R&S plan with the military planning effort, the GCC and staff will have already begun the planning process in response to the GCC's or Secretary of Defense's direction, perhaps initially independent of a decision to undertake whole-of-government planning or response. Ideally, the relevant combatant command staff will have participated in the development of the situation analysis overview and can use this information to inform its planning efforts.

b. While the IPC is deployed to the combatant command they may develop products that inform the combatant command staff. These products may include:

(1) Briefing slides capturing issues for COM and/or CRSG decision and provide a situation update, including proposed changes to the USG R&S Strategic Plan.

(2) Information to combatant command planners on individual civilian agency implementation plans, and MME deliberations.

(3) Generated slides for the GCC on ACT activities and assessments, including those from FACT(s) and USAID Disaster Assistance Response Team (DART)(s) located in the ACT area of operations.

8. Integration Planning Cell Lifecycle

a. IPC structure, composition, and size should change over time to meet the mission of the IPC and the combatant command (or multinational command). An IPC should be deployed as soon as practical to ensure civilian-agency representation within the military planning. In some cases and by mutual agreement, some IPC members may travel to the combatant command early to begin making the necessary arrangements for follow-on IPC members and to begin the planning with relevant combatant command sections. Similarly, civilian agency liaisons may have already established positive working relationships with the combatant command through steady-state work or contingency planning (in a whole-of-government context or through bi-lateral agency cooperation), and these individuals could prove valuable members of the IPC.

b. An IPC will generally experience six phases within its "lifecycle" as outlined below. Personnel composition and organization of the IPC may shift throughout these phases and there will be an ongoing evaluation of combatant command needs that can be met by the IPC.

(1) **Phase 1: Pre-Deployment**. Before deployment, the CRSG should determine initial IPC staff requirements– this might entail deploying certain experts immediately and placing others on standby pending recommendations made by the IPC Team Leader upon arrival at the combatant command. Pre-deployment training should occur during this time.

(2) **Phase 2: Arrival/Familiarization/Initial Effort**. Upon arrival, the IPC Core staff should work with the GCC and staff to determine appropriate IPC structure, composition, and size based on an evaluation of the requirements of the military operational planning process.

(3) **Phase 3: Main Effort/Planning**. The IPC should be at its most robust during this phase when the combatant command is heavily engaged in operational planning and developing/refining planning guidance for deployed units. Subject matter experts and civilian planners familiar with the USG R&S Strategic Plan will be most critical at this stage. As major planning guidance is sent to the field, the IPC should begin to assess who, if any, of their staff should forward deploy to the AMEMB, redeploy to their parent agency, or deploy to the CRSG Secretariat. Composition of the IPC might shift as well during this phase depending on the type of subject matter experts required during different phases of planning.

(4) **Phase 4: Planning Maintenance/Operational Awareness**. When the locus of planning and operations shifts to the field, the composition of the IPC must be re-adjusted based on the requirements of the combatant command and other elements of the IMS that might need visibility into combatant command activities. In general, to avoid duplication of AMEMB efforts, the IPC should start down-sizing during this phase

and shift its focus from heavy engagement in planning to maintaining operational awareness, advising on any future planning the combatant command might be undertaking or regional military-military efforts in support of the USG R&S Strategic Plan, or assist the AMEMB in justifying or clarifying military support requirements (for example, during the "Request for Forces" process). During this phase IPC staff might shift in composition from subject matter experts to more generalist based personnel who can support both planning and operations. Note: It is possible that during a major transition (e.g., from US military to civilian-led operations) the IPC Team Leader and GCC might recommend to the CRSG that the IPC ramp-up again to facilitate planning and communication during this transition and then again down-size.

(5) **Phase 5: Stand-down**. As the operation matures and the role of the combatant command diminishes, some IPC staff should remain at the combatant command to maintain basic advisory, awareness, and reach-back capabilities. Eventually a recommendation should be made to the CRSG by the IPC Team Leader and GCC to stand-down the IPC. At this point, the CRSG will instruct the remaining IPC personnel to either return to their parent agencies or to support the R&S effort in Washington, DC, or the field.

(6) **Phase 6: After-action Review (AAR)**. Throughout the IPC's lifecycle and culminating in the stand-down phase, the IPC leader should direct an after-action review to capture IPC best practices and to document areas for improvement. A central location can serve as the locus for archiving and objectively reviewing the effectiveness of the IPC's contribution. Illustrative questions to address include timeliness of IPC's contributions, adequacy of personnel skill sets, and effective business processes for adding value to integrating the civilian and military response. The AAR should preferably involve soliciting feedback from the combatant command or multinational HQ element, and partners, such as the POLAD, senior development advisor, and interagency staff elements, as appropriate.

9. Combatant Command Logistics, Administration, and Communications Support to the Integration Planning Cell

a. The IPC may not deploy to a combatant command with all the necessary logistics and administrative support it will require to be effective. The GCC will have to provide some measure of both. The IPC will likely deploy with computers, satellite phones, and other basic necessities. In instances where this is not possible the combatant command will be informed of the logistics needs requiring support. OSD will endorse requests for IPC logistics and admin support. Normally, the GCC should be prepared to provide the following:

(1) reserve Hotel/lodging for IPC members near combatant command location;

(2) provide/coordinate for transportation to receive IPC members (as required);

(3) provide welcome packet that includes list of local restaurants, medical facilities, and other area amenities to IPC members;

(4) provide desk/work stations for each IPC member;

(5) provide conference room where IPC can meet as required; and

(6) provide administrative supplies (paper/envelopes/pens/pencils).

b. IPC personnel will arrive, in most cases, with computers and phones. The GCC should be prepared to provide network connectivity and accommodate the following equipment shortfalls when prior notification has been given:

(1) computers and monitors for both NIPR and SIPR Net for IPC members;

(2) printers (both color and black and white) sufficient for IPC members;

(3) FAX capability;

(4) sufficient telephones;

(5) sufficient secure telephones;

(6) photocopier access;

(7) VTC capability;

(8) server storage space for NIPR and SIPR to IPC members;

(9) NIPR and SIPR (with appropriate clearance) Net email accounts for all IPC members;

(10) training to IPC members on combatant command specific information management and information technology tools;

(11) Certify IPC members for use on combatant command NIPR/SIPR nets; and

(12) system maintenance/trouble-shooting capability (as needed).

10. Combatant Command Security Support to the Integration Planning Cell

a. Provide DOS S/CRS and/or IPC members information on passing of security clearances to the combatant command security officer (normally Secret – Level clearance is required).

b. Verify receipt of clearances prior to IPC deployment to the combatant command.

c. Provide security access badges to members of the IPC and access to areas within combatant command appropriate for the individual security level.

d. Provide secure storage of any classified materials.

e. Provide classified material destruction capability.

f. Provide storage of firearms as required for IPC law enforcement members.

g. Provide shipping capability of classified and bulk materials (as required).

Intentionally Blank

CHAPTER VII
MILITARY PARTICIPATION IN THE ADVANCE CIVILIAN TEAM

1. Introduction

a. The ACT assists in the integrating, and in certain roles, the implementing of civilian components of an R&S operation. When the demands of planning and executing an R&S mission are unable to be met by the existing civilian capacity in-country, the CRSG, in consultation with the COM, may deploy an ACT to the AMEMB or, where one is not present, establish a US presence. The ACT is designed to be flexible and scalable; as such an ACT deployed to one R&S crises may not have the same composition or size as another ACT. However, core aspects of the ACT such as mission, structure, processes, and authorities will remain consistent.

b. The ACT is comprised of personnel who deploy to provide additional capacity to existing and/or newly created structures and processes in an R&S environment. They operate under the guidance and authority of the COM. Country-level, whole-of-government structures and processes are the **integrated systems** at the country-level which provide the COM and JTF commander the capacity to integrate activities of all allocated assets in time, space, and purpose to achieve unity of effort. The ACT structures and processes do not exist apart from the COM and JTF commander. They include both new and existing structures, processes, and personnel, and originate from within the embassy and the JTF, when present. ACT personnel provide capabilities and capacities to support and if necessary assist in building integrated structures and processes.

c. The ACT works under the authority to the COM but will have working-level relationships with the CRSG, IPC, and the JTF when deployed. The ACT joins existing AMEMB personnel (if present) to provide specific R&S functions supporting the COM in executing the USG Country Plan. In the absence of a COM the ACT leader may be designated as the COM.

d. There are two scenarios that are most likely for the deployment and location of the ACT. In the first scenario, an AMEMB exists and a Chief of Mission (COM) is present. In this scenario the ACT will deploy to the US embassy and establish itself with the embassy. In the second scenario the US embassy either does not exist or, due to the circumstances on the ground, is vacant and untenable. In this case the ACT will deploy and co-locate with the JTF. The director of the ACT is appointed as COM or a designated COM is identified and the director of the ACT is answerable to the COM.

e. ACT personnel may be drawn from members of the US military. Personnel drawn from the US military should be fully trained and qualified to perform the functions necessary to support the ACT. Members of the US Military will be in the unique position of being part of an element of the IMS under the ultimate operational control of the COM, but being a member of a military unit deployed into theater under the ultimate operational control of a GCC. In these instances careful consideration should be made to determine what functions will be performed by these personnel. If the function is primarily liaison then the lines of authority remain with the sending organization. If however, military personnel are assigned or attached then an early determination must be made as to whose operational control they fall under; the COM or the GCC. This should be clearly laid out and put into writing utilizing a MOU or MOA between the GCC and COM or their designated representatives.

f. The ACT has the capability to perform the following functions for the R&S operation in country and on behalf of the COM:

(1) Integrate Planning and Resource Allocation

(a) Manages the development, maintenance, and revision of the country-level plan.

(b) Ensures a coordinated approach towards mobilizing resources.

(c) Supports the CRSG by monitoring the flow of assistance and in ensuring interagency programs are successfully addressing USG objectives.

(2) Integrate Operations

(a) Manages the sequencing, tasks, and activities related to implementing the R&S operation and plan.

(b) Maintains visibility over all activities and processes of the USG R&S operation.

(c) Provides decision support to the COM and R&S Integration Group.

(d) Facilitates agency and deployed element execution of COM and R&S Integration Group decisions.

(e) Ensures integration with the JTF in country.

(3) Integrate Information Management

(a) Provides a central repository for information, including: creating the capability to find and access information, deciding what information to seek, acquiring information, processing the information, organizing information, communicating information, and accessing information in support of planning and operations.

(b) Creates structures and manages processes to ensure that information is presented in the right way to the right person (or injected into the right process) at the right time.

(c) Facilitates the creation of a COP (for the CRSG, COM, or JTF commander).

(4) Integrate Strategic Communication

(a) Develops the overarching communication plan for the operation that identifies specific messages, recommends source and manner of conveyance (media, internet, posters) and assesses the results.

(b) Facilitates the coordination of embassy and joint force public communication activities.

(c) Serves as the main point of contact for media requests for issues not related to the joint force or its activities.

(d) Works with the CRSG to develop messages for international audiences.

(e) Integrates and enables sub-national messages with FACTs (and any other sub national implementation bodies).

(5) **Direct and Supports the FACT(s)**

(a) Supports the FACTs by providing sector specific reach-back, logistics, communications, contract support, assistance with the host government.

(b) Provide national-level direction to the FACTs as implementing bodies for the R&S Country-Level Plan.

(c) Provides the FACTs with clear statements of their tasks and purposes, informed or refined through consultation with FACT leadership.

(6) **Enabling Support for ACT and FACT Activities**. Supports expanded AMEMB and in-country activities by providing additional capabilities as required for new or additional functions resulting from the R&S operation.

2. Structure

a. The structure of the ACT and the processes it utilizes are derived from the functions it must perform to fulfill its mission. Though the scale and scope of the structure of the ACT will change depending on the R&S effort, the basic elements of the structure and their relationship to each other will not. The ACT structure includes the ACT leadership office, functional offices, an integration structure (the term used to refer to all the MME teams) and agency representation positions.

b. The functional teams are where the R&S-specific functional expertise of the AMEMB is housed. The functional teams may include: leadership, planning, resources, operations, security, strategic communication, situation analysis, monitoring and evaluation, and support. The size of each functional team depends on the R&S operation.

c. Military participation within the ACT structure will most likely occur within the functional teams, the integration structure, and agency representation positions depending on the scope and nature of the mission. This participation may go beyond the traditional security and logistics duties (commonly associated with military capabilities and applications) to include, but not limited to, participation within the integration structure and functional offices such as planning, operations, and situational assessment and analysis. In certain instances the military may be asked to lead an Objective Team, where multiple agencies are involved, within the integration structure. In these cases the military must be prepared to integrate its planning processes into whole-of-government planning processes envisioned in the *US Government Planning Framework for Reconstruction, Stabilization and Conflict Transformation.*

d. Certain capabilities and functions the military possesses may be of use and greatly contribute to various structures of the ACT. Military personnel such as civil affairs, psychological operations, engineers, military police and contracting officers, to name a few, offer a number of capabilities that could benefit multiple offices within the ACT beyond security and logistical applications. DOD civilians and contractors may also offer certain capabilities across multiple ACT offices depending on scope, nature of the mission, and the objectives. These capabilities may include specific subject matter expertise – both sectoral and functional, as well as reach-back to agency and CRSG counterparts to assist in informing strategic planning and transitioning strategic plans to country level planning and execution.

e. **Leadership**

(1) Just as the composition and make-up of the ACT is situation dependent, similarly the ACT leader positions could also vary. It may be possible for ACT leadership to range from a position subordinate to the DCM, to having the ACT leader also serving as COM. In this final scenario, it is important to stress that COM/DCM are distinct and broader functions from that of ACT leader, although one person could perform both functions. The ACT leadership office consists of the ACT leader, ACT deputy leader (at a minimum) and other necessary staff such as a chief of staff and aides. The various functions of the leadership office may be assigned in totality to the ACT leader and deputy leader or apportioned amongst a larger staff. The ACT leader is in charge of this office, though the daily operations of the office are managed by the chief of staff. The ACT leadership office is subordinate to the COM. It has a peer relationship with the JTF senior leadership (typically a Colonel or Brigadier General if the JTF is based on a brigade task force structure or an independent brigade structure) as well as the implementing agencies. It has a coordinating relationship with the CRSG secretariat and IPC.

(2) Critical from the earliest stages will be the need for close communications and coordination between the COM/ACT leader and the JTF commander. The COM has overall responsibility for implementing the R&S operation; and the JTF commander often has the preponderance of resources and capabilities. It is essential that these two principals communicate at all times. Success or failure of a US R&S operation in the field largely will depend on the COM/ACT leader and the JTF commander having a shared operational picture, an agreed plan and vision for its execution, and a shared process for raising and making decisions.

f. **Reconstruction and Stabilization Integration Group (RSIG)**

(1) The R&S Integration Group is a coordination and decision-making body chaired by the ACT leader. In military parlance the RSIG serves as the ACT team leader's 'senior staff'. The group consists of all Objective Team leads, FACT leaders (virtually), and functional team leads. The exact membership of the group is decided by the COM in consultation with the ACT leader and JTF commander (as appropriate). The group ensures unity of effort by integrating all in-country planning and execution across agencies, functional teams, and between the USG civilian and military actors. The RSIG adjudicates agency disputes and makes recommendations to the COM. It guides the work of the Objective Teams and functional teams. The R&S Integration Group and the ACT leader report to the COM. Performing integrating functions will sometimes require the RSIG to direct activities that involve agency equities. Some of the same personnel on the Country Team may be part of the RSIG and the Country Team can participate in meetings between the RSIG and the COM.

(2) **Responsibilities**

(a) Serve the functions of an executive steering committee – the primary senior consultative body for the US R&S mission in-country, make recommendations to the ACT leader and the COM.

(b) Direct the Objective Teams and FACTs on behalf of the ACT leader or COM.

(c) Responsible for cross-objective issues, results, and objectives.

(d) Makes priority, sequencing, and resource decisions, among objectives prioritization and de-confliction between Objective Teams, responsible for managing cross-objective issues, compile and de-conflict Objective Team plans in the drafting of the R&S country-level plan.

(e) Provides non-binding guidance to agencies - guidance may then proceed to COM to make binding as needed, arbitrate between agencies.

(f) Create Objective Teams and sub-Objective Teams as instructed by the ACT Team Leader, create task forces and other cross-objective working level groups as needed.

(g) De-conflict and approve R&S synchronization matrix compiled by the ACT Operations Section.

(h) Integrate JTF and USG civilian response.

(i) Works with relevant IGOs, international and local partners on planning and integration issues, as delegated by the COM.

g. **Integration Structure**

The integration structure is the term used to refer to all the Objective Teams as a collective whole. The RSIG provides oversight of this structure by managing the Objective Teams. This structure is where whole-of-government processes take place to include planning, implementation, and operations. It represents a transformational way in which the USG organizes for an R&S mission. Instead of being organized by **how** the USG independently implements individual agency activities, the integration structure organizes the USG response by **why,** through focused synchronization of activities in time, space, and purpose by organizing MME(s) around outcomes to achieve a stated strategic objective. The number and focus of MME and Objective Teams are determined by the US Strategic Plan for R&S as issued by the CRSG.

h. **Objective Teams**

(1) Objective Teams are whole-of-government teams organized around either cross-cutting issues (e.g. anti-corruption, anti-drug, rule of law, trade) or the major missions elements (MMEs) of the US Strategic Plan for R&S. The mission of the Objective Teams is to conduct planning and implementation management (i.e. operations) to ensure integration of the activities. The Objective Teams are subject to direction from the R&S Integration Group and the COM. The Objective Teams work across agencies to achieve common objectives. Any disputes that cannot be resolved within the Objective Team can be sent to the R&S Integration Group for arbitration.

(2) It is likely that the agency with the preponderance of assets allocated to the Objective Team and/or for whom the subject of the Objective Team is the core competency of the agency will be asked to provide the Objective Team leader. However, the Objective Team leader position could be a whole-of-government position instead of an agency position. Depending on the size of the operation, the Objective Team leader may be assigned to the AMEMB with no additional duties or obligations to his/her home agency. The Objective Team leaders are appointed by the COM in consultation with the ACT leader, CRSG, and JTF commander, as appropriate. The Objective Team leader is also the main representative for the Objective Team on the R&S Integration Group. The Objective Team leader may have staff to assist in the management of the working-group. This staff is provided by the ACT functional teams.

(3) The Objective Teams consists of personnel from a variety of sources to include participating agencies, functional teams, regional sectoral experts, and the JTF. Objective teams are defined by the COM in consultation with the ACT leader and the CRSG, based on the needs of the operation and the R&S Strategic Plan. Existing AMEMB structures that are not R&S related continue to operate; however, existing working-groups that are R&S related should be re-organized or re-named as Objective Teams, as defined by the COM, to ensure whole-of-government integration.

(4) Objective teams are the primary points of integration with sectoral or task organized teams of adjacent JTF, HN, or international elements. Objective teams may convene together with JTF, HN, or multinational structures for planning and implementation management in order to maximize integration. In more complex environments that call for the use of FACTs, the Objective Teams also provide FACTs with the substantive capabilities required to make them effective.

i. Sub-objective Teams

(1) The Objective Team leader may organize the team into smaller sub-objective working-groups. At the heart of these teams are the managers for the programs that will bring about the condition described in the sub-objective statement. In complex environments sub-objective working-groups are likely to be the main working-level unit of integration in the AMEMB. They may also be the point of daily substantive working-level integration with other USG elements in country, HN ministries, JTF planning cells, or UN organizations.

(2) The sub-objective Team is subordinate to the Objective Team leader and a peer to other Sub-objective Teams within its objective area and all other MME(s). Integration and coordination with sub-objective Teams within an objective area are done under the direction of the Objective Team leader. Coordination with other sub-objective Teams outside of the objective area is directed by the ACT Deputy Leader or the RSIG.

(3) ACT functional offices provide additional capacity to the sub-objective Team by providing planning, operations, and other functions. Whole-of-government integration necessitates the JTF planning and execution of tasks assigned to the sub-objective should be coordinated within the confines of the Objective Team and sub-Objective Team structure to ensure unity of effort between civilian and military implementation activities. Sub-objective Teams may require additional subject related expertise. In such cases, the ACT will deploy subject matter experts to advise and assist the team.

j. Planning Team

(1) The planning team provides planning expertise and capacity to the AMEMB. Members of the planning team are allocated to specific Objective Teams to assist in the creation and maintenance of the country-level plan. Planning Officers are whole-of-government planners and do not represent any one department or agency. Planning officers have a role before Objective Teams are established by supporting the situation analysis cell or articulating objectives (aka MMEs). The planning team is the first point of integration for related functional teams of the JTF, UN, HN, or other entities. The planning team works closely with FACT planners to ensure integration of national and sub-national planning as well as ensure the FACT planners have all the tools they need to be successful.

(2) The military possesses significant planning capabilities which can contribute to this team. This will be especially critical when the military is involved in the response effort utilizing whole-of-government planning and the IMS. Ensuring overall planning integration with the JTF of activities that affect the R&S planning and implementation will be a vital function military planners perform in support of this team. Providing planning assistance and support to the Objective Teams and the RSIG for the development of the R&S Country-Level Plan is an example of a requirement where military planners from the JTF or geographic combatant command may apply their planning expertise.

k. **Resource Team**

(1) The Resource Team consists of whole-of-government resource expertise and capacity. The size and composition of this team will depend greatly on the mechanisms used by Congress and the CRSG to fund the operation. For example, in the event the ACT is allocated contingency funding, the Resource Team coordinates the drafting of additional project proposals for approval by the COM and submission to Washington. The Resource Team is not intended to replace existing funding mechanisms already operating in-country, but rather ensures USG resource reflect a coherent policy.

(2) The Resource Team develops integrated and synchronized resource planning and maintains visibility over all funding issues for the COM. The Resource Team Director serves as the financial advisor for the R&S Integration Group, the Country Team, and the Chief of Mission. Members of the Resource Team support the Objective Teams to assist with resource planning, acquisition, and application.

(3) Military personnel detailed to the ACT or operationally controlled by the JFC may be assigned or requested to provide support to the ACT Resource Team. This may occur if Congress appropriates contingency funds to DOD for use in R&S related activities. The Resource Team will integrate the use of these funds to best support Objective Teams to accomplish the objectives stated in the R&S Country-Level Plan. Ultimately, the agency that received the appropriated funds is responsible and accountable for their use per existing laws and regulations. It is for this reason that it is critical the military establish a relationship with this office either through the assignment of a detailee or by tasking the appropriate JTF personnel to support the mission of this office.

(4) Military comptrollers or a designated fund manager, either assigned to or tasked to support the ACT, should assist the Resource Team with budget planning and reporting functions pertaining to their agency fund, providing fiscal accountability, and tracking DOD resources applied to the R&S operation.

(5) Contracting officers, representing DOD or one of its Service components, will be needed to support this team if DOD funds are used - through the execution of a contract relating to R&S activities. These contracting officers will provide needed contracting capabilities, under DOD authority, to support the execution of R&S activities by ACT elements.

(6) Representatives from the JTF Staff Judge Advocate Office may also be requested to assist this team to provide legal expertise as needed concerning matters related to JTF activities and authorities regarding contracting and fund uses applied to R&S operations.

(7) Military personnel detailed personnel to the Resource Team will depend on the size and scope of the R&S operation and the level of military involvement. However, the type of personnel (comptrollers, contracting officers, and military lawyers) mentioned above are in "low-density" military occupation specialty career fields. It may be more feasible for the JTF to designate representatives (e.g. CORs, fund managers) from the existing military detailees assigned to the ACT HQ. The JTF could then task its offices

(Comptroller, Contracting, and Staff Judge Advocate) to support the Resource Team in the form of reach-back for the designated military representatives detailed to the ACT.

l. **Operations Team**

(1) The Operations Team ensures the execution, synchronization, and integration of all R&S activities during the operation. The Operations Team works closely with all ACT elements to enable them elements to carry out their mission in accordance with the R&S Country-Level Plan.

(2) The primary tasks of the Operation Team are to:

(a) Maintain visibility over all activities and processes of the USG R&S operation;

(b) Provide decision support to the R&S Integration Group and the COM;

(c) Facilitate agency and deployed element compliance with R&S Integration Group and COM and decisions; and

(d) Facilitate support/enablement to FACTs.

(3) Personnel from the Operations Team are assigned to Objective Teams to support and maintain awareness of current and future operations. Operations officers coordinate all activities in time, space, and purpose. They are responsible for communicating decisions and direction to implementing agencies for the execution of tasks in accordance with the R&S Country-Level Plan.

(4) The Operations Team supports FACT operations and maintains the flow of information necessary to achieve unity of effort between the USG and other contributing partners. The Operations Team maintains visibility over the actions of all USG entities operating within the jurisdiction of the ACT and ensures that all orders and request for information are executed in a timely manner.

(5) The Operations Team will exchange liaison officers with the JTF to ensure unity of effort and purpose. The burden of facilitating communication between the AMEMB and the JTF will likely be placed on the JTF liaison officer to the AMEMB. The AMEMB will view the JTF as having overwhelming resources in comparison to it. However, this will not limit the utilization of civilian liaisons officers to the JTF for time sensitive and critical operations.

(6) Depending on the scope and scale of military participation in the R&S operation and the requirements of the Operations Team, the ACT may request the JTF to provide communications equipment (computers, network infrastructure, AV equipment), to enable an integrated R&S COP, and the necessary personnel to set-up and maintain this equipment – either by detail or liaison assignment. This will ensure communications connectivity with the JTF and in tracking the movement of military assets affecting the

R&S operation, in time, space, and purpose. Military detailees or JTF liaison officers assigned to support this team may assist in the development and management of systems for collecting, integrating, and disseminating information and reports between the JTF and the ACT.

m. **Monitoring and Evaluation Team**

(1) The Monitoring and Evaluation Team collects data and translates it into information that allows decision-makers to assess the progress of the R&S operation. Individual departments, such as DOD, will maintain their own monitoring and evaluation processes as required by law, however in an R&S operation the COM will require a whole-of-government monitoring and evaluation capability. To do this, the Monitoring and Evaluation Team will utilize existing data collection systems whenever possible, and coordinate with agencies' own requirements for metrics and program reporting.

(2) The Monitoring and Evaluation Team will collect both output and outcome indicators. Team members will provide support and capacity to Objective Teams and will work with the relevant USG agencies to gather metrics data. It is critical that the initial short-term metrics and processes are synchronized with and complement longer-term metrics and processes. This information is one source used by the Situation Analysis Team to determine whether USG actions are appropriately changing the environment to attain USG strategic goals.

(3) Service members detailed to the ACT or military units operationally controlled by the JTF may be requested to assist and support the development and collection of outcome and output metrics to monitor and evaluate the execution of the R&S Country-Level Plan. The proximity of military units, and their ability to maneuver and conduct patrols in hostile environments, make them a valuable resource to collect the data that is necessary to inform the outcome metrics. The AMEMB will coordinate with the JTF through its Joint Assessment Working Group (or other JTF element with similar responsibilities) to collect data pertaining to its R&S activities for whole-of-government monitoring and evaluation purposes.

n. **Situation Analysis Team**

(1) The Situation Analysis Team provides decision-makers and planners with an accurate understanding of the environment, to include the current situation, as well as medium- and long-term trends. The Situation Analysis Team facilitates and supports the development and continual refinement of a common, interagency understanding of the environment. This team is responsible for developing products for the COM, the County Team, the R&S Integration Group, the Planning Team, and Objective Teams. The team consists of whole-of-government personnel working with liaisons from other agencies and the Political Section in the AMEMB. The Intelligence Community plays an important role, as do liaisons with sectoral or regional expertise.

(2) The Situation Analysis Team coordinates closely with the JTF J2, producing joint products and sharing information extensively. The JTF, combatant command, or

other elements of DOD may detail personnel through temporary assignment or send liaison officers to support the activities of this team. These personnel support the various functions of this team by providing analysis perspectives from the JTF, combatant command, and DOD. These perspectives assist the team in developing a whole-of-government analysis of the situation.

o. **Security Team**

(1) Most R&S deployments will require an ACT Security Team. The Security Team plans, develops, implements, and manages security programs to protect USG facilities, information, and personnel deployed in support of the R&S operation. Security Teams operate under existing DOS rules and regulations governing overseas security operations. Where there is an existing AMEMB and a Regional Security Officer (RSO) the ACT Security Team will provide direct support to and/or augment the existing Regional Security Office. The team will operate under existing COM security policies.

(2) A Security Team is staffed and organized to meet the operational and security requirements of the R&S operation. Security Teams are headed by a DS Special Agent Security Officer who reports directly to the ACT Team Leader. Team composition will be tailored for each deployment and may include DS Special Agents, Security Engineering Officers, Security Technical Specialists, Security Protective Specialists, or other DS security professionals and specialists. Teams may be augmented, when appropriate and resources are available, by Marine Security Force/Fleet Antiterrorism Support Team(s) (MCSF/FAST).

(3) In uncertain or hostile environments the Security Team may require additional security assistance, both static and mobile, from the JTF. These environments may require the ACT to co-locate with elements of the JTF inside the confines of their operating bases. In these circumstances Security Team will need to coordinate with JTF base commanders and their security and force protection representatives to ensure proper alignment of security and force protection procedures. It should be noted that the COM still maintains control over members of the ACT regardless of their location on or off of a JTF operating base. The COM can direct members of the ACT to follow the established force protection and security procedures of the JTF operating base at which they may be located.

(4) In permissive environments, where a AMEMB has already been established, the ACT may not co-locate with the JTF. Force protection and security coordination between the ACT and JTF, under these circumstances, become more complex. As these two elements separate, the reporting chain, communications, and authorities become more distinct. Elements of the JTF adhere to the guidance of their commanders largely informed by military risk and threat assessments. Elements of the ACT adhere to the guidance of the COM and the directives and procedures issued by the Security Team. These are largely informed by their own risk and threat assessments, which may incorporate a different set of criteria than the military's threat and risk assessments.

p. **Strategic Communication Team**

(1) When there is significant USG presence in-country, there may be a need to provide direct assistance to the public affairs section of an AMEMB. When there is limited or no USG presence, a Strategic Communication Team may be formed to provide similar functions. The Strategic Communication Team provides the COM, the Country Team, and Objective Teams with added capacity to create, coordinate, target, synchronize, and integrate messages to both HN and international audiences. Additionally, they work with the JTF to ensure unity of message. Public affairs (PA), information operations (IO), psychological operations (PSYOP), and other specialties that support the strategic communication in the joint force will have significant interaction with the Strategic Communication Team.

(2) Strategic communication personnel do not represent any one department or agency. They assist in identifying specific messages and information that needs to be conveyed, selects how the conveyance will take place, and works with the Monitoring and Evaluation Team to measure the results of the effort. The Strategic Communication Team also works extensively with equivalent functions in the FACTs to integrate and enable sub-national messages. This team is also the main point of contact for media requests.

q. **Support Team**

(1) The Support Team provides logistical and administrative support to the AMEMB, the FACT(s), and all related R&S activities and programs. The Support Team may provide direct assistance to the Management Office of an AMEMB or may be a separate entity depending on the operation. Part of the Support Team may be located out-of-country if specific functions can be provided more effectively and inexpensively. Functions located out-of-country may consist of tasks such as voucher processing and human resources paperwork.

(2) When military personnel are assigned to the ACT as detailees or in a liaison capacity support requirements for them will arise. Military personnel detailed or performing liaison functions to the ACT will utilize, as their primary source, reach-back provided by a deployed JTF such as human resources (personnel), finance and other related administrative and support capabilities. If the JTF and ACT occupy separate locations, the Support Team may serve a coordinating function with the support elements of the JTF for these personnel. Depending on the nature and level of military participation within the ACT, JTF support elements may choose to co-locate their own representatives within the Support Team to ensure an adequate level of service is attained for the military personnel assigned to support the activities of the ACT.

3. Joint Task Force Relationship to the Advance Civilian Team

a. The GCC will have a pre-existing relationship with the COM(s) inside the country or region where the R&S response effort is focused. Their relationship is formalized in 22 USC 3927, which states that the COM has "full responsibility" for the direction, coordination, and supervision of all government executive branch employees in the country (except for ... employees under the command of United States area military commander). This pre-existing, "steady state" (Which the military commonly associates with: military engagement, security cooperation, and deterrence activities) relationship with the COM and country team will greatly inform the initial planning of a JTF in support of the R&S operation while participating within the IMS.

b. This ACT is not a standing structure on a country team and its lifecycle will coincide with the activities surrounding the R&S effort. Similarly, the JTF, deployed by the GCC, to support the R&S effort will have a lifecycle that coincides with the planning and implementation activities related to the R&S operation. Both the ACT and JTF will focus its efforts on executing the R&S Country Plan with the ACT taking a lead role while the JTF will primarily serve in a supporting role.

c. There are two likely scenarios, mentioned in the introduction of this chapter, relating to the roles and responsibilities of the JTF and ACT relationship. In the first scenario the ACT will be deployed into the crisis country and will take up residence either in the US embassy compound or in a securable location close by. The JTF will be located either at an airport of debarkation or seaport of debarkation (APOD/SPOD) nearest the national capitol. All capitols with almost no exceptions have APOD(s)/SPOD(s) in close proximity to the city limits; securing them is critical to the follow-on needs of the R&S mission. The JTF will need to create a secure operating environment and lines of communication between the APOD/SPOD and the AMEMB compound. In coordination with the regional security officer (RSO) and diplomatic security (DS), the JTF will assess the operating environment in and around the AMEMB. Securing APOD(s)/SPOD(s) and the AMEMB will be initial tasks for the JTF.

d. Establishing and maintaining lines of communications will evolve. They may begin as satellite phone communications, evolve towards rotary-wing shuttles and then to road links between the two HQ as the security situation matures. Or, dependent on the nature of the threat, they may evolve from satellite phone and radio communications, to ground transport, and then the development of air transport through secure corridors. A critical security task the JTF will assume as soon as diplomatic conditions warrant will be the protection and movement of diplomatic missions to the government entities of the host country. As conditions warrant, this function may be assumed by armed diplomatic security or by a private security contractor under the direction and management of DS and the RSO.

e. In the second scenario, where a US embassy is either not present or vacated, the situation is changed. The JTF will still have responsibility for securing the APOD/SPOD and establishing the JTF presence at and around it. There will not be the responsibility for securing the non-existent embassy until such time as one is established or re-established. The ACT and the COM, in this scenario, will co-locate with the JTF HQ and operate out of its base. The task of providing for the security of diplomatic missions to and from the functioning government entities will be more challenging since APOD(s)/SPOD(s) are usually more distant from government facilities than embassies. Also in this scenario the COM and the JTF commander decide how they wish to be included in each other's daily meetings and briefings. They can either choose to attend themselves or rely on deputies to do so for them. Coordination between the COM and JTF commander are greatly facilitated by proximity in this scenario. In this scenario, it is likely that when security conditions improve, the COM and ACT will choose to locate at a facility closer to the host country's national seat of power. Preparations should be made to enable this transition.

4. Joint Task Force Planning in Conjunction with the Advance Civilian Team

a. The draft *USG Planning Framework for Reconstruction, Stabilization and Conflict Transformation* does not seek to replace the methodologies and processes by which a JTF will plan. Rather, it establishes the methodology and process for developing a Country Plan and provides guidance on what aspects of JTF implementation plans must be shared with other USG participants and the implementation planning team.

b. A JTF will utilize the planning processes outlined in JP 5-0, *Joint Operation Planning*, to devise a plan or order. The joint operation planning process (JOPP) consists of seven steps: initiation; mission analysis; course of action development; course of action analysis and war-gaming; COA comparison; COA approval; and plan or order development. This planning process has served the military well in operations involving the use of conventional warfare. However, recent experiences in R&S operations have exposed limitations in this process. JOPP is mainly centered on the achievement of military objectives. This process does not sufficiently address the whole-of-government approach to planning in environments that are highly complex, confusing, and ill-structured, which more accurately depicts the reality of the interconnectedness between the drivers of conflict in societies embroiled in a conflict. JOPP was not designed to produce a plan that is implemented through an integrated whole-of-government effort, which is necessary to achieve the desired objectives in a highly complex post-conflict environment.

c. The ACT's overall responsibility is to implement the USG Strategic Plan for R&S through development and management of the Country Plan, under the leadership of the Chief of Mission. Country-level planning is an iterative process to synchronize diplomatic, development, economic and defense implementation planning and tasks through a comprehensive approach to achieve the USG R&S Strategic Plan. This whole-of-government process identifies additional planning requirements, potential impediments, and assumptions regarding the environment. It establishes a timeline for implementation, priority tasks, lead and supporting USG agencies, authorities and cross-sector linkages and sequencing. This continuous planning process is the mechanism to communicate feedback, identify resource and logistics requirements, and conduct monitoring and evaluation while ensuring the flexibility of USG operations.

d. The country-level planning process will create specific actions required to be taken by implementing agencies. Under the guidance of the RSIG, the Objective Teams will generate specific action requirements. These are transmitted to the Operations Team, which publishes and sends them to specific implementing agencies assigned to the requirement.

e. All JFC R&S related programs or activities inside a country where an R&S operation is occurring must be coordinated with the whole-of-government planning activities for both the strategic and country-level plans. Under the IMS, a JTF will retain responsibility for tasks or activities assigned to them through the country-level planning process. This includes the planning, management, implementation and monitoring of the activities necessary to complete the task. In non-IMS situations, the JFC will retain normal responsibilities for program management and monitoring.

f. DOD responsibilities for whole-of-government planning as an implementation agency includes:

(1) Providing information on the JTF's implementation plan, the country and operational environment, prior and ongoing assessments, and ensuring that such information is revised once implementation begins;

(2) Ensuring that to the greatest extent possible, JTF implementation planning systems interface with an eventual interagency planning system;

(3) Providing staff, as appropriate, to the IMS for R&S or to an S/CRS-led SPT; and

(4) Carrying out additional implementation planning as required by the CRSG.

g. Military units subordinate to the JTF and assigned the mission to directly support ACT implementation activities (e.g., civil affairs) will likely participate in the planning processes of the JTF as well as the country-level planning occurring at the ACT. These units will have to develop internal mechanisms and reporting procedures to maximize their contributions to both distinct processes without adversely affecting their vital implementation roles and activities and undermining their ability to achieve their assigned objectives under the Country Plan. These types of units will perform the actual function of linking the planning processes between the JTF and ACT through their information gathering, implementation activities, and associated reporting to both elements. In the absence of assigned military units in direct support of ACT implementation activities, JTF liaison officers or military personnel detailed to the ACT could serve some of the functions in linking the planning processes.

5. Joint Task Force Logistics and Administrative Support to the Advance Civilian Team

a. In uncertain or hostile operating environments it may be necessary for the JTF to provide additional logistics and administrative support to the ACT and its implementing bodies in the field. The JFC should coordinate ACT requests for additional support, under the direction and guidance of its commander, through its plans, operations and logistics elements back to the ACT leadership and appropriate staff elements. It is likely that the JTF will receive guidance from the COM and/or the ACT leader for supporting requirements and that the ACT Support Team will coordinate directly with their counterparts at the JTF to properly assign JTF support capabilities to tasks in support of the ACT and its mission.

b. Although not all inclusive, additional support could be requested by the ACT leadership in the following areas:

(1) airlift/sealift of required sustainment materials and supplies, intra-theater air/ground transport of personnel and supplies,

(2) access to military medical facilities for personnel assigned under COM authority, and

(3) providing necessary customer service (e.g., HR, finance) for military Service members detailed to or performing liaison duties with the ACT.

c. Military units assigned the mission to directly support the activities of the ACT will still fall under the operational control of the GCC or one of the GCC's subordinate commanders. Regardless of their mission, these units will follow established service and support procedures pertaining to their own unit's sustainment requirements. In certain scenarios, these units may locate to separate positions apart from the forces assigned to a JTF to better support the ACT and its field implementing activities. Detailed logistics and sustainment plans must be developed and established between the JTF and these distributed units ensuring that they are supplied, equipped, armed, and manned to levels necessary to support the ACT's mission of executing the R&S Country Plan. Appendix B, *Resource Guidance and Sustainment Considerations*, further details logistics and administrative support the ACT may request of the JFC to assist with or provide.

6. Joint Task Force Communications Support to the Advance Civilian Team

a. The ACT will have an organic communications support capability located in the ACT Support Team. Under some conditions the ACT may need additional support from a JTF. The ACT communications structure will need to have a robust capacity and provide the necessary capabilities for the ACT and outlying FACT(s) to support the execution of the R&S Country Plan. However, some countries may have a small or even non-existing US Missions. This will affect the ACT/FACT(s) communication infrastructure requirements and may result in the need to deploy with a large communications package.

b. JTF communications support may be requested under these circumstances. A JTF may be asked to provide personnel and equipment to supplement and add capacity to the ACT communications infrastructure. In a scenario where the JTF HQ and ACT initially co-locate, the JTF communications could be leveraged without significant changes to their internal communications architecture. However, if or when these two elements locate in separate positions the support requested by the ACT and COM may require a more robust support package and result in re-organization of some JTF communications architecture to fulfill the request if and when it is approved. This is also likely to result in personnel and equipment physically re-locating to the site of the AMEMB (ACT) or one of its regional offices - FACTs. This JTF communications support package would likely interface and/or co-locate with the ACT Support Team. It is likely and suggested that a unit, rather than individual personnel, be assigned this type of support task. This would allow for a more complete support package and ensure that personnel are familiar with the equipment as it is organically assigned to their unit. This would also allow for ease of accountability for a commander over personnel and equipment supporting the activities of the ACT, rather than individually detailing personnel and hand-receipting individual pieces of equipment over to the ACT. Another benefit of assigning a unit is that it can bring with it its own life support equipment (i.e. shelter). This aspect would benefit the COM and ACT in the circumstance when it locates at a small AMEMB site where space is limited. The status of these personnel and equipment will need to be addressed in an MOU or MOA between the JTF and COM or their designated representatives and subject to approval of the JTF commander or an appropriate subordinate commander. Appendix F, *Communications,* provides further details on communications support requirements that may be requested of a JTF.

7. Joint Task Force Security Support to the Advance Civilian Team

a. In uncertain or hostile operating environments the ACT Security Team may require additional security related assistance, both static and mobile, from the JTF. Specific requests for mobile security from the JTF may include both tactical convoy ground transport and intra-theater air transport - rotary and fixed-wing. In uncertain or hostile environments additional requests for static security may occur due to limited resources available to DS. These requests must be weighed against others placed on the JTF and any security restrictions related to COM personnel emplaced by the COM and enforced by the RSO and/or DS. Utilizing military forces of the JTF to perform static security at US Mission sites will provide the benefit of increased security for the ACT and COM personnel, but will divert troops from performing security tasks outside the US Mission in support of the R&S operation. Determinations must be made by the COM and JTF commander regarding the involvement of private security to supplement DS and the JTF security tasks - both mobile and static. In the circumstance where the ACT/COM is co-located on a JTF operating base static security duties can be leveraged with the pre-existing security apparatus of the base.

b. Another aspect of providing security support to the ACT and COM from JTF involves communications security. As in any degraded security environment the need for protecting communications and information is of paramount significance. An inability to do so may result in compromises leading to situations where the physical security of JTF and ACT/COM personnel is threatened beyond established force protection levels. The JTF would be able to provide advanced countermeasures to various threats presented to ACT/COM information and communication systems. Appendix E, *Security and Force Protection,* further details possible support requirements that may be requested of a JTF.

Intentionally Blank

CHAPTER VIII
MILITARY PARTICIPATION IN THE FIELD ADVANCE CIVILIAN TEAM

1. Introduction

a. FACT(s) are field elements of the ACT. Their mission is to conduct and integrate USG activities, and coordinate with actors from the international community and local population to achieve unity of effort while executing the R&S country-level plan in their area of responsibility. The ACT provides direction and support to the FACT(s) based on guidance from the COM. In turn, FACT(s) provide the ACT local level implementation capabilities, understanding of unique local environments within an affected country or region, interaction with the populace, and informs critical aspects and pieces of information that make up the COP. The COP is utilized by the ACT and ultimately informs the information requirements requested by the CRSG to assist in crafting and refining policies and supporting strategies and plans.

b. FACT(s) are usually deployed outside of the AMEMB to establish a US presence, provide direct information about conditions on the ground and support R&S operations conducted at provincial and local levels. In this regard, FACT(s) build upon the lessons learned and best practices from PRTs and provide assessments, first-response, and management to the full range of R&S operations. While remaining under COM authority, FACT(s) may integrate with US or foreign military forces when appropriate to maintain maximum US/coalition unity of effort. As required, they may coordinate the field execution of projects that involve not only USG resources, but also UN, other IGOs, NGO, or HN activities.

c. Selected units, elements, or personnel in a JTF with inherent civil-military capabilities (e.g., civil affairs, engineers, military police, and contracting officers) may be assigned to provide support to the FACT in their area of expertise. Reporting and control arrangements such as OPCON and TACON must be established prior to personnel or unit moves between civilian and military elements through the use of MOUs or MOAs. Whenever possible, for ease of management and accountability, commanders should consider detailing a unit (e.g., an engineer platoon) to support a FACT rather than individual soldiers.

2. Structure

a. FACT(s) are task-organized structures. Each FACT must be designed for the context in which it is placed, and for the mission with which it is tasked. FACT(s) are designed to provide FACT leaders with great flexibility in staffing, tasks, and organization, while providing the necessary structure and processes to facilitate whole of government integration. **The FACT can be divided into four basic structural alignments: leadership, integration/implementation, functional, and support**. FACT(s) may contain, or be divided into, subordinate forward-deployed elements. These could take a variety of forms, but should generally respect the FACT area of responsibility concept of following political boundaries. These sub-elements could range in scope and scale from a single individual (working with a military unit) to full-scale teams. Many of the key decisions about FACT structure and organization will be made by the ACT, and when US military forces are present, are dependent on the agreements and understanding between the COM and the JTF commander as well as decisions made by the CRSG.

b. Leadership

(1) FACT leadership provides guidance and direction to the team, serves as the source of authority to knit together a whole-of-government team, and is responsible and accountable for the overall planning and implementation of R&S activities within their AOR to the extent authorized by the CRSG, COM and JTF commander. FACT leadership includes the FACT leader and deputy leader, and may include a chief of staff. The FACT leader provides vision, strategic direction and policy guidance to the FACT.

(2) The **FACT leader** is the senior civilian USG representative in the FACT area of responsibility and may be tasked with providing policy and strategic guidance to US military or civilian agency elements operating within their area of responsibility (during combat operations, a FACT may be in a supporting relationship to a military unit). FACT leaders are field directors for R&S operations within their geographic area reporting to the COM through the ACT leader and DCM. FACT leaders are given operational control over the individual personnel assigned to their FACT and are able to give guidance and direction to their team members. A COM may delegate, in writing, additional specific authorities as appropriate to FACT leaders within their geographic areas. (NOTE: Civilian agencies, particularly the DOS and the USAID use the acronym AOR for areas of responsibility for ambassadors. ACTs and FACTs use the term as an extension of this and are unlike the military where the term is more restrictively used for a GCC area of responsibility.)

(3) The **FACT deputy leader** may serve several different functions, and the deputy may often be dual-hatted with another role (either within the FACT or in another organization operating within the FACT's geographic area). If there is a significant military presence within the FACT or operating within its geographic area, having the senior military person responsible for R&S activities serving as FACT deputy will simplify the coordination and integration of R&S activities. An example of this could be a BCT XO or a battalion XO. A military deputy preserves the military chain of command and personnel rating schemes for any military personnel assigned to the FACT, and could be appointed from within the FACT if there are no military units operating in the FACT AOR. If there are no military units, it is likely that the senior officer representing the largest single military element or organization within the FACT may be appointed as the deputy. An example of this is a civil affairs commander having a dual responsibility of both commanding a unit assigned to support the R&S implementation activities of the FACT and acting as the rater of individual military personnel detailed to the FACT. This role would require an extra challenge of reporting through two different and distinct lines of authority to stay aligned with US Code. The details of this responsibility should be further stipulated in the form of an MOU between the officer's sending organization and the COM.

(4) The FACT may also require a chief of staff function (not necessarily a specific position); someone to oversee FACT internal operations. This function oversees all FACT support activities, as well as assisting the FACT leader and deputy in managing internal mission-oriented processes. When there is a stand-alone FACT that must provide for all of its own support, this role will grow significantly in scope and importance. In cases where the FACT is small in size the function may be an additional responsibility assumed by the FACT deputy or another suitable FACT member.

c. Integration and Implementation Element

(1) A parallel structure to the Integration Structure in the ACT is the FACT Integration and Implementation Element which, like the Integration Structure, is comprised of Objective or Sub-Objective Teams determined by the FACT transformation plan. This element is focused on implementing programs and plans at the sub-national level within the FACT AOR. These plans and programs will align with the Country Plan.

(2) The Integration and Implementation Element Objective Teams are the focal point for FACT planning and implementation activities. The Integration and Implementation Element is where the true task organizing of the FACT happens and is likely to have the greatest interaction with the local populace and leadership of the host country; all other FACT elements serve in supporting roles to its implementation activities.

d. Field Integration Group (FIG)

(1) The FIG integrates and de-conflicts plans and activities between FACT-level Objective Teams and if necessary the Objective Teams of the ACT Integration Structure. It will serve as the larger FACT steering group under the FACT leader. It coordinates with USG elements inside its AOR, such as the military, and other R&S elements from the host country and international community to achieve unity of effort executing the FACT transformation plan. The FIG will constitute the structure in which leadership from the military and the FACT can meet and make decisions relevant to the conduct of R&S implementation activities within the AOR. Leadership from both the FACT and military inside the FACT AOR will require integrated plans and information concerning the employment of resources, manpower, and equipment supporting the Country Plan prior to the conduct of coordinated or integrated civil-military R&S implementation activities.

(2) The exact make-up of the FIG will depend on decisions made by the CRSG, GCC/JTF, COM/ACT and the FACT leader. Normally, the FIG will include all FACT structural element leaders. It advises and assists the development of recommendations for guidance to integrating, implementation, and leadership functions. The FIG is headed by the FACT leader, with the deputy providing day-to-day management. Within the FACT, the FIG is comprised of Objective Team leads, functional section coordinators, support and security coordinators, and others as determined by the FACT leader. The FIG is also a natural connection point for coordination and consensus-building with

military, other USG agencies, and international or host-country actors operating within the FACT AOR.

e. FACT Objective Teams

(1) The FACT Objective Teams plan and conduct R&S activities in the FACT AOR with all USG elements, to achieve unity of effort and accomplish the FACT transformation plan objectives. There are likely to be Sub-Objective Teams, with Sub-Objective Leads within each Objective Team. These Objective and Sub-Objective Teams contain the FACT R&S implementers from each contributing USG agency – including detailed military personnel or units tasked to support FACT R&S implementation activities. FACT Objective Teams are not sector-based (i.e., governance, economics, rule of law), but organized around objectives or outcomes specifically targeting the drivers of conflict and instability dynamics. This discourages organization around agency stovepipes and brings together individuals with the relevant skills to accomplish a common objective. Given the matrix structured nature of the FACT organization, Objective Team members may perform more than one function, or the same function on more than one Objective Team.

(2) Coordination or integration of activities with military units possessing civil-military capabilities operating in the FACT AOR will need to be generated through the commander and staff of the maneuver unit they are tasked to support and that possess operational or tactical control (OPCON/TACON) over their activities. In some circumstances these units may be tasked to directly support an ACT or FACT, however, per US Code, the area commander (or GCC) will maintain operational control (OPCON) over the forces assigned. Military units tasked to support ACT(s) and FACT(s) will require special planning considerations concerning their sustainment – most likely to be arranged with and fulfilled by the nearest MSC in relation to the location of the ACT or FACT. It is likely that units assigned to support the FACT could provide a source of mobility in uncertain or hostile environments for civilian agency personnel (with approval of the COM and RSO). Due to their mobility capabilities, these units may be requested to gather pertinent information related to FACT implementation activities.

(3) Each FACT level Objective Team will have an **objective lead**, tasked with organizing the processes and managing the activities of the team, as well as their own implementation activities. The objective lead will be chosen based on who can best fulfill the role, not on which agency has contributed the preponderance of resources to accomplish the objective. The objective lead will have the responsibility to maintain a relationship with USG elements outside of the FACT with relevant expertise and involvement in their objective area. This role will put them in contact with military units subordinate to a JTF or MSC that have civil-military capabilities or maneuver units conducting security related tasks supporting the R&S operation objectives. Objective leads are responsible for reach-back and coordinating with personnel in the ACT in their objective area (such as the ACT Objective Team) to ensure the activities and outcomes of the objective team remain integrated into the USG R&S Country Plan. In addition to the objective lead, Objective Teams will be composed of SMEs, advisors, implementers, agency program officers, and policy and reporting officers.

(4) **SME/Advisor/Implementers** provide specific knowledge, capacity building, or direct application capabilities to the objective team. They may be provided by individual agency details including military personnel, CRC call-ups and contractors. They receive direction from the objective lead (or leads) they serve under, while exercising the option to maintain reach-back to their sending organization or agency for resource, programmatic and technical matters or for administrative and human resource reasons as stipulated in MOU(s), regulations, applicable laws and code that govern their relationship to the FACT. Examples include a public finance expert assisting in local budget development, or a military civil affairs team leader assisting in an infrastructure related assessment alongside military engineers and development officers from USAID.

(5) **Agency Program Officers** represent agency programs and funds. These officers follow their agency regulations and authorities to manage and implement agency programs supporting the FACT transformation plan and Objective Team implementation activities. Program officers representing DOD work closely with the FACT and ACT resource management offices and any DOD counterparts within those offices such as contracting officers and comptrollers.

(6) **Policy and Reporting Officers** provide awareness of policy decisions in the FACT level Objective Team's area of interest being made at the ACT, AMEMB, or CRSG. They also report on host-country conditions and activities related to the R&S implementation activities. Policy and reporting officers will work on one or more objective teams. They will coordinate with the FACT Strategic Communication section concerning current policy, perceptions, and implications and the KM&R section concerning their participation in the FACT reporting plan.

f. **Functional Areas**

(1) The functional areas of the FACT are not a single structural element, but a cluster of individual sections that report to the FACT leadership. Functional sections provide support in the form of mission-necessary capabilities to the Integration and Implementation Element. The functional sections include, but are not limited to: situation analysis, planning, operations, reporting and knowledge management[4], strategic communication, and resource management. The functional sections are highly scalable in nature. They may consist of one or two people, or may be enlarged as needed. The composition of each section will be described in terms of functional roles to be performed.

(2) These functional sections may request assistance of the JTF for technical matters associated with communications and information systems and related capabilities. This is likely to happen in the case of a significant military presence in support of R&S activities in order to better facilitate communication and information sharing between the military and the FACT. Other technical support may be requested of the military, especially concerning resource management and the use of agency funds and related contracts. Comptrollers, fund managers, authorized pay agents, and contracting officers representing DOD or one of its subordinate elements (including the deployed military forces of the JTF) will be required to monitor the use and disbursement of DOD funds and maintain oversight of contracts awarded utilizing DOD funds. Lastly, as with the other elements of the FACT, further support from deployed military forces in the form of logistics,

transportation, contracting officer representatives and additional security for movement and travel may be requested. This is especially true if or when the environment in which they operate is evaluated to be uncertain or even hostile. Additional logistic and security requests should be coordinated with the FACT leadership to ensure proper coverage to the FACT organization as a whole.

(3) The following is a description of the functional elements and how they may interact with the military. This may take the form of military units operating inside a FACT AOR or military personnel detailed to a FACT.

g. **Situation Analysis Section**

(1) The Situation Analysis Section facilitates whole-of-government analysis of the FACT's AOR to develop and maintain an understanding of the context, dynamics, activities and trends in the AOR among all USG actors. There are four functional roles that this section provides; COP, intelligence analysis, conflict analysis, and area expertise providing regional and national cultural and historical expertise to the situation analysis.

(2) The Situation Analysis Section may coordinate or integrate planning and execution with various military forces either detailed to provide personnel to a FACT, or that a FACT may work closely with. These include, but are not limited to human terrain teams and tactical HUMINT teams, military intelligence fusion cells or "2" shops, civil affairs teams conducting assessment activities, and information collected by maneuver units conducting presence and security patrols.

h. **Planning Section**

(1) The Planning Section facilitates whole-of-government R&S planning for the FACT and other USG participants in its AOR, based on the situation analysis to achieve unity of effort among R&S activities. There are two functional roles in the planning section; planning and metrics. The planning function links the FACT's planning activities to the host country national level Country Plan at the ACT. The metrics function develops useful measurements of inputs, outputs and outcomes for measuring progress and reassessing conditions.

(2) Assisting R&S implementation planning is another area the military can coordinate or integrate activities with the FACT. In addition to military detailees assigned to the FACT, planners from MSCs in the JTF, conducting civil-military operations (CMO) within the FACT AOR should contribute to and align their planning to FACT R&S implementation plans.

i. **Operations Section**

(1) The Operations Section provides support to day-to-day FACT operations and develops the FACT 90-day operations plan to translate whole-of-government planning into whole-of-government action. The Operations Section's size will be affected by the scale of the R&S operation and depend on the FACT providing for its own support, or relying on other actors such as the military when co-located or embedded.

(2) Like the Planning Section, military forces conducting CMO in the FACT AOR must coordinate their activities with the FACT Operations Section. Military units or individuals detailed to the FACT with mission sets that are inherently civil-military may be tasked to directly support this section; specifically the 90-day operations plan development and refinement.

j. Reporting and Knowledge Management Section

(1) The Reporting and Knowledge Management Section will manage the flow of information within the FACT, between the FACT and other USG elements, between the FACT and ACT, and between the FACT and other R&S actors (IGOs and host country) to ensure that the COP remains "common" and that information and reporting requirements are met while also minimizing duplication of effort.

(2) If the information and communications infrastructure is significantly degraded, MSCs may be requested to provide support to the FACT Reporting and Knowledge Management Section. The level of support requested will depend on the package of personnel and equipment that is organic to this section and gaps in capacity and capabilities which will need to be addressed given the supporting infrastructure in the affected country or region. These requests should be weighed against operating constraints that the military is facing, current capability to provide the requested support, and prioritized in coordination with both JTF and ACT HQ. Maintaining communications necessary to support command and control systems within the MSC will be a major planning consideration when evaluating requests for communications support for a FACT.

k. Strategic Communication Section

(1) The Strategic Communication Section facilitates whole-of-government strategic communication assessment and strategy development in conjunction with the joint force and its components for the USG in the FACT area of responsibility and supports the strategic communication assessment and activity requirements of the integration/implementation section.

(2) The functional roles contained within this section are likely to work with and be informed by activities performed by certain units within a JTF such as (PSYOP), IO, and PA. These military elements coordinate with the strategic communication section when crafting messages and planning activities to ensure a synergistic communication effort throughout the JFC's and FACT's AORs.

l. Resource Management Section

(1) The Resource Management Section will coordinate and plan the use of USG resources in the FACT AOR to ensure that resources are tied to the COP and support the transformation plan. This section provides management and execution of any "contingency funds" allocated to the FACT. The section will be highly scalable and flexible depending on the funds allocated to the FACT. If the FACT is allocated significant funds, then it will need a highly capable resource management section. If not, then the section may not be required and the planning section may take on the resource planning function.

(2) The use of R&S contingency funds allocated to DOD must be coordinated with the FACT Resource Management Section for activities conducted in the FACT AOR. Fund managers, comptrollers, and contracting officers who represent DOD will continue to provide stewardship, expert advice, and management of resource related processes and activities concerning the uses of their agency funds. The appointed project leads representing Objective and Sub-Objective Teams will provide recommendations for project prioritization and funding in consultation with the FACT Resource Management Section. Representatives of agency-allocated funds, and host country government officials will determine which fund source is best aligned to meet their objectives. Ultimately, in the case of DOD contingency funds, the approval authority – usually a military commander - will retain the right to approve or disapprove the use of appropriated contingency funds authorized to their command. This decision will be based largely on the objectives laid out in the Country Plan, availability of funds, and project prioritization developed in conjunction with the ACT/FACT, and when appropriate government representatives of the host country.

3. Joint Task Force Relationship to the Field Advance Civilian Team

a. Pre-existing relationships with the COM(s) inside the country or region where the R&S response effort is focused are formalized between GCC(s) and COM(s) within their AOR under 22 USC 3927. This states that the COM has "full responsibility" for the direction, coordination, and supervision of all government executive branch employees in the country (except for … employees under the command of United States area military commander). This pre-existing, "steady state" relationship with the COM and country team will inform and assist the deploying JTF conducting initial planning to support the R&S operation while participating within the IMS.

b. Similar to the deployment and location scenarios of the ACT, there are two scenarios that are likely for the deployment and location of the FACT. In the first a US mission, consulates, and regional offices exist, and a COM is present. In this scenario the security environment allows the FACT to deploy to the existing facilities established at the US mission and stand-up per established procedures. In the second scenario the US mission and associated facilities in country either do not exist or, due to the circumstances (including security threats) on the ground, are vacant and untenable. In this case the FACT will deploy and co-locate, or even embed, with MSC(s) of the JTF on operating bases located inside the FACT AOR.

c. MSC(s) of a JTF, such as BCT(s), are most likely to interact, coordinate or integrate R&S implementation activities with a FACT. Staff elements of the JTF higher HQ will likely contact individual FACT(s) concerning varying topic areas of concern to the larger effort the JTF is supporting. However, these activities should be coordinated through the ACT and include the subordinate military units operating within the FACT AOR.

d. The roles and responsibilities between subordinate units of a JTF and embedded FACT(s), co-located FACT(s), and stand-alone FACT(s) will vary due to their purpose, mission, and organizational design. The structure of an embedded FACT is likely to be much smaller than that of a co-located FACT. In some circumstances, personnel comprising the make-up of an embedded FACT will act in advisory roles to a commander of a MSC while implementing programs with the support of the command. FACT personnel will remain under COM control, but their roles will be infused into and supported by the mission and activities of the MSC. Embedded FACT(s) may collaborate or integrate their activities with larger stand-alone FACT(s) in neighboring FACT AOR(s). Co-located FACT(s) are likely to be larger and more autonomous than embedded FACT(s) and have a larger and more capable support apparatus reducing the support requirements tasked to a MSC through the JTF. A decline in the security environment or deployment of the FACT to a hostile area may lead to a decision to co-locate. The task of providing security to diplomatic missions traveling to and from HN government entities may be more challenging when co-located since JTF operating bases are likely to be more distant from host government facilities than embassies and other US mission facilities. Coordination between the FACT leader and MSC commander and their organizations is facilitated by proximity in this scenario. As security conditions improve a co-located FACT may choose to depart a JTF operating base and stand-alone to work more closely with their counterparts in the host country.

e. The stand-alone FACT will deploy to an existing US mission compound or securable position preferably located near their counterparts in the host country government. It is likely to be significantly larger than an embedded or co-located FACT. This type of FACT will contain a support apparatus, to include security that will likely surpass the number of actual implementers conducting R&S activities. This stand-alone FACT will require less assistance from MSC(s) within the FACT AOR regarding its sustainment due to increased internal support capabilities. In coordination with the regional security officer (RSO) and diplomatic security (DS), the JTF through its MSC(s) will create a secure operating environment in and around the FACT location. Initial R&S support related tasks for MSC(s) are likely to include the creation of and securing lines of communication between the locations of JTF subordinate units and the location of the FACT enabling implementation of R&S activities. Another critical security task MSC(s) may assume as diplomatic conditions warrant, and manpower and resources allow will be the protection and movement of diplomatic missions to and from the government entities of the host country. When conditions allow, this function may be assumed by armed diplomatic security or by armed private security contractors under the direction of the COM and management of DS and the RSO.

f. No matter the type of FACT, a JTF will likely have subordinate units operating in its AOR whose specialization offer a capability to perform implementing tasks in support of the Country Plan, above and beyond traditional security and logistics roles. First and foremost these units support the mission of a military commander; therefore special considerations should be made when tasking these units, or individuals within these units, to directly support the implementation activities of a FACT. Considerations should include the resulting reduced support capabilities available to a commander versus the benefit to accomplishing the objectives in the Country Plan. These military units or personnel should be identified early in the planning process to help determine their roles and responsibilities in direct support of the Country Plan. Determinations should also be made with regard to authorities and command and control relationships to avoid unnecessary confusion and delays in executing the Country Plan. In some cases, where authorities have not been codified, MOUs or MOAs will be needed and approved to determine specific relationships between these specialized units or individual personnel, their JTF HQ, the FACT, and the COM/AMEMB. These MOUs or MOAs will become the basis of identifying and assigning supported and supporting tasks as well as clarifying supported and supporting relationships, roles and responsibilities. The JTF, or higher level echelon or command (such as the GCC or DOD), may request or be requested to assign detailees or liaison officers to FACT(s). The statuses of relationships for these individuals are further specified in Appendix A, *Authorities for Military Participation in Stabilization and Reconstruction Operations*.

4. Joint Task Force/Major Subordinate Command Planning in Conjunction with the Field Advance Civilian Team

a. FACT(s) are responsible for coordinating planning with all US military forces operating in their geographic area to achieve country-level planning objectives. Likewise, MSC(s) of a JTF will coordinate their R&S activities and harmonize their planning for these activities with all FACT(s) operating in their AO. The primary focus of a FACT is local, on-the-ground tactical level implementation activities. However, their assessments, plan revisions, and sub-national field level planning and execution are important and may have implications that affect plans at the operational and strategic levels. The lesson for the operational level planner is to know and utilize the FACT as a potential JIPOE/COP source. FACT(s) contribute to the planning and revisions of the Country Plan and play an important role informing and achieving the objectives in the USG R&S Strategic Plan. Due to their role at the tactical implementation levels in support of the Country Plan it is likely that the FACT and MSC(s) of a JTF will be implementing programs and projects in the same geographic sector that are interconnected. Therefore, these should be coordinated through an integrated planning process as envisioned in the Country Plan.

b. The land component MSC(s) of a JTF will utilize their Service doctrine planning processes to devise a plan or order. For the Army this process is outlined in FM 5-0, *Army Planning and Orders Production*, and for the Marine Corps this process is outlined in MCDP 5, *Planning*. The Country Plan does not replace the processes by which a MSC will plan. Rather, it establishes the process for developing an integrated civil-military plan and provides guidance on what aspects of MSC R&S implementation plans must be shared with the FACT. Military units subordinate to a MSC and assigned the mission to directly support FACT implementation activities (e.g., civil affairs, PSYOP, engineers) will participate in the planning processes under the MSC as well as the implementation planning occurring at the FACT. These units will have to develop internal mechanisms and reporting procedures to maximize their contributions to both distinct processes without adversely affecting their vital implementation roles. These units will perform the actual function of linking the planning processes between the MSC and FACT through their information gathering, implementation activities, and associated reporting to both elements. In the absence of an assigned military unit in direct support of FACT implementation activities then MSC liaison officers or military personnel detailed to the FACT may serve some of the functions in linking the military and interagency planning processes.

5. Logistics and Administrative Support

a. Support requirements for FACT(s) will vary depending on a number of factors to include its mission, objectives, size, locations and the security environment. Current designs of FACT(s) contain a Support and Security Element to manage the requirements to successfully operate. The size of this office is highly dependent on the type of FACT it will support. When appropriate and available this element may receive additional support from the ACT Support Team to enhance its capabilities. A FACT advance party will plan FACT support requirements prior to its deployment and determine responsibilities for providing that support. This may translate into the development of MOUs or MOAs with the military and the establishment of contracts to provide support that is otherwise unavailable.

b. In uncertain or hostile environments MSC(s) may be tasked to provide additional logistics and administrative support to a stand-alone FACT. These units should coordinate FACT requests for additional support using established staffing processes to generate a command decision and then relay the request response back to the FACT staff and leadership. It is likely that the JTF will receive requests from the COM and/or the ACT leader for FACT support requirements and that the ACT Support Team, or FACT Support and Security element, will coordinate directly with their counterparts inside the JTF to properly assign JTF support capabilities to tasks. Co-located or embedded FACT(s) will leverage, to the maximum extent possible, the support and sustainment capabilities and capacities of the JTF operating base where they are located.

c. Additional support could be requested by the FACT leadership in the following areas: Intra-theater air/ground transport of personnel and supplies, access to military medical facilities for personnel assigned under COM authority, and providing necessary customer service (e.g., HR, finance) for military Service members detailed to or performing liaison duties with a FACT. Military units assigned to directly support the activities of the FACT will remain under the operational control of the GCC, the JTF or one of the JTF subordinate commanders. Regardless of their mission, these units will follow established service and support regulations pertaining to their unit's sustainment requirements. In certain cases these units could locate to satellite positions away from JTF operating bases to better support the FACT(s). Detailed logistics and sustainment plans must be established between the JTF and these units ensuring that they are supplied, equipped, armed, and manned to levels necessary to support themselves and the activities of the FACT. Appendix B, *Resource Guidance and Sustainment Considerations*, further details logistics and administrative support the FACT may request of the JTF.

6. Communications Support

a. FACT(s) will have a small communications support capability to manage communication requirements located in its Support and Security Element. Due to the security environment in R&S operations, the FACT may need additional support from the JTF, specifically from communications units of a MSC that are present in the FACT AOR.

The FACT communications structure will need a robust capacity and provide the necessary capabilities to support the execution of the Country Plan. Some countries may have small or even non-existing US Missions. This will affect the FACT(s) communication infrastructure requirements and result in the need to deploy with or request a large communications package. Examples of communications support requirements a FACT may have include non-secure internet, voice, mobile; secure internet and secure voice; IT support; and interoperability capabilities with the military.

b. In some cases the JTF may be requested or tasked to provide personnel and equipment to supplement and add capacity to the FACT communications infrastructure. In situations where MSC(s) and FACT(s) co-locate, communications could be leveraged without significant changes to their internal structures. However, if or when these two elements locate in separate positions the support requested by the FACT may require a more robust support package. This may result in the re-organization of some internal JTF communications structures to include personnel and equipment physically re-locating to the site of the FACT.

c. In these circumstances communications units or sections, rather than individual personnel, should be assigned to support the task. This allows a complete support package to be sent and ensures personnel are familiar with the equipment since it is organic to their unit's MTOE. This also enhances the accountability for a commander over personnel and equipment tasked to support the activities of the FACT, rather than individually detailing personnel and hand-receipting individual pieces of equipment over to the FACT. Another benefit of assigning a unit is that it will bring its own life support equipment (i.e. shelter). This aspect would greatly benefit the FACT when it locates at a small US Mission or other secured site where space is limited.

d. The status of these personnel and equipment will need to be addressed in a MOU or MOA between the JTF and COM or their designated representatives and subject to approval of the JTF commander or an appropriate subordinate commander. Appendix F, *Communications*, further details possible support requirements to be requested of a JFC.

7. Security Support

a. The FACT may deploy with an organic security and force protection capability, depending on security environment, location, its mission, and design. This capability will be managed within the Support and Security Element in consultation with the ACT Security Team. It will consist of personnel from DOS Diplomatic Security (DS). DS may contract services through a private company to supplement their security requirements depending on the needs articulated by the COM, ACT and FACT leadership. In uncertain or hostile environments the FACT leadership in coordination with the ACT Security Team may require additional force protection assistance, both static and mobile, from the JTF.

b. Specific requests for mobile security from MSC(s) operating in the FACT AOR may include both tactical convoy ground transport and intra-theater air transport - rotary and fixed-wing. In uncertain or hostile environments additional requests for static security will probably occur due to the limited resources available to DS in such environments. These requests must be weighed against other requirements and constraints placed on the JTF. Utilizing military forces to perform static security at US Mission sites will increase security for the FACT, but the cost will be the diversion of troops from performing security tasks outside the FACT location in support of the R&S operation. Determinations must be made by the COM and JTF commander regarding the use of private security contractors to supplement DS force protection and security responsibilities. When the FACT is co-located on a JTF operating base static security duties can be leveraged with the pre-existing security apparatus of the base.

   c. Another aspect of security support to the FACT, ACT and COM from a JTF would involve communications security. Degraded security environments require the need for protecting communications and information. This is of paramount significance. An inability to do so may result in compromises leading to situations where the security of JTF and FACT/ACT/COM personnel is threatened beyond established force protection levels. A JTF can provide advanced countermeasures to various threats presented to FACT/ACT/COM information and communication systems. Appendix E, *Security and Force Protection*, further details possible support requirements to be requested of a JFC.

Intentionally Blank

CHAPTER IX
PRE-INTERAGENCY MANAGEMENT SYSTEM
RECONSTRUCTION AND STABILIZATION OPERATIONS
PREPARATION AND PLANNING

1. Introduction

a. The remaining two chapters in the handbook will discuss the role of military participation in R&S whole-of-government planning processes. This is different from the preceding chapters which described the military roles and responsibilities in a management system – not a planning process. Although there are similarities, the remaining chapters should be viewed through the lens of direct participation in whole-of-government planning – which is not the same as participation in a bureaucratic management system that organizes a whole-of-government response.[5]

b. JFCs can be expected to engage in R&S operations for the foreseeable future. The DOD recognizes the importance of readiness for these operations and has placed them on par with the core military priority of war-fighting. Previously, the military had been reluctant to engage in these forms of operations as it was seen as a drain on resources supporting missions that were not military core competencies. The attacks on US targets on September 11, 2001 fundamentally changed perceptions and made it clear the government needed to change the way it addresses crisis overseas. The result, as has been discussed earlier in previous chapters, is the IMS for R&S.

c. When a significant crisis occurs or begins to emerge and the President or Secretary of State decides to activate the IMS for R&S based on a decision by the Principals' or Deputies' Committees and implemented at the direction of the NSC, the CRSG, IPC, and ACT will be stood up, not necessarily in a simultaneous manner, but in a fashion that addresses the specific requirements of the response.

d. The lessons learned from Iraq, Afghanistan, Bosnia, and Kosovo demonstrate that the US must employ an approach in these types of engagements that draws upon the full range of diplomatic, development, defense, intelligence, information, and economic resources available to the USG. The system provides flexible tools to ensure unity of effort as laid out through whole-of-government strategic and implementation planning for R&S. It is intended to facilitate and support:

(1) Integrated planning processes for unified USG Washington-level and country-level plans, including programmatic and contingency operation funding requests.

(a) "Washington-level" is accepted USG interagency terminology that equates to military usage of "strategic" terminology.

(b) "Country-level" is widely accepted terminology in the civilian agencies which is closely related to the military's usage of the terms "operational-level" and "tactical-level". (Note: civilian agencies normally blend operational and tactical levels)

(2) Joint and interagency field deployments.

(3) A joint civilian operations capability including sustainment and shared communications and information management.

e. On a multinational level, nations need to collectively share their analysis of the conflict which will drive identification of the coalition/alliance goal, subsequent strategy and central priorities to achieve the goal – similar to USG processes. It is more beneficial to share conflict assessments and keep differing perspectives in view rather than develop one single multinational assessment which would reflect the lowest common denominator among partners. Since many US partners developed compatible national whole-of-government processes in parallel with S/CRS, efforts to develop a multinational strategy and priorities should be more coherent than in past R&S operations.

2. Pre-Interagency Management System Preparations

a. The GCC, through the JTF commander and its subordinate commanders, will provide a range of services and assistance to the COM and the ACT or FACTs. sGCCs, and the Services that provide the forces to them, will need to institutionalize training concerning the IMS and identify what the likely forms of assistance and support will be. In many countries where an R&S operation is likely to unfold, the diplomatic footprint is either small or non-existent.

b. The JFC needs to consider two focus areas as forces are prepared for potential R&S operations employing the IMS. One area is planning and preparations to support and assist interagency partners with military resources and manpower, which may go beyond the traditional roles of providing transport and security. The other is the training and readiness necessary to ensure military forces, especially staffs and commanders, have the knowledge and understanding to effectively execute R&S operations, either in a lead or subordinate role. This training and readiness needs to include basic understanding of how civilian agencies operate and their "operational tempo" in field situations, which are very different from the military's OPTEMPO.

c. Of utmost importance is training and education. GCCs must develop contingency plans and bring the IMS into every day planning and operations considerations. When the crisis is unfolding and the President or Secretary of Defense has directed a GCC to respond, then it is too late to try to get these procedures and understandings into place.

d. **Support and Assistance to Interagency Partners**

(1) Civilian agencies do not have the volume of resources, either the manpower or materiel, which the DOD can apply to military operations in support of R&S activities. These agencies may need a wide range of assistance, including personnel and units that provide specialized civil military functions. The bulk of the assistance will likely be in the form of logistics, communications, transportation, security and associated manpower needed to address these requirements. Agencies like DOS and USAID are aggressively building civilian capacity to meet this requirement.

(2) A key planning consideration for R&S countries is level of pre-existing civilian USG presence in the field. In a great number of countries AMEMB exist may consist of a handful of US citizens, often fewer than 12, and the rest will be HN nationals employed to work in the embassy. When an embassy does not exist; the US Ambassador of a nearby country may represent US interests. There may be US diplomatic personnel in the capitol, but they will be very small in number. In all of these cases, the COM staff will lack almost everything for R&S operations, from experience dealing with a complex operation to vehicles, communications equipment/capabilities and housing for in-coming R&S operations personnel.

(3) These embassies will also lack the necessary force protection assets, even when a small marine detachment and/or diplomatic security staff are available. These are places where resources, such as 4-wheel drive vehicles, are scarce to non-existent. The ACTs, and any of their subordinate FACTs, may not be able to deploy with the equipment and assets they need to fully operate and cannot expect to obtain them once they arrive in-country. The likely available source for vehicles, communications equipment, shelter, initial food and water, and adequate force protection, especially in the first few weeks of a deployment to support an R&S operation, will be the JTF. Therefore out of necessity, it must plan to provide support and assistance when it is anticipated or requested.

(4) In cooperation with S/CRS, GCCs will need to develop logistics and administrative plans for supporting an IPC when activated and deployed to the geographic combatant command. GCCs will need to develop logistics and administrative plans in conjunction with JTF commanders when deployed and working with ACTs, FACTs and COMs. Plans should be based on capacity and capability of civilian agencies in a given moment in time, as it is constantly changing (thus plans need to be reviewed cyclically). Logistics plans should address all classes of supply and functions (supply, maintenance operations, deployment and distribution, health service support (HSS), engineering, logistic services, and operational contract support). Logistics preparation should include staff responsibilities for supporting the IPC and the ACT/FACT. Assuming that ACT/FACTs and COMs will request and require assistance from JTFs, planning for them in peacetime will ensure the GCCs are prepared to provide the support with minimal impact on military operations in support of the R&S operation.

(5) Planning should include considerations for detailing military personnel to, and tasking military units to support, the ACT/FACT or COM. For command and control reasons, for example, it might make more sense to task a communications platoon to directly support an ACT rather than individual communications personnel. Individuals would require either an MOU or MOA, but a direct supporting unit would remain under the operational controlled (OPCON) of the JTF commander and the JTF would continue to support that unit.

e. **Training and Readiness to Support R&S Operations**

(1) GCCs and the Services will be expected to integrate IMS training, professional development, and planning into all aspects of their readiness programs. Individual planners should be sent to attend the DOS Foreign Service Institute (FSI) R&S

courses. Command and staff from the GCCs and Services must be trained in the IMS concept and periodically receive refresher training.

(2) It will be essential that GCCs and Services have staff officers educated and trained on the IMS. GCCs and Services need to institute regular and publicized initiatives to have planners attend FSI R&S courses or approved equivalent programs at other institutions on an annual or recurring basis.

(3) The GCC and Service staffs must periodically receive IMS refresher training. Once the basics are understood, commander's should ensure their staffs are familiar with the concepts and the internal supporting SOPs established to deal with the various bodies of the IMS. They should be able to do this internally once the individual training mechanisms are institutionalized and working. GCCs should determine how IPC requirements are addressed in their continuity of operations, (COOP) plans. This will also apply to the approach GCCs need to take as JTFs are established and designated to work with COMs and ACT/FACTs.

f. **Exercises**

(1) Every GCC conducts a wide range of exercises on an annual basis. Recent DOD guidance states that major exercises include interagency aspects in order that command personnel become inculcated with both understanding and familiarity with the non-military components of national power. GCCs are strongly encouraged to conduct at least one major exercise annually where the scenario places the GCC in a supporting role to a civilian-led R&S operation. GCCs should conduct exercises in coordination with S/CRS, which must be coordinated through the JS, J7. Exercises can include full-up staff exercises (STAFFEX) or table tops. GCCs should look at these exercises in two different roles; one as the supporting organization to a whole-of-government plan developed by the CRSG or similar interagency policy committee (IPC) or initially as the supported command where DOD is the lead (e.g., a major operation) and the IMS is supporting parallel planning for Phase IV, Stabilization, and eventual transition from DOD lead to interagency lead after cessation of combat operations.

(2) The geographic combatant command staff should exercise and understand that they will not always be the lead planner and may well be a supporting element to a broader plan. As a result, great effort is required to modify how the GCC normally plans operations through JOPES processes and incorporate core civilian agency considerations throughout all operations. This is easier said than done; thus must be exercised - and can be captured in commander's annual and quarterly training guidance.

(3) Effective exercises with a significant R&S component will be a particular challenge for all geographic combatant commands and Services for the foreseeable future. Ideally, every such exercise should be developed well in advance with the involvement of a robust civilian component. However, civilian agencies may lack experience in planning for exercises, limited staff may be available for TDY to a geographic combatant command, or one of its subordinate commands, to plan for, develop, and participate in exercises. Full appreciation in how civilian and military planning must integrate may not be evident. geographic combatant commands, and their components, will need to be innovative and

creative, finding ways to compensate for these challenges. Ensuring that geographic combatant command and Service staff planners have attended FSI training course will be a significant benefit. GCCs should identify one key exercise every year where significant aspects of the IMS are tested. By providing a clear training benefit to civilian agency partners, participation by civilian planners and exercisers can be realized.

3. Triggers for Application of the United States Government Planning Framework and the Interagency Management System

a. It is appropriate to offer an explanation of the triggering mechanisms for determining when whole-of-government planning for reconstruction, stabilization, and conflict transformation is necessary for crisis response prior to the execution and transitioning of activities in an R&S operation. Triggers for the application of the USG planning framework do not apply to normal or "steady-state" planning or for more traditional crisis response to natural disasters such as hurricanes, earthquakes, and tsunamis. The USG has well established procedures and methodologies in place for these types of responses that work and will continue to be relied upon. The USAID Office for Foreign Disaster Assistance, for example, has well established and highly effective procedures to respond to a natural disaster anywhere in the world. The DOD is equally well prepared for national disaster contingencies.

b. An unfolding potential or actual crisis in a region or individual country can be identified and raised for consideration by the Principals Committee (PC), the DC, a COM, or a regional Assistant Secretary. The R&S Interagency Policy Committee can be asked by any of these individuals or committees to consider initiating whole-of-government crisis response planning (CRP) for any crisis that has already begun or is expected to emerge within the next six months. Any decision to leverage USG resources towards dealing with a crisis in a foreign country will ultimately be decided by the President in consultation with Congress. Two types of planning are impacted by triggers and unique sets of criteria. One is contingency planning and the other is CRP.

c. Contingency planning has a lower threshold. Proposals for initiating planning are based on a set of established criteria, which include:

(1) **Importance**: Impact on US national security and foreign policy objectives;

(2) **Magnitude**: Regional impact; potential scale of humanitarian needs;

(3) **Potential for significant US military involvement**: As indicated in DOD's Guidance for the Employment of the Force;

(4) **Likelihood**: Probability of a crisis occurring, as indicated by information and risk assessments such as the Intelligence Community Watch-lists, USAID Conflict/ Fragility Alert, and/or assessments by the UN or other IGOs; or

(5) **Capacity**: Ability of affected country and neighbors to respond effectively to crisis.

d. The R&S Interagency Policy Committee, in consultation with the appropriate DOS Regional Bureau, will consider proposals and make recommendations on how many and which specific countries or regions require whole-of-government planning to prevent, mitigate, or prepare to respond to potential conflict. The R&S Interagency Policy Committee will hold semi-annual "Planning Guidance" meetings to determine USG objectives for the year and to develop the list of countries that will be the subject of Contingency Planning, and a second meeting to review the planning efforts after six months. Participation in the "Planning Guidance" meetings will include the normal R&S Interagency Policy Committee representatives and others as appropriate. The Interagency Policy Committee will forward recommendations to the DC or PC for final decisions on the list of countries, noting concurrence or non-concurrence of the Regional Assistant Secretary and/or the COM. These recommendations will be coordinated with the Director of Foreign Assistance Operational Plan cycle and the Director of Foreign Assistance core country team. To the extent practicable, contingency planning will link to agency planning cycles. S/CRS will maintain a database of the participants in the interagency planning teams for each country to facilitate the formation of CRP teams, should they become necessary.

e. The DOD will be represented by both OSD and the JS and, in turn, through either of these agents, CCDRs can have a voice and inform planning decision-making conducted by this Interagency Policy Committee. Title 10 USC Section 163 designates the Chairman of the Joint Chiefs of Staff (C/JCS) as the spokesman for the commanders of the combatant commands, especially on the operational requirements of their commands - subject to the authority, direction, and control of the Secretary of Defense. In performing such function, the Chairman shall:

(1) confer with and obtain information from the commanders of the combatant commands with respect to the requirements of their commands;

(2) evaluate and integrate such information;

(3) advise and make recommendations to the Secretary of Defense with respect to the requirements of the combatant commands, individually and collectively; and

(4) communicate, as appropriate, the requirements of the combatant commands to other elements of the DOD.

f. PPD – 1 describes the structure of the NSC. It defines Interagency Policy Committees as the day to day fora for interagency coordination. The R&S Interagency Policy Committee is part of the NSC structure. Its membership is stipulated in PPD 1 which directs that each NSC Interagency Policy Committee include representatives from each Department, Office, and Agency determined by the NSC DC. For the DOD representation on the DC includes the Deputy Secretary of Defense or the Under Secretary of Defense for Policy, and the Vice Chairman of the Joint Chiefs of Staff. This translates into both OSD and JS as the DOD representation on the R&S Interagency Policy Committee. If the IMS is established and a country specific R&S Interagency Policy Committee is formed (called the CRSG), it too will have OSD and JS representation. These DOD representatives may invite the affected GCC into the associated strategy development and policy planning. If this occurs special considerations must be outlined and the roles of geographic combatant command participants clearly defined to not interfere with the statutory command relationship between the President of the United States and the CCDR through the Secretary of Defense.

g. CRP is for a crisis that has already begun or is expected to emerge within the next six months. Triggering CRP does not necessarily imply activating the IMS. The threshold for activating the IMS is higher than the threshold for triggering CRP. However, if a major crisis is unfolding and the USG is planning a robust response, activation of the IMS is probable. Like contingency planning, CRP planning can be triggered by the PC or DC or by direct request from the Secretary of State or Defense. Unlike the contingency planning, a CRP effort does not require deliberations in the R&S Interagency Policy Committee. However, a decision of the R&S Interagency Policy Committee can also trigger whole-of-government planning. Given the need for urgent action in a crisis S/CRS will undertake initial crisis analysis. In the evolving doctrine, these initial activities will also include setting initial parameters for the R&S mission in coordination with Principals.

h. Given the need for urgent action in a crisis S/CRS will undertake initial crisis analysis. Following a decision by the S/CRS will form an initial SPT by calling together a group of interagency planners who have been identified by their agencies to be available for participation for such planning. If the IMS were activated, this initial SPT would be joined by more interagency personnel and evolve into the CRSG Secretariat. Likewise, the initial crisis analysis would serve as a starting point for the situation analysis.

i. In addition to the criteria listed above for triggering contingency planning, additional criteria for CRP may include, but are not limited to:

(1) significant actual or potential (near-term) US military involvement;

(2) events with significant potential to undermine regional stability and development progress, (e.g., a coup, economic collapse, severe environmental damage or degradation);

(3) actual or imminent state failure, particularly where the host government is unwilling or unable to respond;

(4) excessive mortality rates;

(5) large-scale displacement of people;

(6) rapid increase in USG-funded civilian programs operating in an R&S environment;

(7) activation of USG agencies' crisis assessment, planning, or response teams (such as a Disaster Assistance Response Team);

(8) embassy drawdown or evacuation in an R&S environment and/or significant threat to US citizens and US facilities;

(9) international or allies' crisis response, such as the formation of a UN peacekeeping operation; or

(10) determination of an impending or actual genocide, ethnic cleansing, or massive and grave violations of human rights.

j. For military planners it is important to know that crisis action planning can, and often will, commence before whole-of-government CRP begins. GCCs will often recognize the initial signs of an unfolding crisis and anticipate orders to take action with preliminary planning efforts of their own. Take, for instance, the historical example of Kuwait. The same day Kuwait was invaded by Iraq in 1990 the CDRUSCENTCOM, General Norman Swartzkopf, ordered his planning staff to expand already on-going contingency planning to free the country with force. Months earlier General Swartzkopf recognized signs in the region that led him to order his staffs to start looking at how the US military, and USCENTCOM in particular, might need to respond to military aggression on the part of Iraq even though at the time there were no overt indications that Iraq was planning on invading Kuwait.

4. Joint Force Commander Planning for the Interagency Management System

a. Context for JFC Participation

(1) R&S operations will be more likely to occur in places with very weak central governments, with strong potential or actual religious, cultural or social conflict, victims of drought, economic mismanagement or places with high corruption and potentially lucrative natural resources. These are considered high risk candidates for the kinds of crisis that could lead to the need for an R&S response. The second group of countries is listed to distinguish between poor countries or countries with weak economies that are, nevertheless, not likely crisis candidates because of relatively stable central governments, no strong latent domestic social, cultural or religious conflict and places with potential economic resources not being squandered through mismanagement and/or corruption.

(2) Due to the nature of R&S operations a JTF will likely be established by the affected GCC. In some circumstances the JTF may already be present in the affected country. This JTF will work closely with the COM, the ACT and any Forward Advance Civilian Teams (FACTs). In some circumstances, particularly when a US embassy is not present in country or conditions on the ground warrant, the ACT will co-locate with the JTF and draw substantially on military resources, but even when the ACT is not co-located, the JTF will likely still be asked to provide assistance and support. In other circumstances an MOA can be signed placing the JTF under direction of the COM, while still retaining Title 10 command relationship authorities. Military planners need to be prepared to respond to these circumstances and all possibilities in between.

(3) In hostile operating environments, US and multinational military forces often possess the only readily available capability to meet many of the local populace's fundamental needs. Human decency and the law of war require land forces to assist the

populace in their areas. The US military has a long tradition of extending help and assistance to impacted populations in crisis areas.[6] Leaders at all levels should prepare to address civilian needs, including identifying people in their units with regional and interagency expertise, civil-military competence, and other critical skills needed to support the local populace and host government. In some cases, to identify these individuals, commanders and their staffs may need to canvas their entire force, not just personnel organic to their HQ, the active component, or in specialized units already conducting civil military operations to locate personnel with the critical skills to provide additional support.

(4) Military forces must defeat enemies and simultaneously help shape the civil situation through stability operations. Shaping the civil situation in concert with civilian USG agencies, IGOs, civil authorities, and multinational forces is important to campaign success. Stability operations may complement and reinforce offensive and defensive operations, or they may be the main effort of an operation. These operations may take place before, during, and after major combat operations and seek to secure the support of civil populations in unstable areas. Forces engaged in an operation dominated by stability tasks may have to conduct offensive and defensive operations to defend themselves or destroy forces seeking to challenge the stability mission. Following hostilities, forces conduct stability operations to provide a secure environment for US, coalition, multinational, and local civil authorities as they work to achieve reconciliation, rebuild lost infrastructure, and resume vital services.

(5) The focus of these combined military and civil efforts is to diminish the means and motivations for conflict, while developing local institutions so they can take the lead role in national and local governance (provide basic services, foster economic development, and enforce the rule of law). Success depends ultimately on the HN and on the interrelationship and interdependence of the ensuing dynamics:

(a) The legitimacy of the government and its effectiveness as perceived by the local population and the international community.

(b) The perceived legitimacy of the freedoms and constraints placed on the forces, both HN and/or coalition, supporting the government.

(c) The degree to which factions, the local population, and other actors accede to the authority of the government and those forces supporting the government.

(6) There are times when hostilities continue to exist in many forms during stability-focused operations because of warlords, tribal competition, ethnic rivalries, outlaws, terrorists, or insurgents. This can leave areas of a country caught in the middle of the transition between major combat and relative stability. Combat operations may be very much "on again/off again" across parts of the country, and there may be areas that have not stabilized significantly and are at risk of "slipping back" if security forces are removed. However, moving these areas further along is beyond the expertise and capabilities of any one department or agency. The military can operate in these unstable areas but has limited development capability. Diplomatic and development agencies have these skills but are unable to operate in these areas using their traditional delivery mechanisms because of the instability threatening their security. Therefore, this complex

environment requires an integrated civilian-military approach focused on achieving sufficient stability to allow reconstruction and development to begin.

b. **Approaches to USG R&S Planning**

(1) Approaches to R&S Planning within the context of the *USG Planning Framework for Reconstruction, Stabilization and Conflict Transformation* include the conflict transformation and whole-of-government approaches. The conflict transformation approach to R&S operations is two pronged in nature. It focuses on building both local institutional capacity and reducing the sources of conflict and instability. The USG has many years of experience in building institutional capacity – to include the military's train and equip programs; however it has limited experience and even more limited success at targeting drivers of conflict. To be successful at transforming conflict, the USG must do more than build institutional capacity; it must also identify and address the sources or roots of conflict and instability through the use of targeted transformational policies and programs to reduce and/or mitigate these sources. R&S planning should serve to develop policies, design programs and measure success in the context of the interplay between these two endeavors.

(2) A whole-of-government approach to R&S recognizes that success requires unity of effort across all civilian and military components of the USG. Integrating the efforts of the USG is necessary for effective coordination with HN authorities, bi-lateral partners, non-governmental actors and multilateral organizations. This approach is driven by the search for those combinations of USG resources and activities that reinforce progress made in one sector or enable success in another. To do this, the interagency community must resist seeing USG resources (e.g., funds, personnel, programs, expertise, equipment) and instruments of power (e.g., diplomatic, military, development, intelligence, economic, strategic communication) as belonging to any one agency, military service or entity. All are parts of a USG whole. Moreover, in complex R&S operations no single sectoral solution is sufficient.

(3) It is imperative that all of the USG participants involved in an R&S operation, at the appropriate level as deemed by their agency, participate in the policy-making and planning process. This will ultimately determine how the various resources and instruments are arrayed as a whole in partnership with the HN and, if present, our international partners. This approach requires "early and high" (i.e., early in the process and at a high level of policy and strategy) level collaboration within the USG as well as with stakeholders from the HN and international community.

(4) A more detailed explanation of whole-of-government planning utilizing the IMS is provided in Appendix E, "Whole-of-government Planning Utilizing the IMS."

c. **Levels of Planning**

(1) The military has detailed and comprehensive planning tools, approaches and methodologies to cover many possible contingencies and circumstances. Civilian agencies do not have a culture of contingency planning similar to that of the military, but the civilian agencies do conduct a range of planning efforts and address a wide scope of

contingencies. This section is intended to offer a basic understanding of the planning process developed by the civilian agencies. It is not JOPES and differs from the way the military plans, but then, the civilian agencies are different from DOD and civilians plan to accomplish different goals. Military planners typically plan for operations in a finite period of time measured in hours or days. Civilian planners do not plan force-on-force engagements and their planning scope typically spans weeks, months and even years.

(2) When a crisis is identified that is in the US national interest both the DOD - particularly the GCCs, and the DOS will establish a crisis response or task force cells that will immediately begin preliminary planning. These planning efforts will continue to function and evolve as interest in the crisis matures and USG policy towards the crisis determines the appropriate level of response. The whole-of-government approach to planning involves three levels. At each level, planning teams produce products that drive the process.

(3) The first level of planning is policy formation, followed by strategic development, which is in turn followed by implementation planning. The process begins with an analysis of the conflict, which drives the identification of the USG policy goal. The policy goal informs the development of a strategy around central objectives to achieve the goal, or MMEs. MME teams then determine the sub-objectives that are necessary to achieve the MME. Development of MMEs flows from a careful and comprehensive assessment of the drivers of conflict or instability as well as the local capacity to address those destabilizing factors. MMEs therefore must be a narrowly-tailored set of outcome statements that are together necessary and sufficient to achieve the overarching policy goal within the stated timeframe. Stating MMEs as outcomes will help planners avoid stove-piped responses based on current capacities.

(4) Collectively, the policy formulation and strategy development levels of planning lead to a USG Strategic Plan for R&S. This strategic plan informs individual agency implementation planning at the field level, requiring revisions to agency implementation plans where they already exist, and the integration of those plans into a USG Country Plan. For military planners the challenge is to take military plans at the tactical level that are often either fully developed or well into the process and align them with IMS implementation plans that will be playing "catch-up" to the military planning efforts.

(5) The methodologies for the three levels of planning are:

(a) **Level One: Policy Formulation**

1. Assess the operational environment to define policy-level assumptions and interests, analyze risk, and determine drivers of conflict or instability.

2. Determine clear and measurable goals of the intervention based on US national interests and transforming the drivers of conflict and instability.

(b) **Level Two: Strategy Development**

<u>1</u>. Harmonize policy goals with available resources and focus policymakers on resource implications that may limit goal achievement.

<u>2</u>. Identify MMEs and assign agency responsibility for sub-objectives and tasks.

<u>3</u>. Create a meaningful evaluation system to measure progress in achieving goals and MMEs.

(c) Level Three: Country-Level Planning

<u>1</u>. Orchestrate the application and integration of all instruments of national power to accomplish policy goals.

<u>2</u>. Integrate US national efforts with those of other international partners and organizations.

<u>3</u>. Create a meaningful evaluation system to measure achievement of sub-objective and the completion of tasks.

(6) Together, policy formulation, strategy development, and country plans form the backbone of the whole-of-government planning process. While these levels are sequential—each providing essential outputs for the next—they should not be seen as completely discrete and linear. The intent of this overview is not to get into levels of detail that are comprehensively provided in the *US Government Planning Framework for Reconstruction, Stabilization and Conflict Transformation,* also addressed in Appendix E, "Whole-of-Government Planning Utilizing the IMS."

d. Planning Process Structure and Focus

(1) The first step in putting together policy options is determining which assumptions are critical to the direction of a USG plan and the ultimate success of USG R&S operations. Besides the causal assumptions (drivers of conflict and mitigating factors) drawn from the Situation Analysis, there are three main categories of contextual assumptions about the strategic environment to consider:

(a) conditions within the country (e.g., electrical infrastructure in major cities will be sufficient and functioning, the security environment will be permissive);

(b) behavior of other regional and international actors (e.g., the European Union will provide sufficient resources to achieve objectives in the rule of law sector, neighboring states will not send military forces across borders); and

(c) resources (e.g., forces/people, assistance, activities) available from the USG (e.g., there will be a $300 million supplemental, 100 civilians will be deployed from the civilian reserve corps).

(2) Drawing on the interagency situation assessment, the SPT should determine which assumptions are critical, and by varying those assumptions, identify two or three alternative plausible contextual scenarios for the plan. Given that a mismatch between goals and resources always spells mission failure, each scenario should make explicit the USG resources assumed, and the time envisioned to meet those goals. These "scenarios" form the basis for the determination of policy options.

(3) The identification of achievable and realistic goals is the next stage in the formulation of policy options. The SPT, which is established at the CRSG, should identify a goal for each contextual scenario.

(4) Following the conflict transformation approach, planners should consider the longer-term objectives for the country when trying to determine shorter-term goals that focus on capitalizing on the two to three year period where political and financial resources are often at their highest levels. The two to three year goal should be to reach the conflict transformation "tipping point" of locally-led nascent peace, where the country is on a sustainable positive trajectory out of conflict, regardless of international assistance. Stated otherwise, the goal would be that the country is beyond major conflict and beyond major security, political, and economic reliance on foreign interveners so that future transformation of the country or region is largely and increasingly in the hands of benign, credible, and legitimate local authorities, with international assistance shifting to a supporting role.

(5) When presenting a goal, the SPT should describe, as clearly as possible, what "success" would look like if the goal was reached. Proposing that country X will be "at peace with itself and on the path to economic growth" is a standard goal that could apply to any R&S country. The strategic planning process should, however, provide senior policy-makers with a more detailed explanation of the goal in order to faithfully convey the challenges that lay ahead. This discussion will also prove valuable when planners begin to outline the necessary benchmarks to be reached and the measures of progress to be observed.

(6) Limiting the scope of the plan helps focus a response strategy on a realizable set of goals and within a manageable timeframe. This helps mission leadership, domestic constituencies, and implementing staff come to a common understanding of the threshold for intervention success, and in turn, down-sizing, transition, or mission exit. The plan should not be based on long-term developmental goals that may require decades of sustained assistance or support, but should nonetheless be informed by and consistent with that perspective. After determining an overarching R&S/conflict transformation goal for each contextual scenario, the SPT must then determine the course of action or strategy that the USG will follow to achieve the goal – the MMEs.

(7) At this stage in the development of policy options, planners should explicitly recognize any critical causal assumptions for each strategy. Causal assumptions are hypotheses about the relationship between action and effect: that by doing X, you will achieve Y (e.g., giving individuals a job will prevent them from participating in an

insurgency, holding an election will give you a more effective local government, or reducing poverty will eliminate conflict). These types of assumptions can also be termed "theories of change." Theories of change are often implicit and unacknowledged in the crafting of plans. The planning process presented here seeks to draw attention to the theories of change that drive planning at each level.

e. **Expanding on the Policy Options**

(1) The SPT should then expand on each policy option into a one page format that outlines:

(a) overarching policy;

(b) policy implications (any changes to current policy, or political/ legislative issues, and policy priority trade-offs);

(c) strategy summary;

(d) conflict transformation strategic goal, i.e., what success would look like;

(e) MMEs;

(f) Causal and contextual assumptions (summary of the drivers of conflict drawn from the situation analysis and contextual assumptions about the country environment, anticipated roles and resource commitments of other actors) and how the assumptions will be verified over time;

(g) USG resource availability, rough orders of magnitude of USG resource needs expressed in a common, agreed lexicon; and

(h) associated risks and opportunities.

(2) While all resource issues may not be fully identified at this stage in the planning process, it is crucial to put potential resource gaps squarely before policymakers as early as possible, so they understand the hurdles in achieving desired policy objectives.

(3) In addition to the one-page briefs on each policy option, the SPT should explain the broader context drawn from situation analysis and reasoning associated with the set of options. One option assumes significantly greater USG resources than the others or one option posits the crisis to pose a greater threat to US national security interests than the other options). Although policy implications for each policy option are briefly discussed in each one-page brief, the narrative should also underscore policy implications and recommendations: any issues of policy incoherence, gaps in capability, or longstanding legislative and policy issues. Together, these overarching and policy option paragraphs form a *Policy Advisory Memorandum*.

f. Preparation of MMEs

(1) Once the DC has approved a policy option, the SPT in Washington, DC identifies MME planning teams from key participants in the interagency community to develop a strategy for each MME. In the field, under the direction of the COM and ACT leader, objective planning teams will also be identified, to begin country-level strategic planning. MME/objective teams function as interagency sub-working groups (sub-Interagency Policy Committee level) charged with developing the USG strategy to achieve each MME, and report to the interagency body under which they are convened (Interagency Policy Committee, CRSG). Generally, an MME/objective planning team is formed for each MME/objective, but in some cases it may be more efficient for a planning team to develop the strategies for multiple MME/objectives.

(2) A MME/objective planning team should bring together each agency relevant to the MME, including regional experts and sectoral and functional experts in R&S and conflict transformation. In addition, the team should include those who understand the processes and requirements involved in employing, prioritizing and sequencing the various instruments of national power that may be useful in the MME strategy (budgeting, logistics, legal, public affairs) taking into account the resources that other nations, IGOs, NGOs, and HN may apply to the problem. This composition ensures an integrated USG strategy toward the MME outcome. MME teams will be Washington, DC-based, and the objective teams will be field-based, and ultimately could be civil-military, international, or coordinated with HN structures. It is advisable that a regional or sectoral expert and a strategic planner co-chair MME and objective planning teams. The participation of a strategic planner as a co-chair of each MME/objective planning team ensures strong vertical integration between goals and tasks, as well as interagency integration of the expertise, tools, and resources within and external to the USG that can be brought to bear on MME/objective strategy development. MME/objective planning teams should be designed to facilitate the maximum gain from coordination among participants, and between regional and functional experts, while minimizing the inefficiencies that could arise from that inclusiveness.

g. Responsibilities for MMEs and Objectives

(1) In some cases, there will be an obvious agency or office to lead an MME or objectives and undertake the bulk of the strategy development for the MME or objectives. Even in such a case planners should be careful to ensure that all equities, capabilities, and capacities, particularly those from agencies with which they are not familiar, are represented on the MME or objectives. MME teams or objective teams will consist of members representing all agencies and departments that have equities in the particular MME or objective. For the military there is a traditional recognition among the USG interagency community that security MMEs or objectives will be in large part initially led by DOD.

(2) Following the comprehensive approach, security sector MMEs or objectives will include representatives from civilian agencies who can offer their insight

and expertise into security sector reform, which encompasses more than just military related security objectives and tasks. Agencies such as the DOS, Department of Justice, USAID, and their respective bureaus will figure prominently in their representation on security sector focused MME or objectives. Just as in other MMEs, particularly at the beginning of R&S operations, military representation and participation will be crucial to support a successful outcome, especially during critical transitions between the military and civilian authorities. For example, a MME or objective focused on restoring basic civil services such as sanitation, power and water may be led by USAID. Because the military will be integrally involved initially in the restoration of these services, DOD will want to have relevant expertise represented on this MME team or objective team.

h. IMS Planning and Implementation for Essential Tasks

(1) Once MMEs are identified, planners refer to the essential task matrix and their functional expertise to develop objectives, sub-objectives and activities necessary and sufficient to achieve the MME outcome. To ensure shared understanding of sub-objectives, the MME team may want to generate a list of illustrative activities for each sub-objective. Like the MME, objectives and sub-objectives should be stated as outcomes with suitable indicators for measuring achievement.

(2) MME planning teams are responsible for completing an *MME Strategy Memorandum* and *MME Overview Presentation* that include the following elements: linkage to the overarching policy/conflict transformation goal; linkage to other MMEs; measures of success; assumptions; impediments to success; sub-objectives necessary and sufficient to achieve the MME; and a resource strategy. Throughout the period of plan execution, MME planning teams are responsible for assessing progress, sequencing, and cross-MME linkages.

(3) The "MME Strategy Memoranda" become part of the overall *USG Strategic Plan for R&S or Conflict Transformation*, and serve as the foundation for the *USG Strategic Plan for R&S Narrative* drafted by the SPT.

5. Organizational Linkages

a. GCCs have three linkages that need to be planned. At the strategic level the CRSG will include representatives from OSD and the Joint Staff. The CRSG will be formed when there is a crisis in a country or region of the world and the President of the United States made a determination that the national interest dictates the USG will respond with a whole-of-government R&S operation. All departments and agencies of the USG participating in the operation are represented in the CRSG.

b. In some circumstances OSD and the JS will invite the GCC to send representatives to inform and participate in CRSG planning and deliberations. GCCs will need to be prepared to send representation of sufficient stature commensurate with the level of participation on the CRSG, but remain cognizant that the Joint Staff and OSD representatives will retain their overall roles of being the primary DOD participants. It is essential that the GCC work closely with the JS to ensure it knows what is emerging from the CRSG and the CRSG knows clearly what information the GCC is gathering pertaining to the subject crisis and what it can and cannot do or provide.

c. At the operational level the GCC must plan to host the IPC. The IPC is an essential component of the IMS and improper utilization of the IPC will be a major detriment to the overall execution of the R&S strategic and implementation plans and will inhibit the effectiveness of military participation in the IMS. GCCs must plan on how best to integrate an IPC into their planning staffs. This should be exercised and rehearsed during peacetime and it needs to be internalized as well as institutionalized. At the time of a crisis, this effort will be too late. Since each command is organized differently, each commander must determine what the best method is for them.

d. Consider the following for reception and integration:

(1) What staff element is responsible for initially receiving and integrating the IPC—J3, J5, JIACG?

(2) How will they do it?

(3) How will they build IPC capability/SME into their staff processes?

(4) Does the geographic combatant command LNO in the Pentagon possess all this information and understand what the command will do and how it will integrate with the IMS?

e. GCCs should determine how IPC requirements are addressed in their COOP plans. They should consider developing an internal handbook, SOP, or similar document that establishes how the command will handle an IPC with reference to, but not limited to, organizational links, communications, and logistics.

f. At the tactical level the GCC will likely form and deploy a JTF to execute military operations. What is new or different is the high probability that the JTF will have to not only work closely with an ACT, it might be operating in a supporting role to the ACT. Similarly, subordinate units of the JTF will have to work closely with field elements of the ACT also known as FACTs, if the determination is made that they are needed. Like the JTF, its subordinate units may be operating in a supporting role to the FACT. Additionally, the GCC must take into account the likelihood that the ACT or the COM or both will need military assets and support in order to carry out their functions.

Intentionally Blank

CHAPTER X
JOINT FORCE COMMANDER RECONSTRUCTION AND STABILIZATION PLANNING AND IMPLEMENTATION UTILIZING THE INTERAGENCY MANAGEMENT SYSTEM

1. Transition to the Interagency Management System in Reconstruction and Stabilization Operations

a. This chapter will address the very challenging issue of executing activities and transitioning them within an R&S operation from military to civilian lead once the IMS has been activated. Relationships between military commanders and civilian leaders will be critical to ensuring smooth transitions. The more civilian leaders and military commanders understand each other, each other's missions or objectives, and each other's capabilities, the easier it will be to coordinate and plan to hand leadership and responsibility from one to the other. These leaders must do everything possible to establish and foster good relationships between themselves and their supporting staffs and, ideally, should endeavor to meet with each other at every opportunity.

b. The military may be the first USG entity to arrive or return to an affected country or region in crisis in many R&S operations. It will have the initial responsibility and leadership for many of the immediate tasks identified in the strategic planning process under the *USG Planning Framework for Reconstruction, Stabilization, and Conflict Transformation*. The most important task will be establishing security and creating conditions that will allow civilian organizations to become fully engaged. While some civilians are likely to be with the military as it deploys into the crisis country or region, their roles will be limited until the situation becomes more stable. As a result, the military can expect to initiate a number of R&S activities.

c. While the US military may be the first USG representative to arrive or return to an affected country, it is likely that IGOs or NGOs and USG civilian agencies under a COM will have been present prior to US military involvement and will likely remain afterwards. They and the local populace will inherit the consequences of any US military actions – good and bad. Being aware of, and when appropriate, collaborating with those organizations and agencies still in country as well as the local populace is essential for long-term mission success.

d. Until interagency CRP is initiated or the IMS is activated, the military will need to lead the planning and implementation process of administering, maintaining, or re-establishing the HN's essential government services. This includes getting power, water, sanitation and emergency service functions operational and beginning the process of managing the activities associated with refugees and internally displaced persons – referred to as dislocated civilians by the military. All of these tasks will transition to USG, international, multinational, or host government civilian control and responsibility. Transitioning is not a linear or country-wide event. It will occur at different times in different places within the affected country or region based on the situation and measures of progress achieved. It will involve many different organizations (both governmental and nongovernmental) that will require different levels of planning – theater strategic to tactical implementation.

e. Transitioning to civilian led R&S operations after the IMS is established will be among the most challenging and time sensitive activities the military and civilian component will accomplish during complex operations. Transition can be related to the military's own "Relief in Place or RIP" operations conducted between military units. Among the most complex of military operations, a RIP requires leadership, timing and absolute sound planning, training and readiness among commanders, staffs and individual service members. These same qualities are a necessity in the much more complex transitions that occur between military and civilian led operations.

f. Transition to a civilian led R&S operation utilizing the IMS occurs when a military commander hands the leadership and major operating responsibilities and associated structures of a complex interagency operation over to an interagency civilian leader (e.g., ACT leader or COM) and assumes a supporting role. In most circumstances a transition may be incremental, both geographically and at different times, involving many subordinate JTF commanders and FACT leaders of an ACT. It is possible for a transition to reoccur from civilian led to military led. However, this would mean the situation on the ground deteriorated to the point where security re-emerged as the most significant challenge and civilians could no longer safely execute their responsibilities.

g. The complexity of a transition from military to civilian leadership stems from two factors. First, in a crisis response utilizing the IMS, the leadership is coming from dissimilar organizations with different cultures, planning horizons and objectives with differing timeframes. Second, while the command or leadership of the overall R&S operation will change from military to civilian authority, component elements of the R&S operation could remain military-led or civilian-led for timeframes that are not linked to the overall transition from military to civilian. For instance, the JTF commander may transition responsibility for R&S operations over to the ACT leader at a time when most of the sub-objectives of the MMEs are still being led and conducted by subordinate military units. However, this in no way will interfere with the command and control authorities the JTF commander exercises over his military forces.

h. For example, public communications activities may initially be managed and led by elements of the joint force early in an R&S operation. Once the ACT has been deployed and established, joint force public communication activities will need to be coordinated with the ACT leader or a designated representative and military communications activities will become a supporting effort. In relative terms this transition will occur early after the IMS is established. Conversely, the transportation responsibilities for the implementing teams envisioned in the IMS (ACT and FACT) will likely be assigned to the military at the outset and may remain a responsibility throughout the duration of the operation. Depending on the situation, the civilian organizations participating in the IMS may not be able to provide their own transportation to effectively support operational needs.

i. An important recurring theme in R&S operations employing the IMS is transitioning responsibility and participation in MMEs; regardless of the division of labor. During a military to civilian led transition military leaders must ensure continuity of the USG contribution to the initial supporting tasks of the crisis response while meeting the needs of the HN government, and its local populace.

j. Maintaining unity of effort is particularly important during transitions, especially between organizations with different capabilities and capacities. Relationships between organizations tend to become strained during transitions; especially between organizations with vastly different cultures and background. Transitions are not a single event happening all at once; instead they are rolling processes of little handoffs between different actors along several streams of activities. There are usually multiple transitions for any one stream of activity over time. Training can significantly facilitate transition activities; however, it is likely that transition training will not be resourced among the civilian components participating in the IMS. Even if the military has trained for these activities, they will probably have not trained with the civilian counterparts they will interact with when deployed.

k. It is imperative that planning for transitions begins early and communications between the organizations that transition is vibrant and two-way. The need for the civilian leaders to understand the military and for the military to understand the civilians is critical to successful unified actions enabling unity of effort. The understanding needs to be focused on what responsibilities will transition and the specific organizations involved. Numbers of personnel, where are they located, current communications, logistics, and transportation capabilities and anticipated needs of each organization involved in the transition need to be taken into account. Minimizing the impact of the transition on the HN and on NGOs, IGOs, and international partners that are engaged with one or both of the transitioning parties should be taken into consideration.

2. Joint Force Commander Planning and Implementation Considerations During Multinational and United States Government Interagency Reconstruction and Stabilization Operations

a. **Focus on the host government**. The primary focus of a military and civilian coalition intervention in an R&S operation should be on developing, supporting and sustaining a legitimate host government through the use of all available instruments of power. This is accomplished in great part by supporting and facilitating the establishment of rule of law and social well being capacities.

b. **Shared Assessments**. The process of developing USG situational assessments and then sharing them with partners is useful to improve communication and facilitate a common understanding of the problem. It is more beneficial to share our national assessments and keep differing perspectives in view rather than develop a single common coalition assessment which would reflect the lowest common denominator among partners and be time and resource intensive.

c. **Strategic Guidance**. Shared strategic guidance is needed early to clearly convey the coalition's focus and intent. It also is necessary to establish coherence and align the appropriate resources and authorities to delegated leaders in theater enabling unity of effort.

d. **Comprehensive Approach**. Comprehensive approaches to analysis, planning, programming and evaluation across organizations are needed for unity of effort. Pursuit of a singular approach is not desired as it will alienate key partners external and internal to a coalition and likely generate a process that seeks the lowest common denominator and marginalizes the unique strengths of the participating organizations in the R&S operation.

e. **Campaign Design and Planning**. Campaign design and planning must focus on the unique situation presented in a particular country or region embroiled in conflict and account for achieving the strategic objectives envisioned in the formulation of a strategy utilizing a whole-of-government approach to planning nested within a coalition's comprehensive strategy. The design of a campaign plan should include the military's role in transitions; transitions from military to civilian control, transitions from civilian to international control, and handover to host government control. It should also include analyses of influential indigenous actors who may support or oppose the society's transformation to a locally led nascent peace.

f. **Measuring Progress and Employing Metrics**. Civilian agencies and the military face a common challenge in measuring results on the ground and evaluating progress toward achieving objectives. Many organizations are able to measure their own programs and project-level activities; however adequate methods have not been implemented to evaluate USG interagency and coalition wide impact of collective efforts. Ultimately, determinations must be made regarding coalition efforts contributing to achieving the strategic objectives.

g. **Maintain a Dialogue**. Active dialogue among civilian and military organizations within and external to the coalition, and at all levels of activity, is important to sharing perspectives. This expands the coalition's scope of awareness, sharpens its situational discernment, and facilitates cooperation among the actors.

h. **Understanding Differences**. Differences in motives, objectives, perspectives and cultures between the varieties of actors involved must be understood and accounted for. This understanding contributes to flexibility in thinking, adaptability in planning and compromise in developing objectives.

i. **Fostering Cooperative Relationships**. Command and control relationships will not likely be established among all participants in the R&S operation. Collaboration conducted among the voluntary civilian and military participants, both internal and external to a coalition, should be based on cooperative relationships rather than restrictive command and control relationships. However, the importance of centralized decision making control in cooperative relationships should be understood.

3. Interagency Management System Actions

a. General Actions

(1) The goal of R&S operations utilizing the IMS is to return "normalcy" in the HN. The response effort needs to be viewed in terms of a long timeframe. The military normally views operations based on specific timeframes; a "from start date to" or "D+", or in terms of deployment rotation schedules, six months, a year, eighteen months.

However, the USG approach is to view events in terms of years or even decades. Whole-of-government planners from agencies participating in the IMS will look at a crisis state in terms of how circumstances were ten or twenty years prior to the crisis and what circumstances should be ten years after the crisis. The crisis itself, if placed on a timeline, might be viewed as a "blip", an anomaly in the timeline's continuum.

(2) Planning prior to a crisis is steady-state planning. The USG has an engagement plan with every country in the world, even with those the USG has no official relationship. The US ambassador to a country has a strategic plan that defines what the steady-state engagement with that country will be. The normal or routine planning, programmatic, and budgeting processes of USG agencies will serve as a start point for the whole-of-government R&S planning process. The SPT of the CRSG Secretariat must become familiar with current plans, programs, and their supporting budgets both for CRP and contingency planning. Each SPT member, drawing from their own agency-specific expertise and reach-back capability, will brief the team on the objectives, assumptions, timeframes, and implementation status of their agency's existing plans, programs and supporting budget processes. Next, the team must consider the implications of the new or potential crisis and identify where existing planning, programs and budgeting does not adequately address the new R&S needs.

(3) Listed below are examples of routine planning, programs, and budgeting processes that planning teams must take into account:

(a) DOD contingency planning and campaign planning;

(b) DOS mission strategic planning and bureau strategic planning;

(c) DOS and USAID foreign assistance planning and programs; and

(d) The President's budget request and Congressional budget cycle.

(4) The initiation of CRP or contingency planning does not stop individual agencies' internal planning and budgeting processes. CRP shifts the responsibility for whole-of-government R&S planning for a given country to the SPT. Individual agencies will continue to plan independently to be able to fulfill both their specific R&S responsibilities within the USG R&S plan and their non-R&S functions. Contingency planning occurs in parallel with steady-state planning.

(5) During a crisis the planning teams will actively plan to return to steady state planning. Because of the complexity of transition, military commanders and civilian leaders will need to work very closely and should treat the transition planning as a distinct effort informing and improving the overall CRP effort. R&S planning and operations are, by their nature, transitional efforts to confront a crisis whose resolution is in the national interest. As the drivers of conflict are addressed and the HN institutional capacity increases, the USG will move to long-term steady-state planning, as represented by mission strategic plans (MSP), military campaign plans, and traditional foreign assistance programs such as country assistance strategies (CAS) and operational plans.

(6) When the R&S Interagency Policy Committee of the NSC, in consultation with the appropriate DOS Regional Bureau, decides to discontinue contingency planning for a country, the whole-of-government planning process described in the planning framework will cease. Contingency planning is a parallel process and does not replace steady-state planning, so the "transition" is just a matter of stopping the contingency planning. Individual agencies should consider the results of the contingency planning and any new guidance from senior officials as they continue steady-state planning in support of USG policy goals for the region.

(7) The main difference between a transition from contingency planning and CRP is that the scale will be larger, particularly if the CRP coincided with a robust USG response effort implemented through the IMS. If the USG deployed additional R&S capacity (civilian and/or military) to the field, key planning and implementing personnel as well as technical experts may be in-country, rather than in Washington. When the CRSG determines that the R&S goal has been met it will stop CRP and individuals who had been part of the CRP teams will gradually rejoin their agencies. Planning for transition from the R&S operation will be a critical component of the planning. This will include the resumption of steady state planning processes such as MSP, CAS, and military campaign planning.

b. Forming the SPT of the CRSG Secretariat

(1) One of the first tasks of the CRSG is to form a SPT, if not already assembled by S/CRS prior to a formal decision to trigger the planning process or establish the IMS. This team fulfills the planning and budgeting functions of the CRSG Secretariat, including conducting an initial assessment and developing policy goals and a strategy to achieve them. This process requires identifying assumptions and priorities, as well as developing a broad resource strategy.

(2) The SPT will consist of the members of the appropriate regional assistance working group (AWG), augmented by S/CRS planners and additional representatives from across the Executive Branch of the USG interagency community as appropriate. The team must include at least two persons designated to deploy as part of the IPC and two persons designated to deploy as part of the ACT R&S implementation planning team. The SPT should also include representatives from those USG agencies responsible for interfacing with the relevant multilateral bodies and as many representatives of implementing organizations as possible, such as the JTF and USAID. While the exact composition of the SPT will vary depending on a number of factors, the success of the team depends upon the convergence of functional, regional and country context, resource, and planning experts.

(3) The SPT will form the core of MME planning teams, and will most likely send liaison members to join the country-level objective planning teams. The planning process will initially constitute a full-time commitment for the members of the SPT; contracted experts may augment the team to supplement planning capacity. In the event of large-scale multilateral involvement, the SPT will coordinate the USG Strategic Plan for R&S with international counterparts, ideally accommodating international participation from close allies or coalition partners. The combination of CRP and the IMS represents

the most complex undertaking for R&S planners. Transition planning will be done by the planners in the field in cooperation with the planners at the CRSG. Transition planning should be treated as distinct plans that are critical to informing the overall strategic and implementation plans because of their uniqueness and complexity. Planners in the field will take the lead in developing transition plans with ACT planners and JTF planners working closely together. Command relationships will be critical to planning for transitions. Civilian representatives will likely not fully understand the military definition of command relationships, but they will understand the need for leadership, coordination and responsibilities at different levels both horizontally and vertically. Developing and fostering the relationship and understanding between the JTF commander, the ACT leader, and COM plus their respective staff is vital to accomplishing transitions with a minimum of disruption and confusion.

(4) An R&S operation likely involving a significant US military presence creates the need to integrate crisis action planning or contingency planning occurring simultaneously at the geographic combatant command with the whole-of-government CRP or contingency planning in Washington and the field. A team of civilian planners called the IPC will deploy to the affected geographic combatant command to ensure this integration occurs. Likewise, a similar type of team may deploy to a multinational planning HQ to integrate USG efforts with an international response.

c. **Development of the Situation Analysis**

(1) Civilian agencies do much, if not most, of their planning at the strategic level. The next four sections look at the development of the Situation Analysis, the formulation of policy, strategy development and country-level planning. These all take place in Washington, except for the last, which spans the levels of execution from Washington to the field. Military planners at the geographic combatant command and JTF levels will not directly participate in the strategic level activities, but their planning and deliberations will influence and inform strategic level situation analysis, strategy development and policy formulation. Both OSD and the Joint Staff will contribute significantly to all aspects of the whole-of-government planning process at the strategic level.

(2) Situation analysis describes the current environment for the R&S operation and is a prerequisite to developing policy options for senior-level review. The situation analysis will draw, where possible, on consultations and information exchanges with US personnel and other multilateral, governmental and nongovernmental partners in the field. Situation analysis for R&S planning should include conducting a comprehensive interagency assessment using, when possible, the Interagency Conflict Assessment Framework (ICAF) that diagnoses the conflict or civil strife. Information generated from prior planning and assessments, as well as existing data and intelligence from interagency partners will be used in the analysis.

(3) The military will participate in the development of the situation analysis at all stages. This process will in almost all cases begin prior to the establishment of the CRSG. The development of the situation analysis is similar in approach to the Army's tactical operations intelligence preparation of the battlefield (IPB) where all sources of

intelligence and information are used to determine enemy strength, disposition, intentions. For situation analysis all of these factors are considered, as are: environmental facts, cultural, ethnic, religious, economic factors that all impact on understanding the environment where the crisis is taking place.

(4) Drawing on the results of the ICAF, the SPT will develop a *Situation Analysis Overview Memorandum* that provides a clear depiction of the drivers of conflict and mitigating factors that reduce civil strife or conflict, and current USG and international efforts. Also depicted are US interests relating to the country and region, the expected actions of key participants (both partners and competitors), gaps in current and expected efforts to address the instability or conflict, risks associated with action and inaction, legal considerations for providing assistance to the country, and critical gaps in knowledge/ intelligence. The SPT uses the *Situation Analysis Overview Memorandum* to help develop policy options for consideration by senior officials.

(5) The *Situation Analysis Overview Memorandum* should be no longer than ten pages and include:

(a) a summary of key US interests relating to the country and region, and the major risks associated with a continuation of current trends;

(b) a brief summary of recent developments and the strategic context, key Drivers of Conflict and Mitigating Factors, and critical knowledge gaps;

(c) a review of international engagement in the country/region, including the impact of past, present and expected HN and international actions, as well as a review of the impact of past and present US actions; and

(d) a review of possible opportunity costs and/or policy tradeoffs to US action (or inaction) and possible US and/or international legal or other impediments to US action.

(6) A shared understanding of the situation is critical to the success of the planning process and ultimately the implementation of the USG Strategic Plan for R&S. The situation analysis serves as the foundational process to forge this shared understanding, identifying the underlying drivers of instability or conflict, the US interests at stake, existing USG and other actors' plans and activities, key assumptions, possible contingencies, anticipated resource availability, intelligence requirements, and the dynamics of the regional and international context. It is the foundation of the consensus-building effort to formulate policy options and develop the strategic plan. This is particularly relevant as parallel military planning and situation awareness is coordinated and de-conflicted with civilian agency planning and situation awareness. The *Situation Analysis Overview Memorandum* produced by the SPT will serve as a mechanism for in-briefing new planning team members and fostering a shared understanding of the situation beyond the SPT to all participating agencies.

d. **Policy Formulation**

(1) The *Situation Analysis Overview* is the basis for second step of the whole-of-government strategic planning process: the articulation of clear policy options with associated risks and benefits in the form of a *Policy Advisory Memorandum* for PC/DC. The *Policy Advisory Memorandum* combines the most important elements of the *Situation Analysis Overview* with an explanation of how differing assumptions about critical planning considerations (conditions within the country, the behavior of other regional and international actors, and resources from the USG and other sources) lead to options for an overarching R&S policy goal and the strategic objectives required to achieve the R&S policy goal. These strategic objectives correspond to the drivers of conflict and local capacity needs and are termed MMEs.

(2) PC/DC respond to the *Policy Advisory Memorandum* by either issuing a *Policy Statement* or requesting new policy options. OSD and the JS are deeply involved and likely to play a leading role in developing many of the options sent to the PC/DC for decision. The *Policy Statement* determines the overarching R&S goal through the approval of one of the policy options. This includes stipulating the critical planning considerations that planners should use as they develop the USG R&S Strategic Plan and providing a preliminary estimate of the USG resources likely to be available for the R&S operation. The *Policy Statement* also designates the US official responsible for implementing the plan and identifies the US agency tasked with leading the planning around each MME supporting the development of the USG R&S Strategic Plan.

(3) The first step in drafting policy options is determining which assumptions, in addition to the causal assumptions drawn from situation analysis, are critical to the direction of a USG plan and the ultimate success of the R&S operation. There are three main categories of contextual assumptions about the strategic environment to consider:

(a) conditions within the country (e.g., electricity infrastructure in major cities will be sufficient and functioning, the security environment will be permissive);

(b) actions of other regional and international actors (e.g., the European Union will provide sufficient resources to achieve objectives in the Rule of Law sector, neighboring states will not send military forces across borders); and

(c) resources (funding, manpower, equipment) available from the USG (e.g., there will be a $300 million supplemental, 100 civilians will be deployed from the civilian reserve corps).

(4) The identification of achievable goals is the next stage in the formulation of policy options. The SPT should identify a goal for each contextual scenario. Planners need to consider the longer-term objectives for the country when trying to determine a shorter-term goal that capitalizes on the two to three year period where political and financial resources are at their highest levels. The two to three year goal should be to reach the conflict transformation "tipping point" of locally-led nascent peace, where the country is on a sustainable positive trajectory out of conflict, regardless of international assistance. Considering two to three year periods in planning will be a departure for many military planners that are familiar with planning timeframes measured in hours and days.

(5) When presenting a goal, the SPT will define, as clearly as possible, what "success" would look like if the goal was reached. Proposing that country X will be "at peace with itself and on the path to economic growth" is a standard goal that could apply to any R&S country and therefore not useful. The strategic planning process should provide senior policy-makers with a more detailed explanation of the desired end state to faithfully convey the challenges ahead. The defined goal will prove valuable when planners begin to outline the necessary benchmarks to be reached and the measures of progress to be observed.

(6) Next, the SPT will flesh out each policy option into a two to three paragraph narrative that outlines:

(a) overarching policy;

(b) policy implications (any changes to current policy, or political/legislative issues, and policy priority trade-offs);

(c) strategy summary;

(d) conflict transformation strategic goal: what success would "look like;"

(e) MMEs;

(f) Causal and contextual assumptions (summary of the drivers of conflict drawn from the situation analysis and contextual assumptions about the country environment, anticipated roles and resource commitments of other actors) and how the assumptions will be verified over time;

(g) USG resource availability, rough orders of magnitude of USG resource needs expressed in a common, agreed lexicon; and

(h) associated risks and opportunities.

(7) Resource issues may not be fully identified at this stage in the planning process. However, it is crucial to put potential resource gaps squarely before policymakers as early as possible so they understand the obstacles in achieving desired policy objectives. The SPT will seek input from all USG elements in the affected country throughout the development of the situation analysis, scenarios, goals, and MMEs. This input may arrive through regional bureau representatives on the team or directly from the COM (or the ACT) to the CRSG.

e. **Strategy Development**

(1) The SPT uses the *Policy Statement* to begin the iterative process of developing the USG R&S Strategic Plan. This plan will determine how the R&S operation will address the prioritization, sequencing and cross-sectoral linkages of USG efforts. DOD will play a significant role in apportioning resources to the mission due to the

significant resources it brings to an R&S operation and because any USG presence in the field is likely to include military personnel. DOD has formalized a process for estimating the cost associated with contingency operations. This process is outlined in DOD 7000.14-R the Financial Management Regulation (FMR) Volume 12 Chapter 23 entitled "Contingency Operations" and would support OSD and Joint staff representatives on the CRSG developing cost estimates for the R&S Strategic Plan.

(2) The preliminary DOD contingency cost estimate, called the pre-deployment estimate, typically is prepared by the Office of the Under Secretary of Defense (Comptroller) (OUSD(C)) and the JS J-8. It projects a rough order of magnitude cost estimate. Typically, DOD components need additional time to develop "ground up" estimates. As an adjunct to this model, the OUSD(C) has established a contingency cost estimating team to develop a more reliable preliminary cost estimate for contingency operations. This team is on call to OUSD(C) and consists of financial managers from OSD, the Joint Staff, and DOD components. It is augmented by operational and logistics planners as needed, to collect information about the operation and to formulate assumptions to support the cost estimating effort.

(3) The SPT is also responsible for synthesizing the constant flow of information from the field into its deliberations on the plan including, where possible, input from HN authorities. As a guiding principle, HN authorities should be engaged, as early as possible, in strategic planning. In extreme instances, where outside actors have assumed authority, criteria for triggering a transfer of authority to a responsible HN government should be established early and reviewed regularly for continuing relevance to changing situations.

(4) The locus of planning during the strategy development phase will depend on the nature of the R&S operation, as indicated in the Policy Statement. More information on the Policy Statement is provided in Appendix E, *Whole of Government Planning Utilizing the IMS.*

(5) The strategy development level of planning is the final step towards completion of the USG Strategic Plan for R&S, which in turn begins the country-level planning process. The completed plan will be submitted to the CRSG and to DC as necessary for approval. Once approved, the USG R&S Strategic Plan and associated guidance can be issued to executing agencies.

f. **Implementation Planning to Develop a Country-Level Plan.** Agencies and participants across the USG have existing capabilities to plan the resourcing and support to implementation of their own agencies' activities. Agency–level implementation plans exist prior to the beginning of the whole-of-government planning process. Agencies will likely begin internal discussions on what revisions to their implementation plans are necessary in parallel with whole-of-government planning processes. In the case of DOD, contingency plans will likely be well underway by the time the USG decides to act on a crisis and establish the IMS. DOD planning will continue, however it must adjust to and incorporate the requirements developed by the whole-of-government planning process employing the IMS. The whole-of-government approach to planning utilizing the IMS does not replace the methodologies and processes by which DOD plans. Rather, it establishes the methodology and process for developing a Country Plan and provides guidance on what aspects of DOD implementation plans must be shared with other USG participants conducting implementation planning. For more information on Country Plan development see Appendix E, *Whole of government Planning Utilizing the IMS*.

4. Coordination at Strategic Level

a. Coordination at the strategic level on transitions is not going to significantly vary from coordination that occurs throughout the R&S operation employing the IMS. The CRSG will have the lead for deciding when transitions will occur based on input from the field, and with the advice and consent of the COM and ACT leader, who will assume leadership roles after the transition has occurred. The overarching R&S goals for the operation are used by the SPT to identify and develop the strategic objectives necessary to accomplish the overarching R&S goals. These strategic objectives are termed MMEs. All agencies and departments with a role in a MME will be involved in the planning and subsequent implementation activities surrounding the MME.

b. A scenario example may have an MME that covers the restoration of the HN power grid initially with DOD in the lead, due to a tenuous security environment, playing a key planning role along with other agencies providing technical advice in developing the sub-tasks for the MME. Eventually, the Department of Energy (DOE) will transition to assume leadership of the subsequent planning and execution of this MME. In time the DOE will transition the responsibility for the power grid over to a HN entity. DOE representatives will participate on the MME planning team from the outset and DOE will deploy the appropriate personnel to the HN to work with the DOD counterparts as soon as possible in order to assume lead responsibility when the CRSG leadership determines based on advice received from the field regarding the security environment.

5. Coordination at Operational and Tactical/Implementation Level

a. Integration Planning Cell (IPC)

(1) At the geographic combatant command operational level the IPC serves the role of synthesizing the military operations planning with interagency R&S planning. Its purpose is to support civilian-military communication and integration of civilian and military planning in order to achieve unity of effort. The goal of the IPC is to provide timely, usable information, advice, and coordination from an interagency perspective to the CCDR. The IPC will not be directly involved in transition planning. Its role will primarily be to help the geographic combatant command staff understand the capabilities, limitations and requirements of the civilian organizations they represent and serve to liaise between the ACT and the geographic combatant command where and when appropriate.

(2) IPC members serve as a bridge between their civilian agencies' Washington and field staffs by addressing the civilian agency gap at the operational level of the military, represented by the geographic combatant command, and ensuring plans and decisions by civilian agencies in Washington and the field are represented and informed by planning and decision-making at the military operational HQ. The IPC members will be

of sufficient stature and possess sufficient knowledge to provide insights into the R&S plans utilizing the IMS and reach-back to their respective parent agencies. The interagency representatives on the IPC are the R&S subject matter experts for their respective agencies and have expert level knowledge of the IMS.

(3) The joint interagency coordination group (JIACG) or its equivalent interagency staff element exists in all geographic combatant commands. They help CCDRs by providing advice and linkages during normal day-to-day activities with the civilian components of our national power (e.g., DOS, the USAID, and other departments and agencies). The IPC is established to facilitate the conduct of the IMS by providing interagency support to plans, operations, contingencies, and initiatives. The IPC does not replace the JIACG or its equivalent. The IPC does not subsume JIACG responsibilities, nor does the JIACG become the IPC. The two organizations will be expected to cooperate with each other. The members of the JIACG should help facilitate IPC integration into the combatant command structure. The JIACG will continue to exercise its advisory function to the commander and members of the JIACG may, if appropriate, serve temporarily on the IPC; however the IPC is specifically sent to the geographic combatant command to facilitate the execution of the IMS supporting the planning and implementation of an R&S operation.

b. **Advance Civilian Team (ACT)**

(1) The ACT, in addition to being headed by the ambassador or a designated leader, is composed of the senior member of each represented department or agency. In a foreign country, the COM is the highest US civil authority. The Foreign Service Act assigns the COM to a foreign country the responsibility for the direction, coordination, and supervision of all government executive branch employees in that country except for military Service members and employees under the command of a US area military commander – the GCC. As the senior USG official permanently assigned in the HN, the COM is responsible to the President for policy oversight of all USG programs. This includes a scenario involving an R&S operation using the established IMS as part of a whole-of-government response to a crisis that may unfold in their country of responsibility.

(2) Country-level whole-of-government structures and processes are the **integrated systems** at the country-level which provide the COM and JTF commander with capacity to integrate the activities of all allocated assets in time, space, and purpose to achieve unity of effort. These integrated structures and processes do not exist apart from the COM and JTF commander. They include both new and existing structures, processes, and personnel, and originate from within the AMEMB (and the JTF if present). ACT personnel provide capabilities and capacities to support, and if necessary assist in building, these integrated structures and processes.

(3) The more extensive the USG participation is in an R&S operation and the more dispersed US military forces are throughout a country, the greater the need for additional coordination mechanisms to extend civilian oversight and assistance. However, given the limited resources of the DOS and the other USG agencies, especially at the outset of a crisis response, military forces often represent the USG in decentralized, diffuse, and oftentimes hostile operating environments. Operating with a clear

understanding of the guiding political aims, military commanders and their subordinates at all levels must be prepared to exercise judgment and act without the benefit of immediate civilian oversight and guidance.

(4) Initially, civilian agencies will integrate into the existing implementation efforts and procedures established by the military in a supporting role due to the security environment and its affect on their abilities to carry out their normal responsibilities. Transitions will occur when practicable with the recommendations of the JTF commander and the ACT leader as more civilian agency personnel and resources enter the AOR and the USG Strategic Plan for R&S and the subsequent USG Country Plan unfold utilizing the IMS.

(5) The military should not remain the lead of any traditional civilian responsibilities for longer than is absolutely necessary. Tasks such a good governance, establishing local medical clinics, security sector reform, local infrastructure restoration, restoring schools are all tasks the military may undertake at the outset of an R&S operation using the IMS, but are all tasks that are civilian led by nature and require civilian leadership as soon as possible. The military may play a key supporting role, such as in security sector reform, but the role should be supporting, not lead. The transitions will be planned in close coordination between the ACT implementation planning team and the JTF planners. The ACT leader and the JTF commander must have a close working relationship that includes daily interface. Determinations will be made between these two leaders when the various transitions should occur and by whom. Their recommendations will be passed to the CRSG in close coordination with the GCC and COM – if the COM is a different person than the ACT leader.

c. **Country Team**

(1) The country team is led by the presidentially appointed ambassador. The makeup of the country team varies widely from country to country, depending on the US departments and agencies represented in the country and the desires of the ambassador and the HN government. The country team, regardless of size, has a range of responsibilities that go on daily in the diplomatic, informational, bilateral military and economic spheres. The largest US embassies with representation in some form from the Departments of State, Defense, Justice and Treasury, as well as USAID, the CIA and the DEA, but many small and medium-size embassies have country teams with much more limited representation. The American citizens in most embassies are outnumbered by the HN nationals that work for the AMEMB and perform most of the routine non-policy related work.

(2) The country team does not have the capacity and may lack the expertise to deal with the challenges of a complex crisis. However, they have the understanding of the society, government, local customs, culture, and language that will be invaluable to the incoming ACT implementation personnel. The ACT is comprised of a group of people who join the embassy staff to supplement capabilities already present at the AMEMB, under the direction of the COM. The ACT is not a separate entity which takes over and leads R&S missions regardless of the country team. The COM will determine the roles and priorities of all members of the country team, those who are permanent assignees on

the team and those, of the ACT, that have come to augment the country team. It is also possible that some country team members could serve briefly as liaisons with the JTF until more personnel have deployed in. When there is no country team in a crisis country— either one did not exist before the crisis unfolded, or the one that was present was withdrawn—the ACT may have to temporarily assume the duties of the country team, in addition to their own duties.

(3) The military, the JTF, will not have transition requirements regarding the country team. At no time will the JTF or another military entity assume the roles of the country team so a need to transition will not occur. The JTF will coordinate closely with the country team and sometimes the lines between the country team and the ACT may be briefly blurred if personnel serve on both. However, this will not affect the overall relationship the JTF will have with either the country team and/or the ACT. The COM may insist on using his/her military advisor in a liaison role with the JTF. If the relationship between the COM and the senior military person in the embassy is good and the COM has trust in the individual, this can serve to facilitate the cooperation between the COM, ACT, country team and the JTF. This liaison function can facilitate transitions as the military advisor will have a measure of knowledge and understanding of the country situation and where US interests lie as the mission moves from crisis to steady state.

(4) The lack of a transition requirement between a country team and a JTF alludes to but does not address the extreme scenario where the US military is an occupying power and the USG has imposed a military government on a foreign country. This topic goes beyond the scope of the IMS and this handbook.

d. Field Advance Civilian Team (FACT)

(1) The FACT level of the IMS is where transitions from military authority to civilian leadership will be most visible. FACTs are stood up "away from the flagpole" in outlying areas or provinces once there is sufficient stability to allow them to establish and commence longer-term R&S activities. In most, if not all cases, FACTs will take over from military units - engineers and special operations forces to include civil affairs will be among those that will have started the implementation of R&S activities. A few exercises are encouraged and recommended while training for such situations. However, it is probable that no formal process will be in place prior to the transition and civilian participation in exercises is likely to be under resourced and compete with other budgetary and program requirements within their respective agencies.

(2) Military commanders and leaders should continue to plan, dispatch, and execute missions while the FACT team members become familiar with the situation. The FACT should gradually begin planning and executing more of the missions in its operational area, initially working with the military components and gradually assuming leadership with military support as appropriate according to a schedule agreed upon between the FACT leader and the military officer in charge. The military will retain responsibility for the missions initially but gradually the FACT will take over and at a point in time mutually agreed upon will assume all mission responsibility. The FACT assumption of mission responsibility in no way diminishes the authority a military commander has over forces assigned or attached to them.

(3) The military will assume a supporting role and will remain in place until mission requirements no longer necessitate the involvement of military forces and their higher HQ make a decision to redeploy. This transition process is often referred to as "left seat, right seat" by military personnel and is traditionally executed during a RIP operation conducted between two or more military units. Military commanders need to be prepared to maintain a military presence with the FACT indefinitely, if the need and justification warrants it.

6. Coordination with Host Nation Public and Private Sectors

a. A JTF deployed to a country or region in crisis as part of a US whole-of-government response will have the primary mission of security. In most cases this will be a broad mandate, security will be a dynamic and challenging suite of operational imperatives. The JTF commander will ensure the security of the military personnel and resources placed under his command, establishing securable operating bases, a HQ, and securing routes of movement for his elements. At the same time the JTF commander must balance the security of the forces under his command with the security needs of the population within the HN. Maintaining a constant security presence, preferably and when appropriate utilizing the tactic of dismounted operations, will greatly contribute to the resumption of normal daily activities of the HN population and allow the deployed JTF to counter messages and actions perpetrated by extremist or insurgent groups.

b. Maintaining a security posture that isolates the deployed JTF from the host-country population, will in the short term provide adequate security to the military forces under command of the JTF commander. However, the security needs of the HN population may be sacrificed using this strategy. It will also become difficult for the JTF to counter the messages and actions of extremist and insurgent groups under this strategy, thus leading to an overall degraded security environment for both the HN population and the forces under the command of the JTF commander.

(1) Sometimes, the more one protects the force, the less it may be secure. Ultimate success in COIN is gained by protecting the populace, not the COIN force. If military forces remain in their compounds, they lose touch with the people, appear to be running scared, and cede the initiative to the insurgents. Aggressive saturation patrolling, ambushes, and listening post operations must be conducted, risk shared with the populace, and contact maintained. The effectiveness of establishing patrol bases and operational support bases should be weighed against the effectiveness of using larger unit bases. (FM 90-8 discusses saturation patrolling and operational support bases.) These practices ensure access to the intelligence needed to drive operations. Following them reinforces the connections with the populace that help establish real legitimacy.

(2) Heavily armed and armored personnel have more difficulty connecting with the population than those who can move more naturally amongst the population. A dismounted soldier not wearing full body armor is more approachable than a mounted soldier or one in full body armor. Military commanders must balance force protection and approachability. In non-permissive (i.e., uncertain or hostile) environments in present

Afghanistan and Iraq, PRT personnel move with armed military escorts, which contributes to the overall security presence. However, the PRT does not conduct military operations, nor do they assist HN military forces. The only security role assigned to a PRT is force protection by providing armored vehicles and an advisor to escort PRT personnel to meetings with local officials. US military assigned to escort civilian PRT members receive training in providing PRT civilian personnel protection under an agreement with DOS. The training is designed to reinforce understanding of escort responsibilities and to prevent endangerment to PRT civilian personnel. US military escorting PRT personnel should not combine this responsibility with other missions. The problem of providing PRT civilian personnel with security is compounded by competing protection priorities, precluding dedicated security teams in most situations and limiting security teams to available personnel.

c. The JTF will implement the operational objectives and guidelines established by the GCC. Policy guidance and the strategic objectives, referred to as MMEs, will originate in Washington, DC. through the CRSG and military specific operational level sub-objectives under each MME will get passed to the JTF commander through guidance and direction from the GCC with the appropriate input from the COM or ACT leader. The COM will occupy a special position and will advise the formation of strategic and operational objectives while keeping appraised of the tactical situation in country from information gathered at the JTF and the resident ACT and country teams.

d. While the COM has no command authority over the JTF commander, the COM nonetheless carries substantial influence as that official with Presidential authority over US policy concerning the HN. Cooperation between the COM and the JTF commander are essential to successful execution of the broad missions of all USG elements inside the affected country. The tasks assigned to the JTF commander as a result of the GCC's operational plans incorporating the MME sub-objectives will significantly broaden the security responsibilities of the military force.

e. A JTF commander can expect to be asked to supplement existing security at the facilities of the AMEMB in the affected country or those facilities that have been designated a temporary embassy. The JTF will be asked to secure lines of communication between its HQ and the embassy. It also may be requested to provide a measure of security to a pre-determined set of critical HN infrastructure, refugee centers, and emergency medical locations.

f. JTF commanders must plan on the likelihood that assigned military personnel will be the only "American face" present on the street in the HN during the first critical hours and days of the USG response. What happens in those first hours and days will set the tone for how the USG presence is perceived by the local inhabitants. In an ideal circumstance, civilian experts in a range of disciplines such as power generation, sanitation, municipal governance, law and courts, police functions, and cultural awareness will all arrive in country with the military force. The reality is that these personnel are probably not going to arrive until days or even weeks later when the main body of the ACT arrives. Until that time the JTF will, out of necessity, be the face of the American presence and will be expected to respond to a range of demands not normally expected by military commanders.

g. The JTF command and staff will have to establish a mechanism for dealing with local leaders and individuals representing tribes, communities, regions and themselves. They will also need to establish a two way dialog with whatever senior USG civilian leadership is present, either the embassy, the COM located in an adjacent country or the US, or through the GCC to the DOS. To deal with the HN's private and public sector the JTF commander needs to establish a CMOC or its equivalent.

h. The CMOC may be located near the JTF HQ where the JTF commander or their designated representative will meet with any private or public sector representatives on a daily basis to determine what assistance the command can offer the HN to further stabilization. The presence of the CMOC, its purpose, and who its target audience is will need to be publicized and distributed out into the HN population by whatever mean is available to the JTF — radio, local TV, local news media and public announcements by the JTF public affairs office or through the use of subordinate military units conducting civil military operations. The information should identify the daily hours when the CMOC is staffed and open. When the security environment is prohibitive to establish normal operating hours the information provided should contain at a minimum who to contact and how to arrange an appointment.

i. CMOCs facilitate the integration of military and political actions. The CMOC is an organization normally comprised of civil affairs, established to plan and facilitate coordination of activities of the Armed Forces of the United States with indigenous populations and institutions, the private sector, IGOs, NGOs, multinational forces, and other governmental agencies in support of the JFC (See JP 3-57, *Civil Military Operations*, for more information on the CMOC).

j. Below the national level, additional CMOCs where military commanders and civilian leaders can meet directly with local leaders to discuss issues and coordinate implementing activities may be established. Where possible, IGOs and NGOs should be encouraged to participate in coordination meetings at CMOCs to ensure their actions are known, de-conflicted, and if possible integrated with USG, coalition, and HN plans.

k. The JTF can utilize the CMOC or its equivalent to better organize its civil military efforts and provide a venue to interface with representatives of the HN. Members of the HN from the public and private sectors will routinely approach the CMOC for a wide variety of reasons. These could be simple requests for assistance or to file a complaint to much larger and complex issues dealing with security, governance, essential services, infrastructure, economics and commerce. It will be important, in all of these factors, to assess the situation and address the issues from the standpoint of military support to stabilization activities to enable a transition to civil authorities utilizing the FACT and ACT structures as they establish and become operational.

l. The JTF is well suited to conduct short term high impact projects that have been coordinated with its higher HQ (the geographic combatant command), the ACT in communication with the CRSG and, when deemed to be appropriate, representatives from the HN. Daily and regular coordination needs to be maintained to ensure projects and programs initiated by the JTF support the longer-term USG strategic objectives or MMEs.

Funding sources will be essential in determining what the JTF can do. As in the past, the JTF commander is expected to receive contingency funds to initiate immediate impact projects below a pre-set ceiling. More costly projects will have to be prior approved on an individual basis. The JTF staff and the CMOC will have to act in a circumspect manner with all individuals claiming to be legitimate leaders until assistance can be obtained to verify claims. IGOs and NGOs can be a very good source of advice on prioritizing quick impact projects and can even serve to promote higher cost larger scale projects, often with the approval and advice of a senior USAID representative at the US Mission and/or the ACT. These projects must conform to governing regulations concerning the use of contracting and funding mechanisms when they exceed pre-set dollar threshold amounts.

m. A well functioning CMOC will see requests for assistance increase and may not be able to support all projects. Careful consideration must be given to the accomplishment of R&S objectives when prioritizing and selecting projects with HN counterparts. The goal is to stabilize first then transition to the appropriate civilian authority for follow-on, longer term R&S and development activities.

n. Lastly, the US Army Corps of Engineers (USACE) can assist in the development and execution of infrastructure related projects – both short-term and longer-term. USACE has a history of working with CMOCs for the development, prioritization and selection of projects. All projects to include those that go beyond short-term and into the longer-term development category most be carefully coordinated with the appropriate authorities from the HN and the USG. The expertise of USACE, if available, can be utilized as a "bridge" for longer term projects that can be transitioned to the relevant civil authorities.

o. The CMOC will be approached by representatives of recognized IGOs and NGOs with advice and requests for assistance, especially transportation requests and security requests. JTF staffs are encouraged to establish dialogs with these representatives and take advantage of the depth of "ground-truth" knowledge these organizations have. Transportation and security requests should be considered in the context of the JTF priorities, mission requirements that resource the USG Country Plan, as well as advice from the ACT and any set or standing guidance from its higher HQ. Granting these requests will require coordination with various elements of JTF operations and logistics staffs and may require a commander's authorization.

p. CMOC personnel may be approached by intelligence and counter-intelligence officials for information derived or produced through interactions with the representatives of the HN. It is important to remember that the main focus of a CMOC is to assist in the activities of engaged military forces as it relates to civil military operations. Intelligence collection methods are a sensitive issue that will be managed at higher levels at or above the JTF level and direction will be provided accordingly based on applicable policies.

q. There will be many types of personnel working within a CMOC and many more actors who will utilize a CMOC for various purposes. Military commanders and senior USG representatives will utilize the CMOC while meeting with senior level counterparts in the HN for a variety of purposes ranging from security to humanitarian assistance needs. Civil Affairs forces and representatives of a commander's civil-military staff will utilize the

CMOC on a daily basis when interacting with representatives from the HN. Depending on the security environment other US agencies and departments may utilize the CMOC – most likely for program and project implementation purposes in coordination with the HN.

r. Another scenario a JTF commander and staff must be prepared for is the necessity to open multiple CMOCs from the JTF level down to subordinate command levels as determined by the commander, the requirements pertaining to the situation on the ground, the number of military forces present, and the geographic footprint of the forces inside the HN. These CMOCs should strive to correspond to their equivalent level ACT and FACT structures. However, this may not be possible as their focus will be toward short-term stabilization tasks to allow for the implementation of the IMS and the reception of the interagency community resident within the structures of the IMS. The USG Country Plan utilizing the IMS should consider the concept of a RIP when transitioning CMOC responsibilities to corresponding structures of the IMS. However, personnel from a CMOC must be prepared to conduct a RIP (on their own) with their relevant IMS counterpart if the implementation plan does not sufficiently address the topic.

s. Once the ACT and FACTs have deployed and established a significant presence inside the affected country the JTF should consider the phasing out of CMOCs. The JTF staff members of the CMOC should be considered for duties liaising with the ACT or even being detailed to the ACT to ensure smooth transition from military CMOCs to the civilian led ACT and FACTs. The transition from CMOCs to ACT/FACTs may not happen all at once due to conditions in the security environment. It is likely that during transition there will be sub-national regions of a country where CMOCs will remain while other more permissive environments at the sub-national level may establish FACTs outside of the ACT HQ. CMOCs and FACTs may even co-exist or co-locate during the RIP.

t. A JTF commander or subordinate commander may opt to continue the operation of a CMOC when circumstances cause the forces of a JTF and civilian authorities to locate in disparate positions. In these circumstances the CMOC will coordinate with ACT/FACTs to ensure their activities remain aligned with and support the R&S objectives of the USG Country Plan. Overall, the JTF commander needs to strive to move forward on stabilization activities and initial reconstruction efforts consistent with USG projected goals and objectives so that a smooth transition is accomplished when civilian members of the ACT and FACTs arrive in the affected country.

7. Military Resources Supporting Civilian Components of the Interagency Management System

a. Resource and Manpower Requirements

(1) Both the GCC and the JTF commanders will need to take into account resources and manpower requirements above and beyond those needed for more traditional military operations. The requirements will be different for every complex R&S operation employing the IMS, however, common threads can be found that can help prior

planning and preparation. Manpower requirements supporting the established IMS will fall in several categories; liaison, tasks to military units to provide operational support, and attachment of individual service members to civilian led elements of the IMS to name a few. Transitions should be treated as distinct activities requiring additional manpower to support its planning teams. Transition planning should be incorporated into the USG Strategic Plan for R&S, the Country Plan, and military plans and resourced accordingly.

(2) Upon initial completion of the strategic plan, the scope of the operation, general numbers and types of civilians being deployed, and general logistics and transportation requirements will become increasingly clearer. Military planners can estimate and prioritize where and when military elements that are performing or assisting civilian tasks can hand over leadership responsibility for those tasks and assume a supporting role or withdraw entirely from involvement. In many cases the military components will assume supporting roles and then phase out over time, they will not execute abrupt handovers. JTF commanders should plan to retain leadership and responsibility for a number of supporting tasks; normally this will include security, logistics, transportation, and communications. The civilian components are not likely to be able to assume responsibility for these until normal steady-state operations are re-established.

b. **Determine Resources**

(1) Resources have been covered in other parts of this handbook. Executing transition operations will have specific demands on both manpower and resources that are somewhat unique. One of the critical objectives of transitions is to maintain a measure of equilibrium with the HN and other actors like NGOs, IGOs, and multinational partners. It will be necessary for military planners to consider a brief surge in manpower and resources during the transition period to ensure no breakdowns occur while maintaining implementation activities. Military planners need to know what civilian personnel are involved in the transition from the civilian agencies and NGOs and what resources they might lack that the military could provide, temporarily, until the transition is complete and the civilian lead has accepted responsibilities.

(2) A scenario to consider is the RIP of a civil affairs unit that is managing the restoration and rehabilitation of a power generating station along with the involvement of technical experts from a military engineer unit to an NGO that is coming into the AO under the auspices of a contract with USAID. The NGO will not have communications equipment with which to communicate with the military units it is relieving or the FACT responsible for the region within which the power station resides. Military planners may be asked to plan to provide a specified number of communications equipment to the NGO and personnel to either operate them or provide some basic training in their use until the transition is complete and they have established their own communications link-up with the FACT and others. This is just one example, for the same scenario there may be a request for several days of rations, vehicles for transportation and even access to potable water. Even a relatively benign transition can present military planners and leaders with unanticipated and complex challenges.

c. Obtaining Manpower and Resources

(1) Transition operations will occur within R&S operations when conditions have been relatively stabilized and reconstruction activities have increased in tempo. Military and civilian planners and leaders will need to work in close cooperation to identify the needs of the civilian components entering the AO. The military will have in place the preponderance of the manpower and resources allocated to address the immediate needs of the crisis. In preparation for transitions to occur the civilian planners, especially at the ACT level, will need to identify manpower and resource needs the civilian agencies cannot fill that will be requested of the military to provide. The military will likely have the skills and resources in place that civilian planners on an ACT may request. Obtaining manpower and resources will need to be conducted by the ACT through formal requests passed to the CRSG and executed using letters of agreement (LOA) and letters of request (LOR).

(2) The military can respond to these requests with the manpower and resources already in the AOR, or with augmentation from the geographic combatant command. For example, a scenario could have civilian agency personnel on an ACT identifying the number of persons with the appropriate skills needed to manage a detention facility in the ACT AOR, but the contract for the right number of contractor personnel with the appropriate skills will not have them in place until several weeks following the transition. The military has been managing the detention facility since assuming control early in the stabilization phase. At the request of the ACT through the CRSG, the military may be tasked by its chain of command to provide a specified number of soldiers with the necessary skills to remain in place until the contractor group arrives. If the JTF does not have other responsibilities for the troops at the detention facility this can be accommodated with organic assets. If there is another mission for these troops, the JTF might have to request additional forces from the geographic combatant command for a short period of time. In all cases requests from the ACT to the JTF for additional resources supporting its operational requirements will need to be coordinated with and cleared by the CRSG and the GCC.

APPENDIX A
AUTHORITIES FOR MILITARY PARTICIPATION IN RECONSTRUCTION AND STABILIZATION OPERATIONS

1. Introduction

It is important to know and understand the authorities surrounding military participation in R&S operations within the context of a whole-of-government approach envisioned in the USG Planning Framework. These authorities are rooted in law and provide a basis for regulations and doctrine that inform military planning and guides the implementation effort of the military contribution to a whole-of-government planning and implementation process. The intent of this appendix is to inform military commanders and staffs of the authorities that are likely to influence military participation in these operations under the context of an established IMS. This appendix, and indeed this handbook, is not intended to be directive or prescribe a one course of action solution to a commander, rather it should be used to inform military planning while utilizing a larger whole-of-government approach. Although the authorities described in this appendix are found in law and regulation and provide a commander and staff with planning constraints, they also serve as a set of guide markers providing an authoritative basis to assist interagency coordination mechanisms and support interagency planning and implementation efforts.

2. Relationships between a Joint Task Force Commander and the Chief of Mission, and by Extension the Advance Civilian Team Leader

a. Authority over US personnel in foreign countries is fundamentally a statutory issue. It is divided primarily between the COM and the applicable senior US Military commander with geographic responsibilities, i.e., the GCC. This clear division of authority is well illustrated in Title 22 USC 3927, which states that the COM has "full responsibility" for the direction, coordination, and supervision of all government executive branch employees in the country - except for employees under the command of United States area military commander." This divided authority is echoed in Title 22 USC 4802, which tasks the SECSTATE with the responsibility to protect all USG personnel on official duty abroad, "other than ... those personnel under the command of a US area military commander."

b. The US area military commander is understood to be the commander of a unified combatant command with geographic responsibilities, as that term is used in Title 10 USC 161-164. Title 10 USC 162 states, "Except as otherwise directed by the SecDef all forces operating within the geographic area assigned to a unified combatant command shall be assigned to, and under the command of, the commander of that command." This GCC is responsible to the SecDef and the President for the performance of missions assigned by them. In accordance with Title 10 USC 164, this includes "sufficient authority, direction, and control over commands and forces assigned to exercise effective command."

c. The nature of this command authority is further delineated in JP 1. JP 1 cites unity of command as one of the primary general principles for command relationships. It states,

"Unity of command requires that two commanders may not exercise the same command relationship over the same force at the same time."

d. Therefore, both as a matter of statute and doctrine, the authorities of the COM and the GCC are separate, distinct, and sufficient within their own realms. This is not meant to breed disharmony in working relationships. In fact, in military doctrine, the concept of unity of command is not meant to be exercised in isolation, but is contextualized within the broader goal of unified action.

e. Unified action synchronizes, coordinates, and integrates joint, single-Service, and multinational operations with the operations of USG civilian agencies, NGOs and IGOs, and the private sector to achieve unity of effort. Unity of command within the military instrument of national power supports the national strategic direction through close coordination with the other instruments of national power.

f. This means that unity of command (specific to the military) and unity of effort (among USG agencies) are mutually reinforcing: "Command is central to all military action, and unity of command is central to unity of effort." So, despite the distinct nature of GCC and COM authority, close coordination is essential to achieving national objectives. In fact, JP 1 assigns to the military commander an affirmative burden to coordinate. GCCs are responsible for coordinating with US ambassadors in their geographic AORs (as necessary) across the range of military operations, and for negotiating MOAs with the chiefs of mission in designated countries to support military operations. There are many MOUs/MOAs existing between GCCs and COMs. Such arrangements are common since they are envisioned by JP 1 as a means to achieve "unity of effort." Many MOUs/MOAs are negotiated and concluded locally. Others, such as those pertaining to security, are forwarded for signature by the Deputy SecDef.

g. Unity of effort is essential to the S/CRS operations. In accordance with the IMS, a deployed ACT serves under COM authority. All ACT team members, including assigned military members, are responsible to the COM. If deployed military forces, such as a JTF, are simultaneously present in-country, their authority runs directly to the CCDR or his designated subordinate military commander with operational control. Although these command chains are separate and distinct, the military concept of unified action requires close coordination between the JTF commander and the COM-directed ACT in order to accomplish the mission.

h. **Authorities Governing the Transfer of Military Forces and DOD Civilian Personnel**

(1) A military unit cannot be transferred to the control of a COM. Per Title 10 USC 162, a military "force" is assigned to a GCC and cannot be transferred to another except by order of the SecDef. In accordance with Title 10 USC 164, the GCC must be a military officer. Although the GCC can delegate OPCON over "forces" assigned to subordinate commanders, they must be officers as well. For example, military "forces" such as a civil affairs team may not be transferred to the control of a FACT and its leader. However, individual members of a civil affairs team may be detailed to a FACT.

(2) Military members and DOD civilian employees may be individually detailed to a COM per the Economy Act and DODI 1000.17. If reimbursable, this detail must be formalized in a written agreement, such as an MOU. If non-reimbursable, a written agreement is preferred.

i. DOD Requirements for Detailing Personnel to an ACT or FACT

(1) DOD personnel may be detailed to other agencies, including bodies of the IMS such as the ACT or FACT, in accordance with the Economy Act of 1932, as amended, Title 31 USC 1535. In DOD, this is further implemented by DOD Instruction 1000.17, *Detail of DOD Personnel to Duty outside the Department of Defense*. Under that Instruction, a "detail" is a temporary assignment of a military member or DOD civilian employee to perform duties in an agency outside DOD with the intent of returning to the Department upon completion of those duties. DODI 1000.17 envisions two types of details – reimbursable and non-reimbursable. Reimbursable details are those for which the receiving agency reimburses DOD for services provided by DOD personnel during the detail period. Non-reimbursable details are those for which DOD receives no reimbursement. According to DODI 1000.17, details must be reimbursable unless there is a clear determination and finding showing that DOD receives the preponderant benefit.

(2) Within the context of R&S Operations, most DOD personnel detailed to an ACT or FACT would inure primarily to the benefit of the COM, who is funded by DOS appropriations. Thus, for these details, DOD must receive reimbursement in accordance with the Economy Act and DODI 1000.17. When DOD desires to change "the size, composition, or mandate" of its staff elements in a US diplomatic mission, it must forward a proposal to DOS in accordance with *National Security Decision Directive (NSDD) 38*. Presumably, any change initiated by DOS that inures primarily to its benefit would be a "reimbursable detail" under DODI 1000.17 and would not require an NSDD 38 request.

(3) COM Control over DOD Personnel Detailed to an ACT of FACT

(a) The Economy Act and DODI 1000.17 do not address the issues of command and authoritative direction. However, since all Economy Act transactions must be made pursuant to a written agreement on a reimbursable basis (see 64 Comp. Gen. 370 (1985)), the issues of control and responsibility over personnel can be resolved in a MOU. Detailed personnel can be directed to follow the orders of the receiving agency, and the performance evaluation can be written to reflect their performance in this regard. However, ultimate control remains with the sending agency (e.g., the GCC), which can revoke the MOU at any time. Similarly, the receiving agency (e.g., the COM), if dissatisfied with the performance of detailed personnel, may return them at any time.

(b) In light of the above, the COM's authority over personnel detailed from DOD is not equivalent to military "command," since the GCC retains this authority at all times. However, for as long as the detailing arrangement is in effect, the COM has the authority described in Title 22 USC 3927, which is described as "direction, coordination, and supervision." Furthermore, Title 22 USC 3927 states, "Any executive branch agency having employees in a foreign country shall keep the COM to that country fully and currently informed with respect to all activities and operations of its employees in that country, and shall insure that all of its employees in that country (except for … employees under the command of a United States area military commander) must comply fully with all applicable directives of the chief of mission."

(4) Requirements for Written Agreements

(a) In most cases, the Economy Act and DODI 1000.17 will require that details to IMS bodies such as an ACT be made on a reimbursable basis. A reimbursable detail must be accompanied by a written agreement. The Federal Acquisition Regulations (FAR) address the required elements for an Economy Act order (see 48 CFR 17.5). The FAR states that Economy Act orders must include (1) a description of the supplies or services required; (2) delivery requirements; (3) a funds citation; (4) a payment provision; and (5) an acquisition authority, as may be appropriate. Further, each Economy Act order shall be supported by a determination and finding (D&F). The D&F shall state that (1) use of an interagency acquisition is in the best interest of the USG; and (2) the services cannot be obtained as conveniently or economically by contracting directly with a private source. The D&F must be approved by a contracting officer of the requesting agency with authority to contract for the services to be ordered.

(b) The establishment of USAFRICOM serves as a ready example. Due to the high number of USG civilian agency detailed personnel and the need for consistency among all agreements, interagency MOUs between DOD and each providing agency were used to document many of the details of support. The USAFRICOM MOUs contain provisions addressing the FAR requirements listed above. However, because some FAR requirements are specific to the individual detailee – such as the description of the person, his/her skills, the services to be provided, and the actual cost to be reimbursed – interagency reimbursable agreements (IRAs) were used as the actual funding document. The MOU and the IRAs together document the USAFRICOM detailing actions required by the Economy Act and DODI 1000.17.

(c) USAFRICOM personnel detailed from USG civilian agencies were also given dual appointments and considered to be DOD employees during their USAFRICOM tour of duty. This action is accomplished by an SF-50, "Notification of Personnel Action."

(d) Non-reimbursable details do not require any of the documents noted above. However, it is common to utilize MOUs to clarify issues, such as access, work space, and support.

(5) **USG Civilian Agency Personnel Detailed to DOD and Relationship to a Military Chain of Command**

(a) USG civilian agency personnel may be detailed to a DOD organization in accordance with the Economy Act. As discussed previously, details can be reimbursable or non-reimbursable. Although the Economy Act does not address command and control, the conditions of the detail, including organizational control, can be addressed in an accompanying MOU. However, even then, the sending agency retains ultimate control over the individual. The terms of the detail addressed in the MOU does not integrate these personnel into a military chain of command.

(b) During the interagency staffing of USAFRICOM, reimbursable details from USG civilian agencies were given "dual appointments" such that they retained their original employment appointment with the sending agency while, simultaneously, receiving a temporary appointment from DOD. There is no statutory prohibition against holding more than one federal appointment. The Dual Compensation Act only precludes a federal official from receiving compensation from more than one office (see Title 5 USC 5533). The Department of Justice, Office of Legal Counsel has opined, "This Office has previously observed that the repeal in 1964 of earlier legislation that prohibited dual office-holding, coupled with the enactment of the current provision barring only dual compensation, impliedly permits the concurrent holding of two offices so long as there is no dual compensation involved" (see 22 OP. O.L.C. 109, 116 (1968)). The practical effect of this temporary appointment from DOD placed those civilians on the employment rolls of DOD, thereby making them DOD employees in accordance with Title 5 USC 2105.

(c) The dual appointment accomplishes two purposes. First, it permits the employee to carry out functions reserved for DOD employees, such as SecDef delegated authority and fiscal decision-making over certain DOD appropriated funds. Second, as DOD employees they become "civilian personnel accompanying a force … who are in the employ of an armed service" for purposes of the NATO status of forces agreement (SOFA) – Article I, paragraph 1b - (and other SOFAs where applicable) and thus entitled to SOFA protections, privileges, and immunities. NATO SOFA protections, privileges, and immunities include: relaxed entry/exit requirements; right to import/export personal property free from customs, duties, and taxes; tax-exemption on income paid by the sending state; claims liability protections, and criminal jurisdiction protection.

(d) Although dual appointments may be useful to integrate USG civilian agency personnel more effectively into a combatant command or a subordinate command (such as a JTF), the resulting relationship would not constitute integration into a military chain of command. A military chain of command envisions a relationship that exists only in the context of Title 10 USC 164 and JP 1. A military chain of command is the uninterrupted flow of authority that extends from the President of the United States, to the SecDef, to the CCDR, to subordinate military commanders, and, finally, to assigned or attached military forces. Civilian employees are not part of this unique military structure. The military chain of command is enforceable through the Uniform Code of Military Justice (UCMJ). Only in very limited circumstances is the UCMJ extended to civilians. This does not mean that civilian employees are not part of the military organization or are, in any way, beyond the military commander's authority. For example, Title 10 USC 802 provides: "(a) The following persons are subject to this chapter … (10) In time of declared war or a contingency operation, persons serving with or accompanying an armed force in the field." DOD employees are subject to the direction of superiors, just as any employee in any other agency.

j. Could an ACT or FACT be transferred to the control of a JTF?

(1) Proposing a transfer of an ACT or FACT to a JTF raises definitional, legal, and doctrinal issues. An ACT or FACT has a specific meaning and mission under the IMS. Both report to the COM. They exist to carry out a mission under COM authority and with DOS appropriations. A JTF is a GCC asset with a separate and distinct mission and chain of command. As such, an ACT or FACT could not be assigned to a JTF without changing their essential character. In other words, they could not be assigned to a GCC unit and retain its nature as a COM-directed entity.

(2) From a legal standpoint, the transfer of civilian units or organizations, such as a FACT, are not specifically addressed in statute, as is the case with military "forces." Thus, authority to transfer civilian entities would be conceptualized as an individual, rather than an organizational, personnel action.

(3) Individual members of a FACT could be detailed to a JTF, either in a reimbursable or non-reimbursable status, depending upon which agency receives the preponderant benefit. However, in either case, the JTF commander would report to the GCC, not the COM. Thus, any attempt to assign a FACT or its individual members to a JTF would result in the FACT losing its character as a COM-responsive entity.

(4) However, a JTF commander may receive a dual appointment by being detailed as an ACT or FACT leader as well as the JTF commander. This model has been used before in domestic circumstances fostering notable efficiencies in information sharing and unity of effort. For example, a National Guard commander, with a National Guard staff (under Title 32), has, in addition to his Title 32 responsibilities, been activated under Title 10 and put in charge of a Title 10 staff. There are practical issues involved with this arrangement, such as keeping funding streams separate, but the model has the advantage of efficiency. To accomplish the dual appointment, the JTF commander could be detailed to the COM as an additional duty and ordered by the GCC to carryout the COM's direction and mission. The detailing MOU can lay out the full parameters of the arrangement, including whether it is reimbursable or non-reimbursable. Ultimately, the JTF commander with the dual appointment remains accountable to the GCC, and the COM's control lies in his or her ability to withdraw from the MOU. This is a one-way option and has not been further described in the overarching *USG Planning Framework for Reconstruction, Stabilization, and Conflict Transformation*. As previously discussed, a civilian ACT or FACT leader could not receive a dual appointment as a JTF commander.

3. Foreign Assistance

a. Foreign assistance encompasses any and all assistance provided to a foreign nation on behalf of the USG (63 Comp. Gen. 422, Appendix A (1984)). Generally, it can be broken down into three categories: (1) security assistance, (2) humanitarian assistance, and (3) development assistance. The DOS is the USG agency primarily responsible for funding and conducting foreign assistance. There are two exceptions for DOD to this general rule. First, DOD can fund and train foreign military forces if the purpose of the training is interoperability, safety, or familiarization of those forces with US military forces.

Second, DOD can fund or conduct foreign assistance if Congress enacts a DOD appropriation and/or authorization for that purpose (see US Constitution Articles I, § 9, cl. 7; IV, § 3, cl. 2). Absent one of these two exceptions, DOD cannot fund or conduct foreign assistance on behalf of the USG.

b. Examples of Select Appropriations that allow DOD to Conduct Foreign Assistance Specific to Iraq and Afghanistan

(1) Congress has appropriated funds for DOD to conduct foreign assistance in certain situations. In Iraq and Afghanistan, Congress authorized and appropriated specific funds for use in both security assistance and humanitarian assistance.

(2) Security assistance is foreign assistance provided to another nation's military or police forces on behalf of the USG. It generally involves funding, training, and equipping those forces. The two DOD security assistance appropriations in Iraq and Afghanistan are the Iraqi Security Forces Fund (ISFF) and the Afghanistan Security Forces Fund (ASFF). The 2005 Defense Emergency Supplemental Appropriations Act established the ISFF and ASFF and the 2008 Consolidated Appropriations Act (CAA) continued funding for them. These appropriations authorized DOD to provide assistance, which included providing equipment, supplies, services, training, and facility and infrastructure repairs to the military and police forces of Iraq and Afghanistan.

(3) Humanitarian assistance is foreign assistance provided directly to the population of another nation by the USG. Specific to Iraq and Afghanistan, the Commander's Emergency Response Program (CERP) provides appropriated funds directly to commanders of operational units allowing them to meet the humanitarian and reconstruction needs of the civilian population in their areas of operation.

(4) The initial CERP program was funded with millions of dollars of seized Iraqi funds that were recovered by US forces during the early stages of the war in Iraq. By September 2003, the Coalition Provisional Authority (CPA) realized that these recovered funds would not last beyond the end of the year. As a result, Congress authorized the use of DOD O&M appropriations to fund the CERP program at the request of the President. The 2004 National Defense Authorization Act authorized the use of $500 million of DOD O&M funds for CERP projects in Afghanistan and Iraq. Since November 2003, Congress has continuously reauthorized CERP through the DOD O&M fund. Examples of CERP projects conducted in Afghanistan and Iraq include water distribution projects, sanitation services, electricity projects, health care efforts, education programs, rule of law and governance initiatives, and civic clean-up activities.

c. Examples of Select Appropriations that allow DOD to conduct Foreign Assistance not Specific to or Outside of Iraq and Afghanistan

(1) There are three humanitarian assistance appropriations that authorize DOD to conduct humanitarian assistance activities. They are the Overseas Humanitarian Disaster and Civic Aid (OHDACA) appropriation, the Humanitarian and Civic Assistance (HCA) authorization, and the CERP authorization. This section will discuss OHDACA and HCA as they are not specific to Afghanistan or Iraq. Operational units outside of

Afghanistan and Iraq are limited to existing OHDACA appropriations and HCA authorizations while conducting full spectrum operations.

(2) The primary purpose of the OHDACA appropriation is to provide funding for humanitarian de-mining operations. However, the OHDACA appropriation contains a set of authorizations that allows DOD to use OHDACA funds for other types of humanitarian assistance operations. These operations include transporting humanitarian relief supplies, making excess non-lethal supplies available for humanitarian relief, and providing humanitarian assistance. The 2009 National Defense Appropriation Act appropriated $83.273 million to be used for OHDACA programs worldwide.

(3) The HCA is an authorization that allows DOD to conduct humanitarian assistance operations using DOD O&M funds (Title 10 USC S § 401). Pre-planned HCA and de minimis HCA are the two types of humanitarian assistance operations conducted under the authorization.

(4) Under Title 10 USC § 401, pre-planned HCA includes: (1) medical, surgical, dental, and veterinary care provided in areas of a country that are rural or are underserved by medical, surgical, dental, and veterinary professionals, respectively, including education, training, and technical assistance related to the care provided; (2) construction of rudimentary surface transportation systems; (3) well drilling and construction of rudimentary sanitation systems; and (4) rudimentary construction and repair of public facilities. Pre-planned HCA is available for world-wide use, but the authorization contains several restrictions that make it difficult to access. These restrictions include: (1) HCA may not duplicate other forms of US foreign assistance; (2) the use of HCA requires service level approval; (3) the use of HCA requires DOS concurrence; and (4) operations conducted using HCA must promote specific operational readiness skills of the members of the armed forces who participate in the activities. Funding for pre-planned HCA comes from Service level O&M funds.

(5) De minimis HCA provides authority for operational unit commanders to react to "targets of opportunity" while conducting authorized military operations world-wide. These activities must be small in scope and must involve only negligible costs. De minimis HCA is undefined, but the general rule is "a few soldiers, a few dollars, for a few hours." DODD 2205.2 limits the amount of funds spent on de minimis HCA to $2500 per operation, unless an exception to the policy is granted which may allow up to $10,000 per operation. Funding for de minimis HCA comes from unit level O&M funds.

d. **DOD Funded Security and Stabilization Assistance**

(1) Operational units, outside of Afghanistan and Iraq, conducting military-to-military security assistance training during steady state operations may use appropriated funds from the "Program to Build the Capacity of Foreign Militaries" authority found in Section 1206 of the 2009 National Defense Authorization Act. This authority allows DOD "to build the capacity of a foreign country's national military forces in order for that country to conduct counterterrorism operations; or participate in or support military and stability operations in which the United States Armed Forces are participating." The authority also allows DOD "to build the capacity of a foreign country's

maritime security forces to conduct counterterrorism operations." Its use, however, is severely restricted. Use of "Section 1206" funds requires the approval of the SecDef, the concurrence of the SECSTATE, and Congressional notification. The current authorization for this fund is capped at $350 million and is available for new obligations until 30 September 2011.

(2) Another fund, referred to as "Security and Stabilization Assistance," is appropriated to DOD and provides services and transfers defense articles and funds to DOS for the purposes of facilitating reconstruction, security, or stabilization assistance to a foreign country. Specifically, "the Secretary of Defense may provide services to, and transfer defense articles and funds to, the SECSTATE for the purposes of facilitating the provision by the SECSTATE of reconstruction, security, or stabilization assistance to a foreign country." Section 1207 of the NDAA for fiscal year 2009 extends the authority to 30 September 2009 and increases the funding of this authorization per fiscal year to $100 million plus $50 million for use in the country of Georgia. According to congressional reports, the original intent of Section 1207 was to be a temporary authority and that DOD should not provide long-term funding in order to enable the DOS to "fulfill its statutory requirements." Use of this fund requires the SECSTATE to coordinate with the SecDef in the formulation and implementation of programs for reconstruction, security, or stabilization assistance to a foreign country involving the provision of services or transfer of defense articles or funding to DOS from DOD. Also, a Congressional notification from the SecDef is required when this authority is exercised. This notification is prepared in coordination with the SECSTATE. S/CRS at DOS has developed additional guidance for the "Section 1207" process.

e. Funding for PRTs: Examples of Current and Previous Funding Mechanisms Supporting Interagency Implementation Activities

(1) As an element of an ACT, the FACT is deployed to establish a US presence and provide information about conditions on the ground to support R&S operations conducted at the provincial and local level. In this regard, the FACT and the ACT, through its higher HQ association with the FACT, are an evolution of the PRT informed and improved by lessons learned gained from analyzing their design and operations. This section describes the various funding mechanisms that have been made available to PRTs as an example of how USG civil-military teams have applied different funds appropriated to different departments to achieve unity of effort supporting shared objectives in R&S operations. This section is not intended to suggest, prescribe, or make recommendations on what future funding mechanisms will be available for the ACT and by extension the FACT. It should be used for informational purposes only.

(2) Initial funding for the Afghan PRT operations came from DOD's OHDACA appropriation. The PRTs used OHDACA funds to dig wells, build schools, and repair medical clinics. The OHDACA funds, however, were difficult to use and limited in their application to basic humanitarian needs projects. The PRTs found this funding mechanism did not provide them with the means necessary to complete more significant projects such as repairing infrastructure, training and equipping security forces, and developing the rule of law. Additionally, the Afghan PRTs found that the projects they were able to complete with OHDACA funds were identical to those that were being completed by various NGOs.

(3) In early 2004, DOS and USAID began to fund Afghan PRT operations by channeling reconstruction aid through the DOS Economic Security Fund (ESF). At about the same time, Congress authorized the use of DOD O&M funds for CERP projects in Afghanistan. Currently, the Afghan PRTs conduct the majority of their reconstruction projects with the DOS ESF funds and use CERP funds as a supplement. Both sources of funding have greatly enhanced the Afghan PRT's ability to achieve their primary mission of assisting the provincial governments.

(4) Initial funding for Iraqi PRT operations came from the appropriated Iraq Relief and Reconstruction Fund (IRRF). This fund was drawn to a close, so the majority of reconstruction funds are now being channeled through the DOS's ESF. The PRTs are also using DOD O&M funds via the CERP authorization. Currently, the Iraqi PRTs fund the majority of their reconstruction projects with ESF funds, while CERP funds are used to supplement these projects. A recent initiative has been the creation of the Iraqi Commander's Emergency Response Program (ICERP) fund. This program is funded by the Iraqi Government and the use of the fund is similar to the CERP. In conjunction with the Government of Iraqi, these funds have been utilized by coalition forces for funding of reconstruction projects.

(5) The funding model is slightly different for the embedded PRT or ePRT because of the subordination of the ePRT to units below that of the JTF. The relationship between the ePRT and the brigade or regimental commander provides the ePRT with greater access to CERP funds. The ePRT team leader, in coordination with select staff members, evaluates potential projects and makes recommendations to the commander for prioritization and funding. As a result, the majority of ePRT operations are funded with CERP. In many instances this project prioritization has involved the input of host country representatives and the production of project prioritization lists.

(6) Since the aforementioned funds are appropriated to different departments for different uses that are distinct yet complimentary, coordination measures for their use must be in place to avoid duplication of effort or set-backs to another agency or host country sponsored program. Most interagency funding coordination measures for PRT operations in Afghanistan and Iraq have been developed in-country with higher level departmental guidance and congressional oversight and are specifically tailored to the conditions in which they operate.

f. Use of DOD Funds in Support of ACT or FACT Activities and Programs

(1) When funds are appropriated to an agency, that agency is accountable for their proper use. The Purpose Statute (Title 31 USC 1301(a)) and the Anti-Deficiency Act (Title 31 USC 1517(a) and 1341(a)) provide the basic fiscal law standards and require that funds be used only within the time period of fund availability, for the appropriated purpose, and in the amount permitted by the appropriation. Although DOD conceivably could agree to an arrangement whereby the agreement or the coordination of another agency is a pre-condition to obligation of DOD funds, it could not cede its responsibility or accountability for DOD appropriations to another agency. This responsibility must be exercised prior to obligation and expenditure of funds.

(2) Employees of executive agencies, who are specifically authorized by the head of his or her agency to certify vouchers for payment, are responsible to ensure the legality of a voucher and the correctness of the facts supporting it. This responsibility cannot be transferred to another agency. Once the voucher is certified, disbursing officers from various agencies may disburse funds as appropriate if they determine the voucher is in proper form and computed correctly on the facts certified. Title 31 USC 3325 indicates that disbursing officials may "disburse money only as provided by a voucher certified by (a) the head of the executive agency concerned; or (b) an officer or employee of the executive agency having written authorization from the head of the agency to certify vouchers." In addition, Title 31 USC 3528 states that "a certifying official certifying a voucher is responsible for; (1) information stated in the certificate, voucher, and supporting records; (2) the computation of a certified voucher under this section and section 3325 of the title; (3) the legality of a proposed payment under the appropriation or fund involved (4) repaying a payment – (a) illegal, improper, or incorrect because of an inaccurate or misleading certificate; (b) prohibited by law; or (c) that does not represent a legal obligation under the appropriation or fund involved ...." Also, Title 10 USC 2773a states that departmental accountable officers may be held financially liable for illegal or erroneous payments resulting from their negligence. DOD Directive 7000.14-R, Vol. 5, ch. 33 (April 2005), paragraph 3307 provides: "Departmental accountable officials shall be pecuniarily liable for illegal, improper or incorrect payments that result from information, data or services they negligently provide to a certifying officer, and upon which, the certifying officer directly relies in accordance with the provisions of [Title] 10 USC 2773a."

(3) For example, a FACT team leader could not tell a FACT member with certifying authority to certify a voucher for payment that is not legally proper under the appropriation or funds involved. Similarly, the FACT team leader could not have authority to direct a fund certifier to authorize the obligation of funds. However, FACT team leaders may participate in determinations of spending priorities, to include approval or coordination of requirements. Conceivably, a FACT member could receive a dual appointment and gain fiscal authority in more than one agency. This would have to be resolved on a case-by-case, agency-by-agency basis, and is mentioned here only as hypothetical possibility. Competent civilian or military legal advice on the proper, lawful expenditure of funds is indispensible. Violations of certain fiscal legal standards can carry personal financial and criminal liability for responsible officers and commanders.

(4) Since ACT and FACT activities are, by definition, conducted at the direction of the COM, DOD is not appropriated funds to specifically support their activities. An ACT or FACT cannot be operated with DOD appropriated funds without specific legal authority. At present, there is no such specific authority. However, security, logistic, sustainment, and other missions may be accomplished by DOD upon reimbursement by the DOS under an Economy Act order. For example in Iraq, where part of the DOD mission is to provide security, DOD provides security (including some forms of transportation) on a non-reimbursable basis (see MOA concerning PRTs between the Deputy SECSTATE and the Deputy SecDef, dated 22 February 2007).

4. Interagency Acquisition and Contingency Contracting

a. Interagency Acquisition (see FAR, sub-Parts 17.501 and 17.502, (2009)) is defined as a procedure by which an agency needing supplies or services, called the requesting agency, obtains them from another agency, called the servicing agency. The Economy Act authorizes agencies to enter into mutual agreements to obtain supplies or services by interagency acquisition. This Act may not be used by an agency to circumvent conditions and limitations imposed on the use of funds. Acquisitions under the Economy Act are not exempt from the requirements of Contractor Versus Government Performance. The Economy Act may not be used to make acquisitions conflicting with any other agency's authority or responsibility.

b. **D & F Requirements and Ordering Procedures (see FAR, sub-Parts 17.503 and 17.504, (2009))**

(1) Before placing an Economy Act order for supplies or services with another government agency, the requesting agency shall make the D&F as required. Competent legal advice on all questions regarding expenditure of appropriated funds is advisable. In the case of Economic Act orders, legal review is mandatory. The servicing agency may require a copy of the D&F to be furnished with the order. The order may be placed on any form or document that is acceptable to both agencies. The Economy Act order and D&F are the same as the process previously described in the written agreement or MOUs for services provided by interagency detailees.

(2) As stated in the FAR, the Economy Act order must include (1) a description of the supplies or services required; (2) delivery requirements; (3) a funds citation; (4) a payment provision; and (5) an acquisition authority, as may be appropriate. Further, each Economy Act order shall be supported by a D&F. The D&F shall state that (1) use of an interagency acquisition is in the best interest of the Government; and (2) the services cannot be obtained as conveniently or economically by contracting directly with a private source. The D&F must be approved by a contracting officer of the requesting agency with authority to contract for the services to be ordered.

c. **Payment Procedures for Economy Act Orders (see FAR, sub-Part 17.505, 31 March (2009))**

(1) The servicing agency may ask the requesting agency, in writing, for advance payment for all or part of the estimated cost of furnishing the supplies or services. Adjustment on the basis of actual costs shall be made as agreed to by the agencies. If approved by the servicing agency, payment for actual costs may be made by the requesting agency after the supplies or services have been furnished. Bills rendered or requests for advance payment shall not be subject to audit or certification in advance of payment. If the Economy Act order requires use of a contract by the servicing agency, then in no event shall the servicing agency require, or the requiring agency pay, any fee or charge in excess of the actual cost (or estimated cost if the actual cost is not known) of entering into and administering the contract or other agreement under which the order is filled.

d. Fiscal Law Constraints

(1) Appropriated funds are subject to three basic fiscal constraints: time, purpose, and amount.

(2) The **time constraint** includes two major elements. First, appropriations have a definite life span. Second, appropriations normally must be used for the needs that arise during their period of availability. The general rule is that current funds must be used for current needs.

(3) The **purpose constraint** commonly referred to as the purpose statute (Title 31 USC §1301(a)), prohibits spending money on objects other than those for which appropriations were made. Funds must be expended for the purpose established by Congress. The Necessary Expense Doctrine states that expenditures must (1) be logically related to the appropriation; (2) not prohibited by law; and (3) not otherwise provided.

(4) The **amount constraint** is of paramount concern. DOD must ensure compliance with the Anti-Deficiency Act (Title 31 USC 1517(a) and 1341(a)), or ADA, which prohibits obligating or spending money before it is appropriated or in amounts in excess of the amount appropriated. It is a criminal act to knowingly enter into or authorize government contracts in the absence of sufficient government funds to pay for such contracts. A knowing and willful violation of the ADA is punishable by a fine of up to $5000, two years in prison, or both. In addition, if a violation occurs, the matter must be investigated and a written report must be filed with Congress.

e. Who can obligate the government? When spending public funds, DOD must substantiate its requirements and strictly control its contracting function. Officially appointed individuals who have express written authority to bind the USG to a contractual agreement accomplish this control. The contracting officer is the only agent who represents the government in this capacity. This unique personal responsibility means supervisors, commanders, and others having administrative control over contracting officers must avoid directing contracting officers to take action that might violate laws or contracting regulations.

f. **Finance and Contracting Relationship**. The contracting and accounting and finance relationship is extremely important when it comes to obtaining documentation to support commitments or payments made by the paying agent. This relationship continues to be important when it comes time for the accounting and finance agent to reconcile the funding document for a contract. Close coordination between the contracting officer and the funding agent is necessary to determine actual obligations so the funding document for a contract will be accurately reported to the supporting accounting and finance personnel.

5. Contingency Contracting

a. Contingency contracting is defined as the process of obtaining goods, services, and construction via contracting means in support of contingency operations. This definition includes four types of contingencies: major theater wars, smaller-scale contingencies, noncombat contingency operations, and domestic disasters or emergency relief.

b. **Contingency Contracting Officer (CCO)**

(1) The purpose of the CCO is to acquire supplies and services needed by the war-fighter to support essential missions in response to a crisis, contingency, or declaration of war. CCOs can support contingencies within CONUS or OCONUS to include responses to major accidents, natural disasters, enemy attacks, and the use of weapons of mass destruction. When CCOs are deployed to declared contingencies, the flow of contracting authority may change based on the maturity of the location, theater of operation, and established command and control.

(2) JFCs must ensure the presence of competent uniformed or civilian legal advisors on their staffs. Legal review of complex questions regarding fiscal law is frequently advisable, and is often mandatory. Antideficiency Act or other fiscal compliance investigations and findings can be distracting and potentially crippling disruptions to the focus of operations.

c. **Planning for Contingency Contracting**. JFCs use the JOPP in developing plans for the employment of military power to shape events, meet contingencies, and respond to unforeseen crises. The JOPP is an adaptive, collaborative process to provide actionable direction to commanders and their staffs across multiple echelons of command. It helps commanders, their staffs, and the CCO organize their planning activities, share a common understanding of the mission and commander's intent, and develop effective plans, orders and contracts. The JOPP includes all activities that must be accomplished to plan for an anticipated operation—mobilization, deployment, employment, and sustainment of forces. The contingency contracting support phases are closely aligned to the phases in the JOPP. See JPs 5-0, *Joint Operation Planning*, and 4-10, *Operational Contract Support*, for more information.

d. **Support to R&S Operations**

(1) Contingency contracting support to R&S operations may include support to implementation of an interagency plan under a whole-of-government approach. Contract oversight will be needed to ensure proper coordination between the Services and prevent duplication of effort among government agencies. Contracting support to R&S operations can be a tremendous challenge to the JFC, especially when the JFC mission requires significant contracting support to major reconstruction actions and restoration of essential government services. Normally, this effort will be done in support of the COM, but in some cases may be done in direct support to the JFC.

(2) Contracting will be essential to the effectiveness of the R&S operations and both the JTF commander and the COM will need to remain cognizant of their responsibilities under the Foreign Corrupt Practices Act (FCPA) which only applies to US personnel. While risks associated with contracting are minimized in a US only operation, there are special concerns when coalition forces are also present, especially when these

personnel are used in contracting procedures. Coalition partner personnel are not subject to the provisions of the FCPA, so their activities relative to the conduct and oversight of US-funded procurements must be closely monitored.

(3) For example, US personnel cannot charge a potential bidder to either receive a copy of a solicitation or for submitting a proposal. However, other countries allow such conduct, and absent ethics training and certification consistent with the laws applicable to expenditure of US funds, violations of US integrity guidelines will occur, whether unintentionally or otherwise. COMs and JFCs, as a minimum, should ensure that all contracting officers and indeed anyone with authority to disburse US funds have received training and certification for this responsibility. The procedures for managing contracting and US funds disbursement during R&S operations will evolve and adopt best practices from lessons learned. JTFs will be challenged to ensure those designated with these responsibilities are trained, certified, and familiar with the complexities of contingency contracting, including FCPA.

e. **Support to Implementation of Interagency Plans.** In many contingency operations, interagency support may be limited in scope and may not pose a significant challenge to the JFC. However, in some stability operations this support can be much more significant, such as a contingency operation when the IMS has been triggered. In most cases, a lead Service will provide this support through theater support contracts, Civil Augmentation Program (CAP) task orders, or a combination of both. The key to success when providing contract support to the implementation of an interagency plan is to establish clear expectations and channels of communication to collect requirements as early as possible in the planning cycle between the supported organization and servicing agency's contracting office.

f. **Lines of Authority**

(1) Figure A-1 below ("lines of authority") illustrates the difference between command and contracting lines of authority. Contracting authority differs from command authority. Contracting authority does not follow the same line of authority as command authority to include OPCON and TACON. However, it does follow a similar path of administrative control.

(2) CCOs receive their contracting warrants from a source of contracting authority, not command authority. During contingency operations, contracting organizations within the operational area will be staffed with senior contracting officials (SCO) through whom all contracting authority will flow. There will be at least one chief of contracting office (COCO) reporting to each SCO. The COCOs are forward deployed to the theater of operation and are staffed with CCOs and CCO-appointed representatives who provide contracting support to their customers.

(3) CCO-appointed representatives may fulfill their role as part of an additional duty assignment. They may perform their representative duties from a different geographic location then the CCO. For this reason the representative must maintain near constant communication with the CCO. The representative's primary duty must not present or create a conflict of interest with their additional duty as a representative. As with a

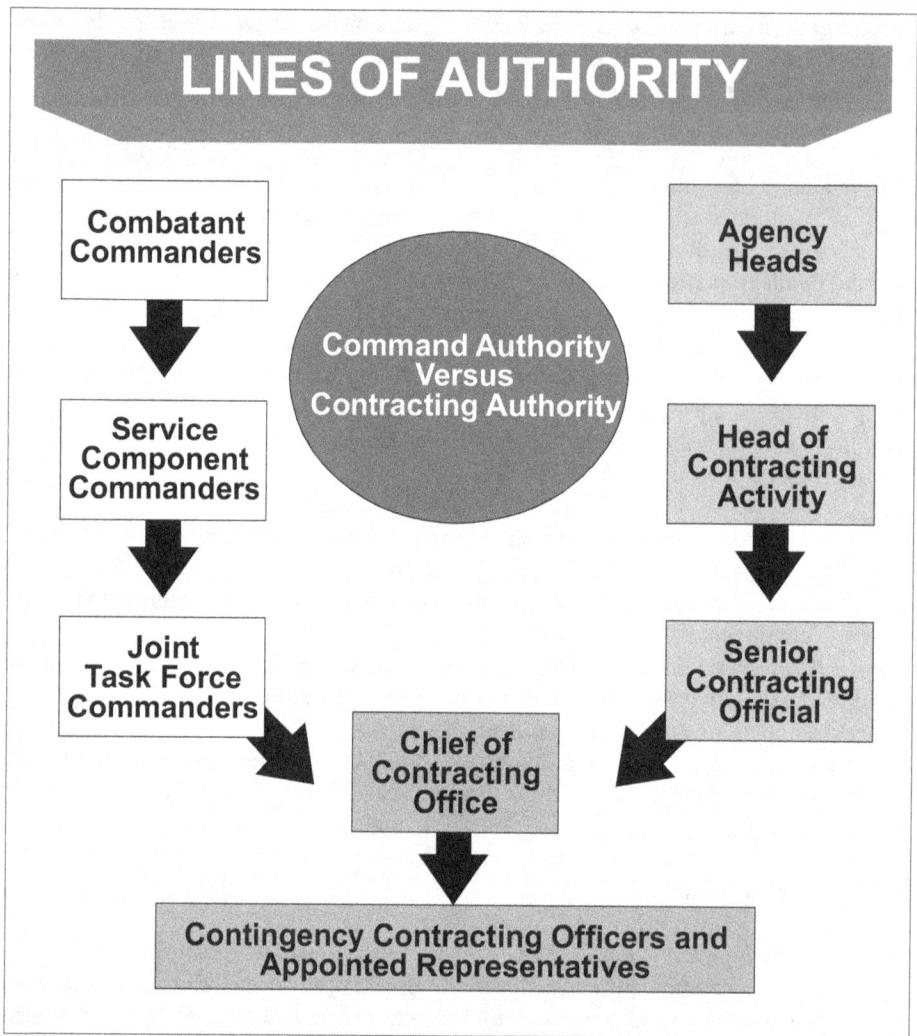

Figure A-1. Lines of Authority

contracting officer, the unique personal responsibilities of a CCO-appointed representative means supervisors, commanders, and others who have administrative control over them in their role as a representative must avoid directing them to take actions that might violate laws or contracting regulations. The relationship between a CCO-appointed representative and their operational command can be especially complex. In their primary duty, outside of being a CCO-appointed representative, they are subject to traditional command authority. In their additional duty they are subject to both command authority and contract authority. When selecting an individual to become a CCO-appointed representative, both the command and the nominated representative must know and delineate the roles derived from both authorities and consider the affect it will have on the performance of the representative's primary duty.

g. **Joint Theater Support Contracting Command**

(1) In larger or more complex contingency operations, the JFC may require more oversight than can typically be provided through the lead Service organizational option. Operational conditions that may drive this option could include, but may not be limited to:

(a) extremely complex operation that requires direct control of theater support contracting by the JFC;

(b) mission is of long-term duration;

(c) mission is beyond the capability of a single Service;

(d) mission that requires significant coordination of contracting and civil-military aspects of the JFC's campaign plan; and

(e) significant numbers of different Service forces operating in the same area or joint bases served by the same local vendor base.

(2) Since GCCs do not have their own contracting authority, the Joint Theater Support Contracting Command's HCA authority would flow from one of the Service components, normally the executive agency or lead Service component responsible for the operational area.

(3) The Joint Theater Support Contracting Command (see Figure A-2), by design, is a Joint command that has command and control authority over designated Service component theater support contracting organizations and personnel within a designated support area. A Joint Theater Support Contracting Command would perform the same functions as a lead Service contracting organization, but would report directly to the JFC.

(4) There is not a formally approved, set model for a Joint Theater Support Contracting Command. In general, The Joint Theater Support Contracting Command will be stood up only for major sustained operations. As seen in recent operations, these sustained operations may include major reconstruction and transition to civil authority mission requirements in addition to the standard joint forces support mission requirements. In these major, long-term stability operations, it may be desirable to stand up a Joint Theater Support Contracting Command with separate SCOs responsible to support joint forces, HN forces or transition operations, and reconstruction support.

h. **SCOs for HN, Transition, and Reconstruction Support**

(1) It is important to highlight the roles and responsibilities of the SCO for HN and transition support and the SCO for reconstruction support within the context of R&S operations.

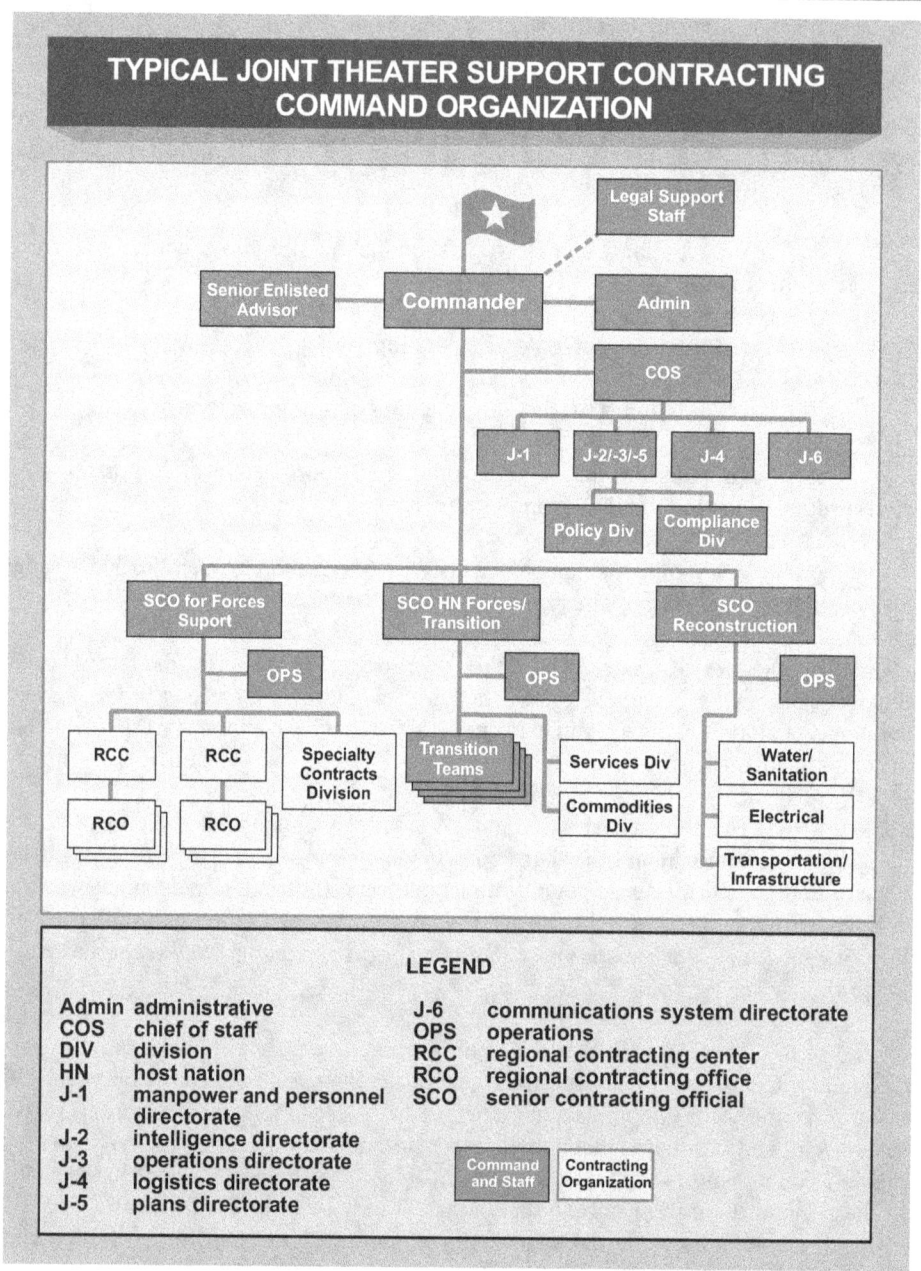

Figure A-2. Typical Joint Theater Support Contracting Command

(2) The SCO for HN and transition support is responsible for planning, coordinating, and managing theater support contracting actions in support of the JFC mission to develop, organize, train, equip, and sustain HN security forces. This SCO is also responsible for providing training and transition assistance to HN security forces (and other HN governmental agencies as directed) to facilitate developing and sustaining their own contracting support capabilities.

(3) The SCO for reconstruction support is responsible for planning, coordinating, and managing theater support contracting actions for the civil reconstruction mission. This SCO may directly support the US COM and by extension COM directed organizations such as an ACT or FACT. The SCO for reconstruction generally will have multiple sector specific support contracting organizations. These may include the following areas: water, sanitation, electricity, transportation, oil production, and other related functions related to essential services and critical infrastructure.

(4) These SCOs can provide SME advice and input to all levels of planning and implementation described in the USG Planning Framework that would require the use of DOD contracts. These SCOs may contribute to DOD participation in the operational and strategic level processes outlined in the framework to better inform courses of action for decision and the contracting mechanisms that will support the objectives developed for MMEs that DOD will contribute to or lead.

6. Theater Support Contracts

a. Theater support contracts are contracts that are awarded by contracting officers in the operational area serving under the direct contracting authority of the Service component, special operations force command, or designated Joint HCA for a designated contingency operation. During a contingency, these contracts are normally executed under expedited contracting authority and provide supplies, services, and construction from commercial sources generally within the operational area. Theater support contracts are the type of contract typically associated with the term contingency contracting. Also of importance from the contractor management perspective is that local nationals make up the bulk of the theater support contract employees.

b. Civil Augmentation Programs (CAP)

(1) CAP plans for the use of civilian contractors during contingencies or in wartime to augment the logistics support of selected forces. Typically these programs could apply in all phases of contingency operations. The Army, Navy, and Air Force each have a CAP contract. All three of these civilian augmentation programs support US Joint operations worldwide. They prevent the dilution of military forces that would occur if the military had to provide the required services and support. However, these contracts are expensive. They should be used only when it is not appropriate for military personnel to provide needed services and functions.

(2) The Army's CAP is referred to as the LOGCAP, and is the type of CAP that is most likely to be utilized to support the implementation of an interagency plan during an overseas contingency operation. LOGCAP is designed to provide general logistics and minor construction support to deployed Army, joint, and multinational forces, and interagency organizations under the control and direction of the COM. The LOGCAP has been routinely used with significant success in supporting the range of military operations for over a decade.

Intentionally Blank

APPENDIX B
RESOURCE GUIDANCE AND SUSTAINMENT CONSIDERATIONS

For the Military Contribution to the Comprehensive Resource and Management Strategy and the Country-Level Resource Plan

1. Summary

a. The construct of this appendix follows the form of the Comprehensive Resource and Management Strategy template in the *USG Planning Framework* for ease of input. This strategy supports the design of the USG R&S Strategic Plan and informs the development of the subsequent country plan.

b. The MME Resource Strategy, which is an element of the MME Concept Memorandum, will contribute to the development of the Comprehensive Resource and Management Strategy. The MME Resource Strategy outlines the following:

(1) total resources (funding, operational) required for the MME broken out over sub-objectives;

(2) available funding and funding targets by sub-objective, mapped to the program areas of the Foreign Assistance Framework;

(3) any potential or actual resource gaps, and prioritization for filling them;

(4) anticipated international contributions by sub-objective; and

(5) any resource restrictions.

c. The military contribution to the Comprehensive Resource and Management Strategy will inform the military input to the Country-level Resource Plan. This plan is an element of the Country Plan. The purpose of the Comprehensive Resource and Management Strategy is to present an integrated approach for addressing resource requirements among participating agencies and departments in a R&S response effort as identified by MME planning teams. The strategy enables coordination with the Office of Management and Budget (OMB) and participating agencies and departments concerning required reprogramming or supplemental funding requests. It also serves as a start point to signal the beginning of the mobilization and deployment process to meet the requirements of the Country Plan supporting the strategic objectives contained in the USG R&S Strategic Plan.

d. The strategy provides senior policy decision makers and strategic planners the rough order of magnitude (ROM) estimate of resource and management costs to achieve the R&S conflict transformation goal for the USG R&S Strategic Plan. An iterative process will ensue as decision-makers align resources and goals, adjust timelines, pursue international burden-sharing, and otherwise adjust plans. The CRSG SPT will endeavor to make available funds that are more effective, agile, and focused on agreed policy goals.

The SPT will clarify for policymakers the tradeoffs between goals and limited resources as the iterative resource planning process moves forward. Figure B-1 below offers a depiction of the military contribution to the resource strategy development.

e. If the CRSG designates the DOD as an MME lead, it is likely that the DOD will assign the Joint Staff (JS) as the MME process lead. However, participation in the IMS within the CRSG and MME teams requires both the OSD and JS to assume roles and perform planning functions that are not part of the JOPP, nor defined in JOPES. Previous experimentation validated the JS as the appropriate US military organization to be the process lead to ensure MME concepts are supported by geographic combatant command planning and implementation. It is expected that representatives of the JCS J4, J5, and J8 will contribute to the development of a DOD-led MME concept to provide estimates for requested military resource and logistical support.

f. Related to JCS J-4 participation in this process is the role of the JS Director for Logistics. The Joint Staff Director for Logistics assesses logistic implications of

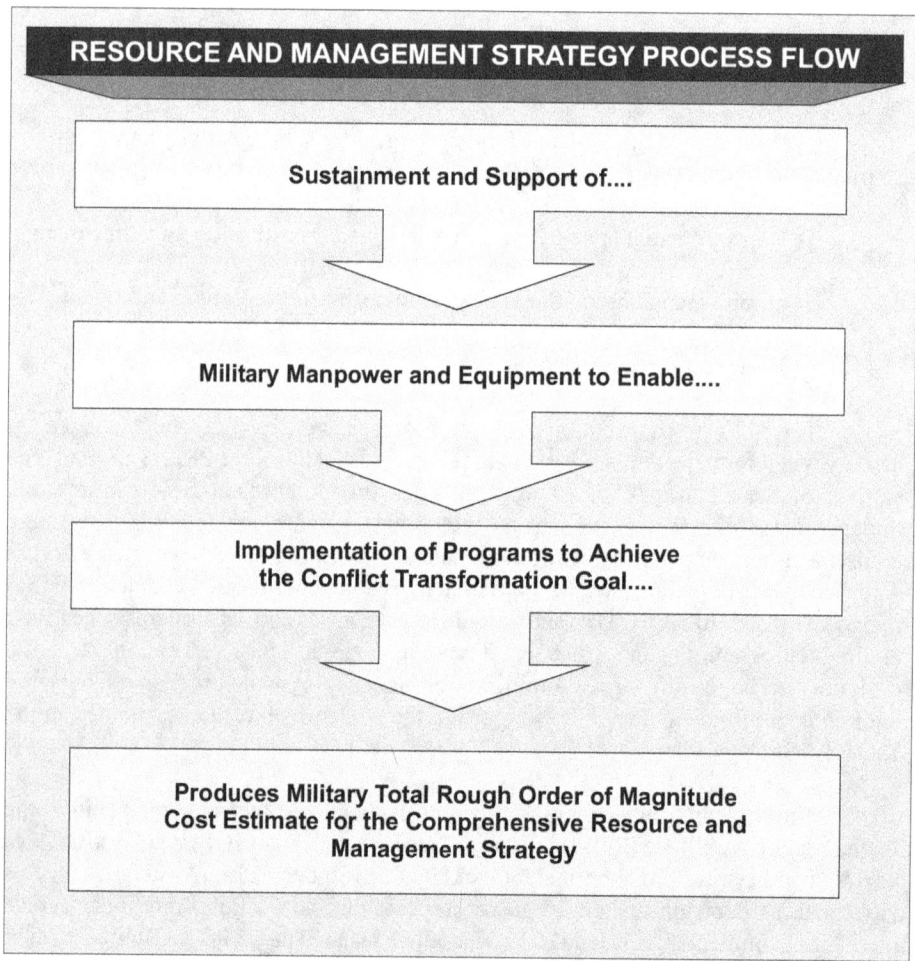

Figure B-1. Resource and Management Strategy Process Flow

contemplated operations from its Joint Logistics Operations Center to the interagency forum and represents or accompanies the CJCS in interagency meetings dealing with logistic issues. While the involvement of the director is not likely to occur at the MME or CRSG SPT level, military resource and logistics recommendations made by the CRSG requiring a decision of the NSC Deputies' Committee (DC) or Principals' Committee (PC) will likely involve the director's input.

g. In concept development during time-sensitive situations utilizing Crisis Action Planning (CAP), such as an IMS triggering event, a Planning Order (PLANORD) or Alert Order (ALERTORD) may be the first strategic guidance received by the affected GCC. Strategic guidance is used to formulate politico-military assessments at the strategic level; develop and evaluate military strategy and objectives; apportion and allocate forces and other resources; formulate concepts and strategic military options; and develop planning guidance leading to the preparation of courses of action. The end product of the military strategic guidance planning function is the supported GCC's mission statement. JS participation on the CRSG will inform the resource and logistics elements of the PLANORD or ALERTORD transmitted to the affected GCC.

h. Strategic guidance derived from the USG Planning Framework will include the USG R&S Strategic Plan and its MMEs containing strategic objectives needed to accomplish the conflict transformation goal envisioned in the plan. The affected GCC will craft military objectives that support national strategic objectives, like those contained in the USG R&S Strategic Plan, with the advice and consent of the CJCS and SecDef. GCC resource and logistics planners will contribute to the concept development products derived from a PLANORD. These products include an approved course of action and commander's estimate containing termination criteria, supportability estimates, and (if time available) an integrated TPFDD of estimated force and logistic requirements by operation phase. It will be important for GCC resource and logistics planners to align resource and logistic support requirements to meet MME strategic objectives and sub-objective tasks assigned to the military. Here the role of the IMS IPC plays an important part. If already deployed to the affected GCC, resource and logistics planners may utilize the advice of the IPC to assist with harmonization of civilian and military plans based on their expert knowledge of the USG R&S Strategic Plan. The IPC will inform military planning processes, including resource and logistics planning, to achieve unity of effort and mitigate the effects of applying duplicative civilian and military resources to the same problem.

i. Command, contracting, and funding authorities are critical and required to implement the military component of the Comprehensive Resource and Management Strategy. These authorities are rooted in law and provide a basis for regulations and doctrine. These authorities guide the military contribution to the Country-level Resource Plan. Appendix A, "Authorities for Military Participation in Reconstruction and Stabilization Operations," explains in greater detail the relevant authorities needed to implement a resource and management strategy.

2. Baseline of Current Operations

a. The second part of the strategy is to develop a baseline of current operations. The purpose is to explain the current operations, foreign assistance footprint, and budget of the USG within the affected country. If US military forces are already present in-country an accurate accounting and status of the force and its equipment and facilities will be needed to inform military planners contributing to the development of both the USG R&S Strategic Plan and the Country Plan.

b. Also, any DOD funds authorized and allocated for use in stabilization, security, and reconstruction activities inside the affected country need to be accounted. The current status of funds, to include related programs and projects, should be updated to inform the baseline assessment of current operations being conducted by the military in the affected country. A military force HQ already present in-country will need to provide input, to provide greater detail, regarding the status of the force, its readiness, status of funds and any programs and projects currently being implemented.

3. Allocation and Reprogramming of Current Department of Defense Resources

a. The purpose of the third part of the strategy is to explain how current USG resources will be used to achieve the goals in the USG R&S Strategic Plan. For DOD this may involve the allocation and reprogramming of funds by account and year and utilizing existing funding and programs that are consistent with the USG R&S Strategic Plan. The reprogramming of funds is likely to occur at the Service, JS, or OSD level informed through their participation on the CRSG and higher level NSC committees while involving the input of the relevant GCC and force provider.

b. Overseas Humanitarian Disaster and Civic Aid (OHDACA) appropriation, Humanitarian and Civic Assistance (HCA) authorization, and section 1206 and 1207 funds in the National Defense Authorization Act for 2009 serve as examples of existing DOD funding and programs that may be consistent with a USG R&S Strategic Plan. The authorized uses and purpose of these funds may enable programs to assist DOD with accomplishing strategic objectives and sub-objectives assigned under the USG R&S Strategic Plan. See Appendix A, "Authorities for Military Participation in Reconstruction and Stabilization Operations," for more information and references regarding these funds and their uses.

4. Additional Military Resources Required

a. The purpose of the fourth part of the strategy is to explain new USG resources required to implement the resource and management strategy and how these resources will be requested over time and by type. Military input into this part of the strategy will include rough order of magnitude (ROM) support requirements, supplemental and new budget requests, additional military capabilities required, and oversight requirements. The military contribution to meet the requirements in the Comprehensive Resource and Management Strategy will largely focus on the forces available and the related funding and programs to be executed for such a force to accomplish the strategic objectives or sub-objectives assigned under the USG R&S Strategic Plan.

b. **ROM Support Requirements**

(1) The ROM support requirements include an estimate of resources required to support deployed military forces. It is not uncommon for military logistics and support operations to begin prior to or concurrent with whole-of-government planning. Thus military logistic planners and their concepts of support need to remain flexible and sensitive to the ever evolving joint and interagency operational requirements and changing force structure and organization of the joint force and IMS teams. At the geographic combatant command level, planning begins with the receipt of strategic guidance or a planning directive and continues as the GCC develops a mission statement. Planning activities include identifying assumptions, planning forces, mission and desired end state. Military logisticians should identify critical joint and interagency logistical assumptions. During mission analysis joint logisticians must provide critical information to operations planners on the guidance contained in military strategic logistical documents such as the *Joint Strategic Capabilities Plan* (JSCP) (Mobility and Logistic supplements) and related or supplemental publications.

(2) The CJCS is responsible for transmitting the SecDef's order to the relevant GCC when a contingency operation, utilizing the IMS, is to be executed (via Deployment Orders and Execute Orders). Those orders will include a funding paragraph outlining financial guidance as directed by the USD(C) Comptroller and USD (P) Policy. In turn, PLANORDs or ALERTORDs from the CJCS constitute authority for a GCC to expend funds available to that GCC and authority to direct a Military Component to expend funds available to that Component for forces assigned to the GCC.

(3) There are three different types of funding estimates that are developed and used during the course of a contingency operation. The **pre-deployment estimate** is used to assess various operational assumptions and to inform the go/no-go decision making process; the **budget estimate** is used to define and defend requests for reprogramming or additional appropriations; and the **working estimate** is used during execution of the operation against which the Military Departments measure actual costs, and which can be used as the base for determining the changes in cost that would result from changes to the operational plan. The first two estimates are likely to be utilized to inform the military input to the USG Comprehensive Resource and Management Strategy during the early stages of whole-of-government planning addressed in the USG Planning Framework. This is because the strategy is geared toward both a ROM estimate and allocations and reprogramming of current funds to achieve the objectives in the USG R&S Strategic Plan.

(4) The pre-deployment cost estimate usually is required on short notice, sometimes within hours of notification. This estimate is the most difficult and unreliable of the three estimates due to lack of supporting information. The preliminary estimate typically is prepared by the Office of the Under SecDef (Comptroller) (OUSD(C)) and the JS J-8 using a cost model that uses major incremental cost drivers such as modes of transportation, operation duration, force deployment/phasing, and environmental conditions to project a ROM cost estimate. As an adjunct to the cost model, the OUSD(C)

has established a Contingency Cost Estimating Team to help develop more reliable preliminary cost estimates for contingency operations. This team is on call to OUSD(C) and consists of financial managers from the OSD, the Joint Staff, and DOD Components, and augmented by operational and logistics planners as needed, to collect information about the operation and to formulate assumptions to support the cost estimating effort. This team and its cost estimate should contribute to the military contribution to both the Comprehensive Resource and Management Strategy and Implementation-level Resource Plan formulated by DOD representatives on the CRSG.

(5) This Budget Estimate is based on specific GCC operational plans, troop levels, location, and operating circumstances. The respective Military Services, via their financial management and logistics staffs, use data provided by the GCC and the in-theater Service Components to derive a projected incremental cost estimate for submission to OUSD(C). Data provided is examined in detail by the OSD and JS to determine the extent to which variations in the plan have been considered in developing the cost estimate. Time permitting, and on an exception basis, information briefings may be solicited from the staffs of the relevant GCC (and/or service component commands) to detail anticipated requirements and factors that may prove useful in enhancing the development of the cost estimate. As a standard procedure in developing cost estimates, the military components shall utilize all available sources of relevant information and ensure that the field commands and HQ personnel have applied the lessons learned from cost estimates associated with previous operations. The budget estimate will inform the justification for reprogramming funds or request for additional DOD appropriations.

c. **Supplemental or New Budget Requests**

(1) Military input to supplemental requests and reprogramming to support the requirements laid out in the Comprehensive Resource and Management Strategy of the USG Planning Framework will center on the resource planning activities conducted by the OSD and JS representatives on the CRSG. Input from the affected GCC and other relevant military organizations per the budget estimate process will inform supplemental and new budget requests. Related to this is the important role the CCDRs serve in the defense-wide Planning, Programming, Budgeting, and Execution (PPBE) Process. Per CJCSI 8501.01A, CCDRs have the opportunity to provide input and comment in all four phases of PPBE to ensure their commands attain the best mix of forces, equipment, and support.

(2) CJCSI 8501.01A further states that the DOD PPBE process is the SecDef's central framework and decision making process for resource allocation. The purpose is to plan a defense strategy which meets a threat, programs resources to fit a strategy or capability, and prepare a DOD budget in support of these programs. The process is based on objectives, policies, and strategies derived from national security directives signed by the President. The planning in support of PPBE tends to be deliberate with defined processes and time periods geared towards the President's Budget. This process may not fully support the demanding and dynamic requirements for resource planning in support of an IMS triggering event. However, many of the same directorates, offices, components, and commands in DOD with PPBE responsibilities will contribute to the

cost estimate procedures for such a crisis. These procedures are detailed in the Financial Management Regulation Volume 12, Chapter 23, "Contingency Operations."

(3) In the past Congress has appropriated funds to DOD to conduct security, stabilization, and reconstruction activities during contingency operations. These funds were specific to an operation and their purpose, time period of use, and amount were well defined. In the context of a whole-of-government approach to R&S planning, the use of operation specific funds allows for flexibility. However, they may also duplicate another agency's programs of implementation creating a series of unintended consequences. As a result, the CRSG should be informed and weigh-in on any individual agency or department requests to Congress for additional funding appropriations. The goal is to avoid duplication of effort and ensure that resources a matched to the appropriate agency or department tasked to implement the strategic objectives as defined in the USG R&S Strategic Plan. Recent examples of funds appropriated to DOD for a specific operation in the areas of security assistance and humanitarian assistance during R&S implementation activities include: Iraqi Security Forces Fund (ISFF), Afghanistan Security Forces Fund (ASFF), and the CERP. For more information on these funds see Appendix A, "Authorities for Military Participation in Reconstruction and Stabilization Operations."

d. **Military Capabilities Required**

(1) Force planning is an activity associated with plan development. At the GCC, the Commander will guide planning through the issuance of a PLANORD or similar directive. The primary purposes of force planning are to: influence COA development and selection based on force allocations, availability, and readiness; identify all forces needed to accomplish the supported component commanders' concept of operations with some rigor; and, effectively phase the forces into the operational area.

(2) In crisis action planning, such as an IMS triggering event, force planning focuses on the actual units designated to participate in the planned operation and their readiness for deployment. The supported commander identifies force requirements as operational capabilities in the form of force packages to facilitate sourcing by the Services, USJFCOM, USSOCOM, and other force providers' supporting commands. The supported commander typically describes required force requirements in the form of broad capability descriptions or unit type codes, depending on the circumstances. The supported commander submits the required force packages through the Joint Staff to the force providers for sourcing. The supported commander will review the sourcing recommendations through the GFM process to ensure compatibility with capability requirements and concept of operations.

(3) Support planning is another activity associated with plan development. The purpose of support planning is to determine the sequence of the personnel, logistic, and other support required to provide distribution, maintenance, civil engineering, medical support, and sustainment in accordance with the concept of operation. Support planning is conducted in parallel with other planning, and encompasses such essential factors as executive agent identification; assignment of responsibility for base operating support; airfield operations; management of non-unit replacements; HSS; personnel management; financial management; handling of prisoners of war and detainees; theater civil engineering

policy; logistic-related environmental considerations; support of noncombatant evacuation operations and other retrograde operations; and nation assistance. Support planning is primarily the responsibility of the Service component commanders and begins during concept of operations development.

e. **Oversight and Advocacy Requirements**

Standard procedures, instructions, and regulations already established within DOD to ensure fiscal accountability and that provide for budget planning and accounting functions should be followed by all DOD organizations and military commands that receive appropriated funds for use in the R&S response effort. DOD representatives on the CRSG whose responsibilities involve PPBE should maintain oversight on the expenditure of funds ensuring that DOD is focusing its resources on the objectives assigned under the USG R&S Strategic Plan. These objectives or sub-objectives are contained in the MMEs of the strategic plan. The DOD representatives with PPBE responsibilities should also act as advocates for the proper use of the appropriated funds and for the authorities that govern the military resources being utilized to accomplish the assigned objectives contained in the strategic plan.

5. Constraints and Mitigation Actions

a. The purpose of the fifth part of the strategy is to summarize the constraints, opportunities, and critical steps to implement the strategy. This section will focus on legislative constraints and other implementation challenges that may impact the resource strategy. It will offer an explanation for requesting new authorities and a mitigation strategy in the event the request is denied. Finally, the section will summarize the broad outlines of the DOD contribution of a congressional strategy supporting the Comprehensive Resource and Management Strategy.

b. **Legislative Constraints**

(1) Many legislative constraints effecting the military contribution to the resource strategy involve statutory authorities. The authority over the use of USG resources in a foreign country is a fundamental statutory issue. This authority is primarily divided between the COM and the applicable GCC per Title 22 USC 4802. The GCC is responsible to the SecDef and the President for the performance of missions assigned to them. To accomplish this Title 10 USC 164 states that the GCC is given the resources to provide "sufficient authority, direction, and control over commands and forces assigned to exercise effective command."

(2) When appropriated funds are concerned, the agency that the fund is appropriated to is accountable for its proper use. The Purpose Statute and the Anti-Deficiency Act address the fiscal law standards governing the use of appropriated funds. Overall, they require that funds be used only in the time period of fund availability, for the appropriated purpose, and in the amount permitted. Again, competent legal review is mandatory.

c. Explanation of Requests for New Authorities and Mitigation Strategy

(1) The authorities of the COM and the GCC are separate, distinct, and for the most part sufficient within their own realms. This is not meant to create disunity between the US military and USG civilian agencies. For the military, unity of command is not exercised in isolation, but is contained within the context of the broader goal of unified action. During the implementation of the USG R&S Strategic Plan, unified action requires the close coordination between the JTF commander and the COM-directed ACT and FACT to accomplish the strategy objectives in order to achieve the conflict transformation goal.

(2) Since ACT and FACT implementation activities are conducted under the direction of the COM, DOD has not been appropriated funds to specifically support them. DOD appropriated funds cannot be used to operate an ACT of FACT without specific new legal authorities. However, the use of Economy Act orders can act as an enabler for a mitigation strategy in the event the requests for new authorities are denied for individual agencies or departments participating in the IMS. For example, security, logistic, sustainment, and other support missions may be accomplished by DOD on a reimbursable basis from the DOS through the use of an Economy Act order. Each Economy Act order must be accompanied by a determination and finding approved by a contracting officer from the requesting agency with authority to contract for the services to be ordered.

(3) Any requests for new agency or department resource authorities to accomplish the objectives of both the USG R&S Strategic Plan and the Country Plan must involve the input of the CRSG. This will ensure the right resources are matched to the appropriate agency or department to avoid duplication of effort.

d. **Congressional Strategy.** The DOD contribution to the congressional strategy for the Comprehensive Resource and Management Strategy supporting the objectives of the USG R&S Strategic Plan will involve the input of the CRSG and higher-level NSC decision making bodies when necessary. Through the PPBE process the DOD has developed mechanisms to influence legislation. The department and its representatives on the CRSG may utilize this process as a guide to contribute to the congressional strategy contained in the Comprehensive Resource and Management Strategy. For further details see CJCS Instruction 8501.01A, *Chairman of the Joint Chiefs of Staff, Combatant Commanders, and Joint Staff Participation in the Planning, Programming, Budget, and Execution System.*

6. Country-level Resource Plan Development

a. The sixth part of the strategy focuses on supporting appendices; however, this section will depart from the template and address the military contribution to the Country-level Resource Plan.

b. The strategic resource decisions derived from the Comprehensive Resource and Management Strategy will influence the design of the Country-level Resource Plan. The

IPT and LPT on the CRSG will work together to develop the Country-level Resource Plan. As an element of the Country Plan, the plan outlines in detail how personnel, assigned to IMS teams (IPC, ACT/FACT) will deploy into theater, the establishment of support systems, and the pre-positioning of stocks. The plan will address resource requirements, to include constraints and limitations. It will also describe HN resources and the non-financial resources that international partners may bring enabling the USG to coordinate its response to its fullest potential.

c. The Country-level Resource Plan will include supporting annexes. The annex containing the schedule for IMS staff rotations and training plans will ensure requisite knowledge of the Country Plan and USG R&S Strategic Plan is instilled in deploying personnel, and that all know their role and where it fits into the associated planning and implementation processes. The annex for financial management, contracting, audit, and legal activities will describe program of implementation contracts, timelines for their establishment, and analyses for gaps or duplication. Lastly, the annex for information sharing will describe how information will be shared and what elements of the Country Plan will be distributed to other actors (HN, coalition partners, IGOs and other international organizations) contributing to the R&S response effort.

d. Following the approval of the Country Plan; however, often much earlier, initial procurement action will begin based on the expected actions required. USG funded contracts and grants can be drawn up and requests for proposals issued to facilitate immediate action upon deployment. USG humanitarian assistance commodities and teams can be pre-positioned to be immediately available for deployment. Detailed planning between the CRSG Secretariat logistics planners and military planners on the CRSG, and when appropriate the GCC, should begin to prepare for support requirements enabling the establishment of the ACT or FACTs. Additional support requirements will be needed and perhaps shared or leveraged in the event the ACT or FACTs embed with the military.

e. The military contribution to the Country-level Resource Plan should describe the military logistics responsibilities in support of the Country Plan. The plan should identify the responsible USG process owners, the coordination framework, and funding responsibilities. The military possesses core logistic capabilities that may contribute to the logistics requirements defined in the Country-level Resource Plan. These core logistic capabilities areas include deployment and distribution, supply, logistic services, operational contract support, and engineering. Figure B-2 below relates specific US military core logistic capabilities to the implementation of a whole-of-government plan for a R&S response effort.

f. The output of the Country-level Resource Plan should provide the process, procedures, guidelines, and tools to inform military joint operational level resource and logistics planning during a whole-of-government operation. To do this the plan should identify the lead USG agency for a specific logistic capability which corresponds to a capability needed to accomplish an objective stated in the Country Plan. The plan should describe the mission, objectives, supported and supporting relationships between participating agencies, and a description of the logistic support responsibilities provided by the joint force. The strategic guidance in the form of a PLANORD, ALERTORD, or WARNORD sent to the applicable GCC should incorporate elements of the Country-level

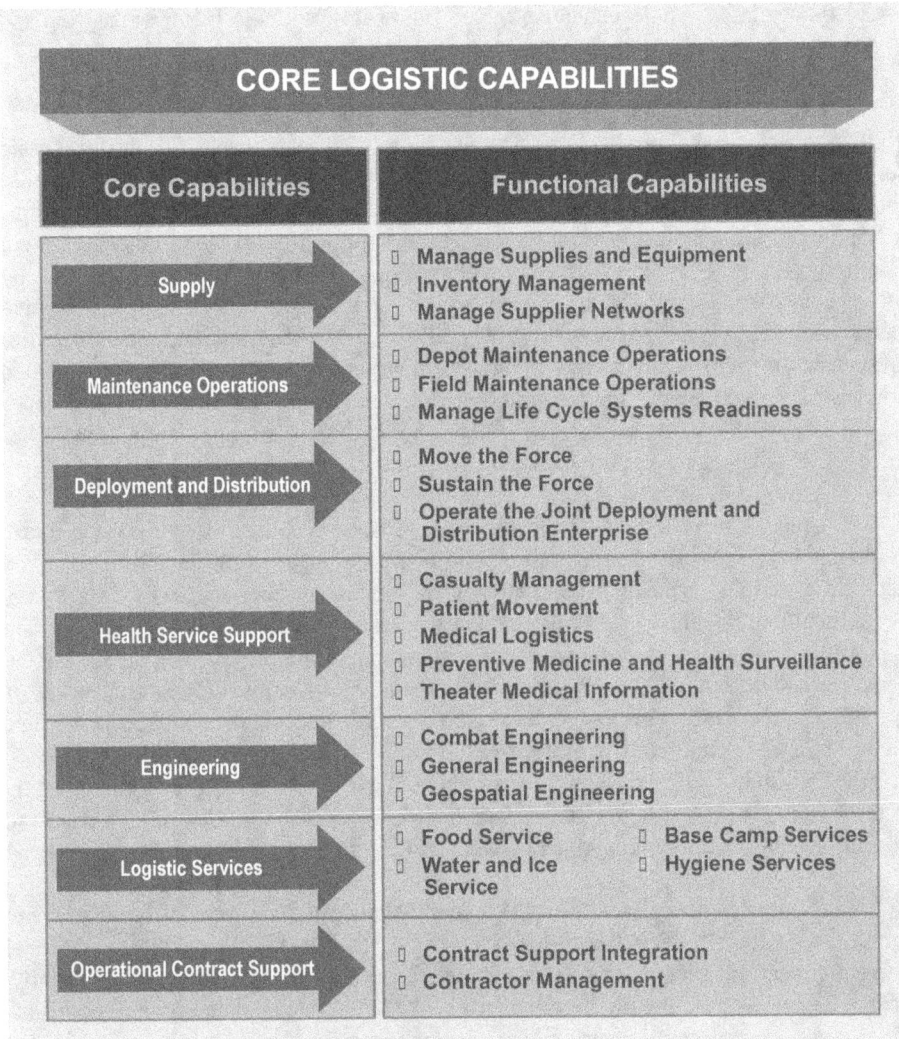

Figure B-2. Core Logistic Capabilities

Resource Plan relevant to operational level resource and logistics planning. This guidance should provide sufficient direction for whole-of-government collaboration, planning, and crisis response to the joint force as it works with participating agencies in the IMS.

g. The Country-level Resource Plan should restate the Country Plan civil-military collaboration framework between the IMS implementation bodies, COM, AMEMB Country Team, and the joint force specific to the crisis. The plan should identify and describe resource and logistics functions coordinated through CMOCs established by JFCs or coordinated through IMS implementation bodies (ACT/FACT) established at the direction of the CRSG. This description should include logistics planning guidance concerning the movement of resources for participating agencies, to include the joint force. The resource plan should incorporate a strategy for contracted air and surface movements, military air and sealift, final distribution, and guidance for local purchases. Lastly, when applicable, the resource plan should include the agreed framework with the HN for reception and distribution.

h. Military forces have long coordinated with the HQ and field elements of USG civilian agencies in the arena of foreign affairs. Within a theater, the GCC is the focal point for planning and implementation of theater and regional military strategies that require interagency coordination. The GCC should consider the ways distribution operations are applied. Initial concepts of operations and the supporting distribution concept will require review to assess the feasibility and consider the impact of related activities by interagency participants with regard to distribution and logistics. For example, primitive seaport and airport facilities may limit the ability to move required amounts of supplies and constrain the collective effort. Planning information for logistics regarding the affected country may be obtained from the country team, which usually is in contact with relief organizations in the crisis area. If the IMS has been established, implementation bodies like the ACT may also be off assistance in providing information.

i. According to joint doctrine, the CMOC may be utilized to assist a military commander in anticipating, facilitating, and coordinating civil-military functions and activities pertaining to the local population, government, and economy. The CMOC may be useful in coordinating with HN distribution infrastructure and other physical distribution capabilities. However, in some situations it may be unacceptable or damaging to local economies for the United States to acquire or procure materiel inventories in a country or in nations immediately surrounding the crisis area while they are trying to recover from a natural disaster or conflict. Therefore, direct or indirect refinement of the military mission and the distribution concept should be coordinated with the USG agencies participating in the IMS to identify and minimize mutual interference and coordinate strategic aims to accomplish the objectives contained in the USG R&S Strategic Plan.

j. Existing logistics capabilities that enable deployment operations are in place in the DOS, USAID, and DOD. These may be utilized to facilitate the deployment of personnel and equipment assigned or detailed to IMS teams such as the ACT or FACT. Presently, using Economy Act order written arrangements, like MOUs, and fund transfer mechanisms, all of these platforms could be shared in various scenarios.

k. For the DOS and USAID, two offices have been identified with capabilities to provide deployment services to IMS team personnel. The Office of Logistics Management (A/LM) in the DOS offers a variety of services to include: procurement of goods and services; contracting; vendor management; shipping and distribution of goods and materials; warehousing and inventory management; and a purchase card program. Through the Office of US Foreign Disaster Assistance (OFDA), USAID supports an equipment training and storage facility that keeps communication and field equipment in stock. These include office kits, armored vests, and vehicles stockpiled in prepositioned locations. The vehicles are normally used to support a Disaster Assistance Response Team (DART) rapid deployment. USAID also supports a transportation office that arranges transportation for employees and equipment.

APPENDIX C
MEMORANDUM OF UNDERSTANDING/AGREEMENT BETWEEN MILITARY AND CIVILIAN COMPONENTS FOR A WHOLE-OF-GOVERNMENT EFFORT

1. Introduction

a. MOU or MOA are developed and signed between the military and civilian components of US national power to document and establish authorities and limitations when the military supports civilian operations, particularly when military resources, both materiel and manpower, provide capacity to non-military elements. It is especially important to establish clear relationships during IMS whole-of-government efforts that involved components of multiple US departments and agencies. By law the authority over US personnel in foreign countries is divided between the COM and the applicable senior US military commander with geographic responsibilities (i.e., the GCC). These authorities do not change when a whole-of-government approach is envisioned or executed. A military unit cannot be transferred to the OPCON of a COM or any other civilian entity such as an ACT. Individual military and DOD civilian employees can be detailed to a COM or ACT, but even in these cases it is a matter of practicality for an MOU or MOA to be put into effect that defines the responsibilities of the COM or ACT for the DOD individual as well as the obligations of the DOD individual to the gaining organization.

b. In most whole-of-government efforts it is envisioned that a JTF, or its equivalent, will be the principal military component involved. A JTF commander may be required to negotiate and conclude MOUs or MOAs, but for the most part it is probable that any MOUs/MOAs that will be concluded will be at the GCC level or higher. Most will likely be concluded at the national level between DOD and its counterparts at DOS, USAID, DOJ. JTF commanders should know about MOUs/MOAs and this appendix offers guidance on what MOUs/MOAs need to address. The most likely circumstances where a JTF commander would be expected to develop and sign a MOU/MOA would be unexpected instances when military personnel or services are being placed under the direction of a civilian ACT director or a COM or in support of a non-American multinational leader such as a NATO force or a UN operation. Such an MOU/MOA would spell out the support being agreed upon and the responsibilities of the non-military or non-American entity towards those US military assets, including care and feeding, reimbursement, any rating/evaluation responsibilities and termination of MOU/MOA instructions.

2. Structure

MOUs/MOAs do not have a prerequisite format or structure, but most follow generally two familiar structures. One is set up in "articles", which is familiar to diplomatic and international readers, and the other offers a structure that is more familiar to military readers, starting with a purpose, then references, background and then named paragraphs that lay out the terms and details of the MOU/MOA. Following are good examples of each type of these MOUs/MOAs.

3. "Articles" MOU/MOA

a. An Articles MOU is typically drafted by IGOs, such as NATO and the UN, or by some of the departments and agencies of the USG such as DOS or USAID. An Articles MOU will normally come under a cover letter from one signatory to the other. The letter will state the purpose for the MOU, such as establishing a liaison officer from an agency to a CCDR's HQ. The letter will also very briefly summarize the reason why the MOU is being established. The letter is almost always one page long and is signed by a senior leader of the organization, such as a secretary or deputy secretary.

b. The reason an Articles MOU is called this is because every section of the MOU is a numbered article with a title. The structure is not standardized; however, the following format represents MOUs of this type and covers the sections one can expect to find in an Articles MOU/MOA.

(1) **Article I, Parties and Purpose** – Identifies the parties covered by the MOU and clearly states why the MOU is being put into effect.

(2) **Article II, Background** – Identifies what led to the need for the MOU/MOA

(3) **Article III, Authorities and Scope** – Identifies relevant laws, department and agency policies and regulations and applicable federal regulations that the MOU/MOA is in compliance with.

(4) **Article IV, Objectives** – Identifies the stated goals or objectives the MOU/MOA is established to accomplish.

(5) **Article V, Specific Responsibilities of the Parties** – Usually the longest and most detailed section of the MOU, this section goes into the specifics of what responsibilities each party to the MOU/MOA has to the other during the life of the agreement or understanding. This section will spell out a level of detail such as "USAID Representative to serve on the HQ USEUCOM staff as the Senior Development Advisor to USEUCOM." And "Provide the USAID Representative with the proper authorities and credentials to interact, on behalf of USEUCOM, with US federal agencies…" Normally Article V is divided into subsections in which the responsibilities of each party are listed. This is done for ease of identifying the responsibilities by party.

(6) **Article VI, Amendments** – Identifies when and under what conditions the MOU/MOA can be amended.

(7) **Article VII, Resolution of Disagreements** – This section normally relates to the Authorities article in that it specifies the validity of the MOU or sections of it if some part should be later found to be in conflict with statues or directives that take precedence over the MOU/MOA. This section also identifies procedures that will be followed if a disagreement develops between the parties that cannot be resolved by them alone.

(8) **Article VIII, Implementation** – Identifies when the MOU/MOA goes into effect, for how long and whether it can be extended and how this is to be done.

(9) **Article IX, Termination and Review** – Identifies when or how the MOU/MOA will be terminated.

c. For the purpose of showing a graphic example, the following articles of an MOU between USAID and USEUCOM is provided, the signature blocks are left out:

ARTICLE I
PARTIES AND PURPOSE

1.1 This Memorandum of Understanding (MOU), between the United States Agency for International Development (USAID) and the United States European Command (USEUCOM), hereinafter known as the Parties, is to strengthen the planning and operations of the Parties through improved coordination and joint actions for the purpose of improving national security, execution of foreign policy and growth of the economy of the United States, matters of concern to the missions of both Parties. This MOU leverages the resources available to the Parties in the USEUCOM Area of Responsibility/Area of Interest (AOR/AOI) and maximizes cooperation.

1.2 This MOU accordingly provides for a USAID Representative to be assigned to and employed at HQ USEUCOM as a civilian member of the staff and sets forth the general relationship and responsibilities between the Parties. The Parties agree that the USAID Representative's specialized and unique technical knowledge provides an essential contribution towards the fulfillment of HQ USEUCOM 's mission.

ARTICLE II
BACKGROUND

2.1. The Secretary of Defense approved the concept of a Joint Interagency Coordination Group (JIACG) to operate regionally at the unified command level. Pursuant to that approval, Commander USEUCOM has established a JIACG that includes an assignment of a representative from USAID.

ARTICLE III
AUTHORITY AND SCOPE

3.1 This MOU is entered into pursuant to U. S. Department of Defense (DOD) Instruction 4000 .19 and under the authority of the Economy Act of 1932, as amended (31 United States Code 1535); adheres to the Federal Acquisition Regulation (FAR) ; and is in compliance with DOD Directive Instruction 4000.19, and applicable USAID rules and regulations.

ARTICLE IV
OBJECTIVES OF MOU

4.1 To ensure that the Commander (CDR) USEUCOM is informed in a timely manner of pertinent USAID information and initiatives, relative to the purpose of this MOU.

4.2 To provide effective interface, cooperation and coordination between USEUCOM and USAID and other agency organizations coordinating US national activities within the USEUCOM AOR/AOI, including the analysis and dissemination of such related information, where appropriate.

4.3 To ensure that the CDR, USEUCOM and USEUCOM HQ staff is given prudent advice, guidance and recommendations relative to USEUCOM's interaction and interface with USAID on pertinent matters within the USEUCOM AOR/AOI.

4.4 To ensure that USAID is provided all pertinent intelligence and information relative to events and activities in the USEUCOM AOR/AOI that fall under USAID authorities.

4.5 To provide USAID a single point of interface and ready access to the CDR, USEUCOM and USEUCOM HQ senior staff. Interface and interaction with CDR, USEUCOM and staff will be through the JIACG.

4.6 To ensure that USAID is cognizant of the USEUCOM mission, capabilities and resources that are available for USAID to carry out its missions in the USEUCOM AOR/AOI.

4.7 To define logistical, administrative and infrastructure support to be provided by USEUCOM for the USAID Representative assigned to HQ USEUCOM.

4.8 To establish the general guidelines, consistent with DOD and USAID rules and regulations, to be used for the sharing and protection of information and intelligence between USEUCOM and USAID.

ARTICLE V
SPECIFIC RESPONSIBILITIES OF THE PARTIES

5.1 USAID, through its Office of Military Affairs (OMA), will:

5.1.a Identify a USAID Representative to serve on the HQ USEUCOM staff as the Senior Development Advisor to USEUCOM. USAID will initially identify a Personal Services Contractor (PSC) of appropriate experience to fill this position. The assignment of the PSC will be for a period of two years, with the option, upon mutual consent of the Parties, to extend for an additional year. The USAID Representative's position is intended to be permanent, but the PSC contract is time-limited. USAID will fill this PSC position, subject to the availability of funds for this purpose, approval by the Federal Republic of Germany (BRD) under the North Atlantic Treaty Organization Status of Forces Agreement (NATO/SOFA), approval by the BRD of the proposed PSC contract, approval by the BRD of the individual identified by USAID to fill the position, and an executed contract with a suitable candidate.

5.1.b Authorize the USAID Representative as the primary point of contact for USAID in the USEUCOM AORJAOI, and establish direct liaison between the USEUCOM and USAID.

5.1.c Subject to the availability of funds for this purpose, provide funding to USEUCOM for all necessary equipment for USAID-unique or specific connectivity through USAID's personal services contract with the USAID Representative to USEUCOM, and ensure that it is in place upon arrival of the USAID Representative .

5.1.d Be responsible for the administrative requirements of the USAID Representative, including all appropriate pay and employee benefits , to include permanent change of station (PCS) expenses, medical and dental costs, and school tuition for dependents as provided for in the personal services contract between USAID and the USAID Representative to HQ USEUCOM, or as may otherwise be provided for in accordance with the terms of the USAID Representatives ' status with USAID .

5.1.e Ensure that the USAID Representative has a valid TOP SECRET security clearance, training and means to ensure the appropriate handling and dissemination of DOD classified and sensitive information . SI/TK/G/H and NATO COSMIC TOP SECRET ATOMAL certification is required. If the USAID Representative has a valid TOP SECRET clearance, but is not certified for SI/TK/G/H or NATO COSMIC TOP SECRET ATOMAL, USEUCOM will provide training for such certification.

5.1.f Be responsible for providing all funding for USAID-specific missions and training requirements through the personal services contract between USAID and the USAID Representative to HQ USEUCOM, or as may otherwise be provided for in accordance with the terms of the USAID Representatives' status with USAID.

5.1.g Provide the USAID Representative with the proper authorities and credentials to interact , on behalf of USEUCOM, with United States federal agencies, relevant foreign agencies and intergovernmental organizations.

5.1.h Be responsible for writing any USAID-required performance reports for the
USAID Representative to USEUCOM.

5.2 The USEUCOM will:

5.2.a Provide necessary infrastructure support, including office space , office furniture, to include a desk , chair, file cabinets/drawers or the equivalent , non-USAID unique communication means, computer connectivity , telephone services, associated equipment and administrative supplies for use by the USAID Representative.

5.2.b Reimburse the USAID Representative ' s travel , training , and other associated mission support costs for the USAID Representative 's USEUCOM-specific activities and training.

5.2.c Ensure that the USAID Representative has reasonable access to HQ USEUCOM staff and staff meetings.

5.2.d Assign the USAID Representative to the Chief, JIACG, with specific tasking authority , where appropriate, over the USAID Representative .

5.2.e Maintain administrative control of the USAID Representative. Chief, JIACG, an agency of the US Forces, will ensure the activities of the USAID Representative will be governed by the principles established in the Arrangement relating to the provision of Analytical Support Services concluded on 29 June 2001, as amended. Specifically, Chief, JIACG, will ensure that the USAID Representative shall exclusively serve the US Forces and that he/she will only be engaged if he/she is not, at the time of his/her engagement, ordinarily resident in the territory of the BRD and that continued privileged status will continue only for so long as he/she has not become ordinarily resident. While entitled to such privileged status, the USAID Representative shall enjoy the same exemptions and benefits as those granted to members of the civilian component of the US Forces, unless the US restricts such exemptions and benefits. When no longer entitled to privileged status, the Chief, JIACG will take the necessary steps to withdraw such exemptions and benefits.

5.2.f Consistent with relevant statutes and regulations, provide support to the USAID Representative. Such support may include, but is not limited to, issuing ration and identification cards and ensuring entry to installations, the Post Exchange, Commissary and Morale Welfare and Recreation activities, access to military medical facilities (on a space-available basis, with all costs paid by USAID, subject to the availability of funds for this purpose) and access to Department of Defense Dependents (DODD) Schools (on a space-available basis, with all tuition and expenses paid by USAID, subject to the availability of funds for this purpose) .

ARTICLE VI
AMENDMENTS

6.1 This MOU may be amended at any time by written agreement between the Parties.

ARTICLE VII
RESOLUTION OF DISAGREEMENTS

7.1 Nothing herein is intended to conflict with current and relevant statutes, Department of Defense, USEUCOM or USAID directives. If the terms of this MOU are inconsistent with existing directives of any of these agencies, then those portions that are deemed inconsistent shall be invalid, but the remaining terms and conditions not affected by the inconsistency shall remain in full force and effect. At the first opportunity for review of this MOU, all necessary changes will be accomplished either by an amendment to this MOU or by entering into a new MOU, whichever is deemed expedient to the interest of both Parties.

7.2 Should disagreement arise on the interpretation of the provisions of this MOU, or amendments and/or revisions thereto, that cannot be resolved at the operating level, the area(s) of disagreement shall be put into writing by each party and presented to the other party for consideration. If agreement on interpretation is not reached within thirty days, the Parties shall forward the written presentation of the disagreement to respective higher officials for appropriate resolution.

ARTICLE VIII
IMPLEMENTATION

8.1 This MOU shall become binding and effective upon signature of authorized representatives of the Parties .

8.2 The Parties agree that the USEUCOM Deputy Commander and the USAID Administrator have authority to sign on behalf of their respective organizations

8.3 The Parties agree that the USAID Representative will be deployed to USEUCOM following the execution of a personal services contract between USAID and the USAID Representative to USEUCOM an d the completion of all required approvals by the BRD.

8.4 Both Parties agree that this MOU will be effective for an initial period of two years, with the option, upon mutual consent of the Parties, to extend for an additional year. Subsequent extension of this MOU will be by mutual consent of both Parties.

8.5 Duplicate originals of this MOU will be provided to both Parties.

ARTICLE IX
TERMINATION AND REVIEW

9.1 This MOU may be terminated upon mutual agreement by both Parties, or upon written notice to the other party by the undersigned or their successors. Both Parties agree to give 90 day written notice of intent to terminate this MOU.

9.2 Both Parties agree to review this MOU every year, or sooner if mutually agreed, and make any changes mutually agreed upon, if any.

4. "Military" or Traditional Memorandum

a. An MOU/MOA that uses structure more typical of military publications or memoranda is typically drafted by DOD entities, including CCDRs. Such MOU may have a cover letter, but more often than not they start out going right into the content of the MOU/MOA. The first paragraph of the MOU/MOA is a "Purpose" paragraph which serves the same objective as the letter in an Articles MO/MOA.

b. Like staff memorandum found throughout the military establishment, the MOU/ MOA here reflects a similar structure, each section is numbered and titled. The content of the MOU/MOA is similar to that of an Articles MOU/MOA, only the structure is different, though like the Articles MOU/MOA, it is not necessarily standardized. The following format represents MOUs of this type and covers the sections one can expect to find in a military or traditional MOU/MOA.

(1) **Purpose** – Identifies the reason for the MOU/MOA, including specific operational requirements, authorities and responsibilities.

(2) **References** – Identifies relevant regulations, agreements, directives, laws that the MOU/MOA is compliant with.

(3) **General Provision** – While not necessarily found in all MOUs/MOAs, this paragraph is used when an MOU or MOA is intended to cover multiple entities, such as are depicted in the following PRT example MOU.

(4) **Areas of Agreement** – This paragraph is usually divided into sub-sections including: Authority, which spells out which entities are responsible for leadership and guidance of subordinate entities; Performance Reporting, which identifies who will conduct evaluations; Regulations and Policies, which defines under which superior agent policies and procedures the subordinate entities will operate; Concept of Support, which identifies who will provide support and in what form that will be; as well as other sub-sections to address topics that are determined by the signatory parties (see the following example).

c. Although in structure this MOU/MOA is different from the Articles MOU/MOA, the content is very much the same and one can be used as a template for the other in that each holds those essential elements needed in both. The following example MOA that was established between the DOS and DOD on the subject of PRTs is provided, again, signatures have been left out.

EXAMPLE MOA BETWEEN USG DEPARTMENTS

1. PURPOSE:

The purpose of this Memorandum of Agreement (MOA) is to specify operational requirements, authorities, and responsibilities shared between the US Mission-Iraq (USM-I) and the Multi-National Forces-Iraq (MNF-I) or successor organizations for Provincial Reconstruction Teams ("PRTs") in Iraq. The PRT program is a priority joint Department of State (DOS)-Department of Defense (DOD) initiative to bolster moderates, support US counterinsurgency strategy, promote reconciliation and shape the political environment, support economic development, and build the capacity of Iraqi provincial governments to hasten the transition to Iraq self-sufficiency. Each agency agrees to support the program to the maximum extent provided for in this MOA.

The MOA supplements the agreements and authorities listed under 'References" below and does not amend, revise, or change these agreements or authorities except as specified herein.

2. REFERENCES:

a. Memorandum of Agreement between Department of Slate and Department of Defense for Support Services in Iraq, dated June 10, 2004.

b. Memorandum of Agreement between Department of Slate and Department of Defense Regarding Physical Security, Equipment and Personal Protective Services dated June 10, 2004.

c. US Mission Baghdad/MNF-I coordinated cable 4045, dated 010330Z Oct 2005, Action Plan to Build Capacity and Sustainability Within Iraq's Provincial Governments.

d. National Security Presidential Directive (NSPD) 36: United States Government Operations in Iraq, dated May 11, 2004.

e. Memorandum of Agreement (MOA) between Commander, US Central Command, and Chief of Mission, US Mission Iraq Regarding Security Responsibility, dated June 28, 2004.

f. The Economy Act (3) USC Section 1535

g. Title 22, United States Code, Sec. 3927: Chief of Mission Authority.

h. President 's Letter of Instruction to the United States Ambassador to Iraq.

i. Supplemental Agreement to the Memorandum of Agreement between Commander, Multinational Force-Iraq, and Chief of Mission, US Mission Iraq Regarding Security Responsibility on PRT Security Responsibilities and Requirements, dated November 9, 2006.

3. GENERAL PROVISIONS:

a. This MOA covers all PRTs, including Regional Reconstruction Teams (RRTs), Provincial Support Teams (PSTs), and embedded PRTs, all of which are hereafter referred to collectively as PRTs, existing or to be established in Iraq.

b. This MOA is not intended to identify each and every support requirement or to prejudice the ability of the Chief of Mission (COM) or Commander, MNF-I to make requests for support not specifically slated herein. Rather, this MOA is intended to address the majority of support issues and to provide baseline direction for support responsibilities.

Except in emergency circumstances, requests for additional support beyond that provided for herein will take the form of a written request from the COM to the Commander, MNF-I or from the Commander, MNF-I to the COM, as specific circumstances dictate. Such requests may be for reimbursable or non-reimbursable support.

c. This MOA will be implemented consistent with available funding and applicable law. The parties' ability, as a practical matter, to implement this MOA depends on their ability to obtain adequate supplemental funding for this purpose.

4. AREAS OF AGREEMENT:

a. Authority:

(i) PRTs are a joint Department of State-Department of Defense mission, and they operate under joint policy guidance from the COM and Commander, MNF-I, harnessing both civilian and military resources against a common strategic plan. The PRT/BCT will function as one team. Together they will receive guidance from both COM and Commander, MNF-I that will follow a common plan for their joint AOR.

(ii) The Department of State will lead PRTs and is responsible for recruiting, hiring, and managing civilian PRT personnel.

(iii) Embedded PRTs will also coordinate their activities with the paired PRT in their area (e.g., the existing Baghdad and Anbar PRTs, which will maintain primary responsibility for provincial-level engagement). The COM and Commander, MNF-I will jointly decide whether PRTs are considered paired with or embedded in military units for purposes of this memorandum.

(iv) The COM provides political and economic guidance and direction to all PRTs. The BCT Commander will exercise his authority over security and movement of personnel for PRTs embedded in military units based on security concerns but will not direct members of the PRT as to who they should see, nor deny the members of the PRT the ability to make contact with certain interlocutors, based on a judgment of priorities other than security.

(v) All parties will coordinate closely in the development of relevant guidance on PRT activities, not only to deconflict relevant activities, but more importantly so that all activities work together toward the common goal of bolstering moderates, supporting US counterinsurgency strategy, and strengthening the capacity of provincial governments to accelerate the transition to Iraqi self-reliance.

(vi) Any disputes between BCT Commanders or other military commanders and PRT leaders concerning he policies, procedures, or activities of PRTs will be submitted promptly to the COM and Commander, MM-I or their senior representatives for resolution.

(vii) All military personnel providing support to PRTs will fall under the UCMJ authority of their respective chains of command as determined by the appropriate command relationships.

b. Performance Reporting:

(i) PRT Team Leaders are responsible for the overall performance of their joint civil-military team and will monitor the individual performance of all members oft heir team. Evaluation reports will be prepared in accordance with Mission policy and employing agency policy.

(ii) MNF-I units provided in direct support to the PRT will follow their internal rating chain. DOD and Military Department Service regulations and procedures will be followed.

c. Regulations and Policies:

(i) PRTs will observe COM directions, rules, policies and procedures: to the extent applicable. In relation to matters of security for which Commander, MNF-I is responsible, PRT members will comply with MNF-I safety and force-protection measures as provided in Reference 2.i. above.

(ii) Each PRT member who is a Federal employee remains an employee of his or her department or agency and subject to the regulations, policies, and procedures of that department or agency to the extent not inconsistent with COM or Commander, MNF-I requirements. Military personnel shall continue to observe MNF-I regulations in their personal and professional conduct in support of the PRT mission.

(iii) Each PRT member who is made available through an institutional contractor will be responsible for performing his/her PRT duties in accordance with the statement of duties prescribed in the contract and shall be subject to the general guidance of the department or agency that awarded the contract, to the extent not inconsistent with COM or Commander, MNF-1 requirements. Further, any conflict between the terms and conditions of the contract under which institutional contractors are employed, their specific agreement with their employer, and COM rules, policies, and procedures should be resolved prior to their assignment to a PRT.

d. Concept of Support:

(i) PRTs are critical elements in achieving the goals of the USG in Iraq. As such, they will be provided the highest level of support available, and the support PRT members receive will be without distinction based on their home organizations, or whether they are USG employees, contractor personnel, or foreign nationals, except as otherwise provide herein or by separate agreement or contract.

(ii) DOS will be responsible for providing, or reimbursing DOD for, all operational support and life support for PRTs, consistent with sections e and f of this MOA. "Operational support" means necessary facilities and facilities services (e.g.: office space, office supplies, and related equipment and services), logistic and infrastructure support (e.g., facilities upkeep and management), and basic utilities/services (e.g., power water, sewer, fire protection, drainage, waste management, hazardous material management, and environmental services). "Life support" includes lodging, food, water, bath and sanitation, and any morale, recreation and welfare facilities or services (e.g. laundry services, food service operations, postal operations, check cashing, and army & Air Force Exchange Service (AAFES) mail order service).

(iii) DOD will be responsible for providing on a non-reimbursable basis all inter theater air and ground transportation and associated support to PRTs, consistent with the terms of Annex A of this MOA.

(iv) DOD will be responsible for providing all medical support including necessary primary care to PRTs collocated with US military units, as well as medical evacuation and mortuary services as required for PRT personnel regardless of locations. PRT contractors and foreign government personnel will be provided medical support, medical evacuation and mortuary services in accordance with the terms of applicable contract provisions or agreements. DOS or the relevant contracting agency, as appropriate, will reimburse DOD for medical support, medical evacuation, and mortuary services provided to PRT members. DOS will be responsible for any arrangements for PRT primary medical care at non-collocated PRTs and for primary care for civilian PRT members in the International Zone.

(v) Communications and information systems support to non-collocated and paired PRTs shall be provided to PRTs consistent with the terms of Annex B of this MOA. At embedded PRTs, DOD will provide communications and information support, and DOS will reimburse.

(vi) For PRTs located on Mission facilities or on Non-US Coalition facilities, the COM or his designee will have overall decision authority on the PRT location. For PRTs collocated with US military units, the responsible Major Subordinate Command will have overall decision authority on the PRT location, facilities management, and administrative and logistic support. The COM and the Commander, MNF-I, or their designees, will coordinate regarding PRT locations.

(vii) DOS and DOD will finalize reimbursement procedures for life and operational support within 30 days of signature of this MOA.

(viii) If factors arise that affect the continued maintenance of a PRT at a specific location, its status, or the provision of support, the Commander, MNF-I and the COM, or their designated representatives, will consult with each other and with their respective chains of command so that appropriate alternative arrangements can be made.

(ix) To facilitate PRT operations, PRT members will be issued appropriate facility access badges in accordance with the applicable security policies. PRT members will hold an appropriate security clearance, background investigation, or employment verification check based on the requirements of the assigned position. Verification will be established through security channels.

e. Support Levels and Funding for PRTs Collocated with US Militant Units:

(i) DOD will provide operational and life support for PRTs collocated with BCTs or other US military units, regardless of whether such support is organic to the military unit except as provided in subparagraph (v) below. DOS will reimburse DOD for such support.

(ii) DOD will provide all support specified in this MOA for PRTs collocated with BCTs or other US military units at the levels provided to MNF-I personnel of similar grade at similar locations.

(iii) DOD will provide operational and life support for PRT contractor personnel serving on PRTs collocated with US military units on a reimbursable basis. In the case of a DOD contractor, DOS will reimburse DOD for the cost of such support. In all other cases, the contracting agency will reimburse DOD for the cost of such support.

(iv) Foreign government personnel assigned to PRTs will be provided the same level of support as other PRT members, subject to the terms of funding arrangements as agreed in the particular case in view of the mission of such personnel and any governing agreement with their respective countries.

(v) DOD is responsible for funding repair and maintenance of all DOD equipment and vehicles: and DOS is responsible for funding repair and maintenance of all DOS equipment and vehicles. All maintenance support provided by DOD for DOS equipment and vehicles will be reimbursed by DOS.

f. Support Levels and Funding for PRTs Not Collocated with US Military Units:

(i) DOS will provide operational and life support for PRTs not collocated with US military units on a non-reimbursable basis: except as provided in subparagraph (v) below, unless arrangements are made for DOD to provide such support on a reimbursable basis, or unless a coalition partner agrees to provide such support.

(ii) DOS will provide any support for PRTs not collocated with US military units at the levels provided to DOS personnel of similar grade.

(iii) Except where the contract provides that the government will provide support, arrangements will be made for contractors serving on PRTs not collocated with US military units to reimburse the non-DOD service provider directly (i.e., DOS or Coalition partner as applicable) for the operational and life support they receive. Where the contract provides that the government will provide support, the contracting agency will reimburse the non-DOD service provider for the cost of such support.

(iv) In cases where DOD provides operational and life support for PRT contractor personnel serving on PRTs not collocated with US military units, such support will be provided on a reimbursable basis. In the case of a DOD contractor, DOS will reimburse DOD for such support. In all other cases, the contracting agency will reimburse DOD for the cost of such support.

(v) Foreign government personnel who are PRT members will be provided support on the same basis as other PRT members, with funding arrangements as agreed in the particular case in view of the mission of such personnel and any governing agreement with their respective countries.

(vi) DOS is responsible for funding repair and maintenance of all DOS equipment and vehicles. All maintenance support provided by DOS for DOD equipment and vehicles will be reimbursed by DOD.

g. Transitional Arrangements:

(i) DOD will pay salary costs for the initial DOD staffing for the PRT surge, anticipated to include 129 positions for a period not to exceed 12 months. DOS will fund all non-DOD agency salary costs for PRT positions thereafter, to the extent that funds are made available to DOS specifically for this purpose.

(ii) DOS will initiate measures to identify replacement personnel for the 109 specialist positions DOD will fill during Phase II. Where advantageous for achieving the PRT mission, DOS will be prepared to replace all of these DOD-provided specialist personnel no later than 90 days after receiving funding for that purpose. In any event, DOS will be prepared to replace these DOD-provided specialist personnel within 12 months of their deployment.

5. ANNEXES:

   A. Air and Ground Transportation Support
   B. Communications and Information System Support
   C. Appendix 1: Communications Support Matrix

6. EFFECTIVE DATE, MODIFICATION AND TERMINATION:

This Memorandum of Agreement will become effective upon signature by both Parties. PRT support extended prior to signature of this MOA will be inclusive. MNF-I and US Mission-Iraq will review this MOA annually for currency and applicability. This MOA may be amended in writing as mutually agreed by the Parties.

Intentionally Blank

APPENDIX D
WHOLE-OF-GOVERNMENT PLANNING UTILIZING THE INTERAGENCY MANAGEMENT SYSTEM

1. Introduction

The IMS R&S is a whole-of-government approach to dealing with a crisis in a foreign country or region where the US national authority has determined a USG response is in the national interest. The system is not designed to respond to natural disasters or emergencies such as tsunamis, earthquakes, drought, floods. For these kinds of situations the USG has proven procedures and methodologies that will be brought to bear. A whole-of-government response can be initiated or mobilized by the NSC, SECSTATE, SecDef, or the regional bureau assistant secretary from the DOS. "Triggers" that can be referenced to mobilize a whole-of-government response are covered elsewhere in this handbook. Currently there is no single procedure or form that is used to mobilize a whole-of-government operation. Initiation can be the result of a verbal or memorandum written directive from either the PC or the DC or from a directive from either the SECSTATE or SecDef. Once initiated whole-of-government planning is managed from the national level by the CRSG. The CRSG is responsible for developing and promulgating a USG R&S Strategic Plan. At the country level an ACT will augment the COM's country team and take responsibility for developing and implementing a Country Plan that is based on the Strategic R&S Plan.

2. Whole-of-government Planning for Crisis Response and Contingencies

a. The IMS is designed to respond to crisis in a foreign country or region. It all begins with planning. R&S planning is undertaken in support of achieving transformation in the specified country or region undergoing or projected to undergo violent conflict or civil strife. The goal of this approach, referred to as "conflict transformation," is to reach the point where the country or region is on a **sustainable positive trajectory**, where it is able to address on its own the dynamics causing civil strife and/or violent conflict. This requires simultaneously supporting sources of social and institutional resilience as well as other factors that mitigate civil strife and violent conflict while reducing the drivers of conflict. A fundamental principle of conflict transformation is that, over the longer term, the HN must develop its own capacity to ensure stability and conditions for economic growth – those conditions cannot be imposed from outside. The *USG Planning Framework for Reconstruction, Stabilization, and Conflict Transformation* is designed to address two related but distinct activities: **CRP** and **contingency planning**. A major crisis response would require significant and complex humanitarian, security, reconstruction, governance, and economic efforts utilizing all the instruments of US national power. R&S operations are not limited to situations where the US military will be or is currently conducting combat operations. Contingency planning would be a more limited planning effort for the purposes of preparing for a potential event. Both employ the same planning framework but to differing levels of detail and with different time demands and personnel constraints.

b. CRP addresses an imminent or existing crisis with R&S and/or conflict transformation implications. CRP may be done with or without triggering the entire IMS.

c. Contingency planning addresses potential future R&S crisis in a country or region over a two to three year period. Contingency planning may also produce recommendations for preventative actions that can be integrated into existing USG planning processes, such as the MSPs, country assistance strategies, and combatant command campaign plans.

3. Specific Steps in the Planning Process

a. The following sections, comprising the remainder of this appendix, rely on explanations for planning processes provided in the *USG Planning Framework for Reconstruction, Stabilization, and Conflict Transformation*. The Planning Framework establishes a four–stage process: **situation analysis, policy formulation, strategy development, and country-level planning**. These stages should be viewed as a planning cycle, with each stage informing revisions and changes to the others. For example, challenges encountered in the implementation stage may require a re-examination of policy or a revision of the USG R&S Strategic Plan.

b. A guiding principle of whole-of-government planning is the inclusion of all relevant USG agencies in the planning process. To facilitate this inclusion, the R&S Interagency Policy Committee or CRSG will be notified when whole-of-government planning for reconstruction, stabilization and conflict transformation has been triggered.

4. Situation Analysis

a. After triggering whole-of-government R&S planning, a SPT is assembled that includes the members of the appropriate regional foreign AWG augmented by planning, geographic (including in-country expertise) and functional experts from across the USG as appropriate. The first task of the SPT is to analyze the current environment for the R&S operation. This will draw, where possible, on consultations and information exchanges with US personnel and other multilateral, governmental and nongovernmental partners in the field.

b. Situation analysis is an on-going activity that assembles data and strategic information from across government partners and builds a knowledge base on vulnerable countries. Situation analysis for R&S planning purposes should include the performance of a comprehensive interagency assessment using, whenever possible, the ICAF that: (1) diagnoses the conflict or civil strife, and (2) completes a pre-planning mapping of current efforts against drivers of conflict and mitigating factors. Information generated from any prior planning and assessments, as well as existing data and intelligence from interagency partners will be used in the analysis and mapping.

c. Drawing on the results of the ICAF, the SPT will develop a situation analysis overview that provides a clear depiction of the drivers of conflict and mitigating factors that mitigate civil strife or conflict, current USG and international efforts as well as US interests relating to the country and region, the expected actions of key actors (both partners and competitors), gaps in current and expected efforts to address the instability or conflict, risks associated with both action and inaction, legal considerations for providing assistance to the country, and critical gaps in knowledge/intelligence.

5. Policy Formulation

a. Once the decision has been made to go forward with a crisis response the CRSG develops policy options for the NSC DC or PC in the form of a Policy Advisory Memorandum. The policy formulation builds upon the situation analysis and offers clear policy options, usually two or three distinct viable options are offered. These options are composed of overarching goals and strategic objectives and associated risks and benefits. Assumptions, such as resources that will be made available and the level of security requirements, are included in the policy formulation, as are critical planning considerations, such as timeframes for manpower to deploy and moving budget and funding sources to support the strategy goals. The goals and objectives will be laid out to correspond to the drivers of conflict and local capacity needs. This is critical since failure to address the drivers of conflict will result in the root causes of the conflict not being removed. The goal of the operation will be to restore HN abilities to manage their own affairs effectively.

b. The options for policy are described in a policy memo for the DC. A critical component of the memorandum is the "order of magnitude" estimate of the resources which would be required to achieve each of the proposed policy options. The format of the Policy Advisory Memorandum is not standardized and will vary from one R&S operation to the next. However, every memorandum includes:

(1) a narrative laying out policy options;

(2) an explanation of the broader context and reasoning associated with the set of options;

(3) issues of policy incoherence, gaps in capacity, or longstanding legislative and policy concerns;

(4) a request for designation of the USG representative "responsible" for implementing the USG R&S Strategic Plan;

(5) the contextual scenario (assumptions about the country environment and anticipated roles/resources of other groups);

(6) the overarching policy goals;

(7) what success would look like;

(8) the MMEs (and associated causal assumptions-theories of change);

(9) the USG resources requirements (rough order of magnitude); and

(10) associated risks.

c. Figure D-1 is an example of a Policy Option that would be included in a Policy Advisory Memorandum.

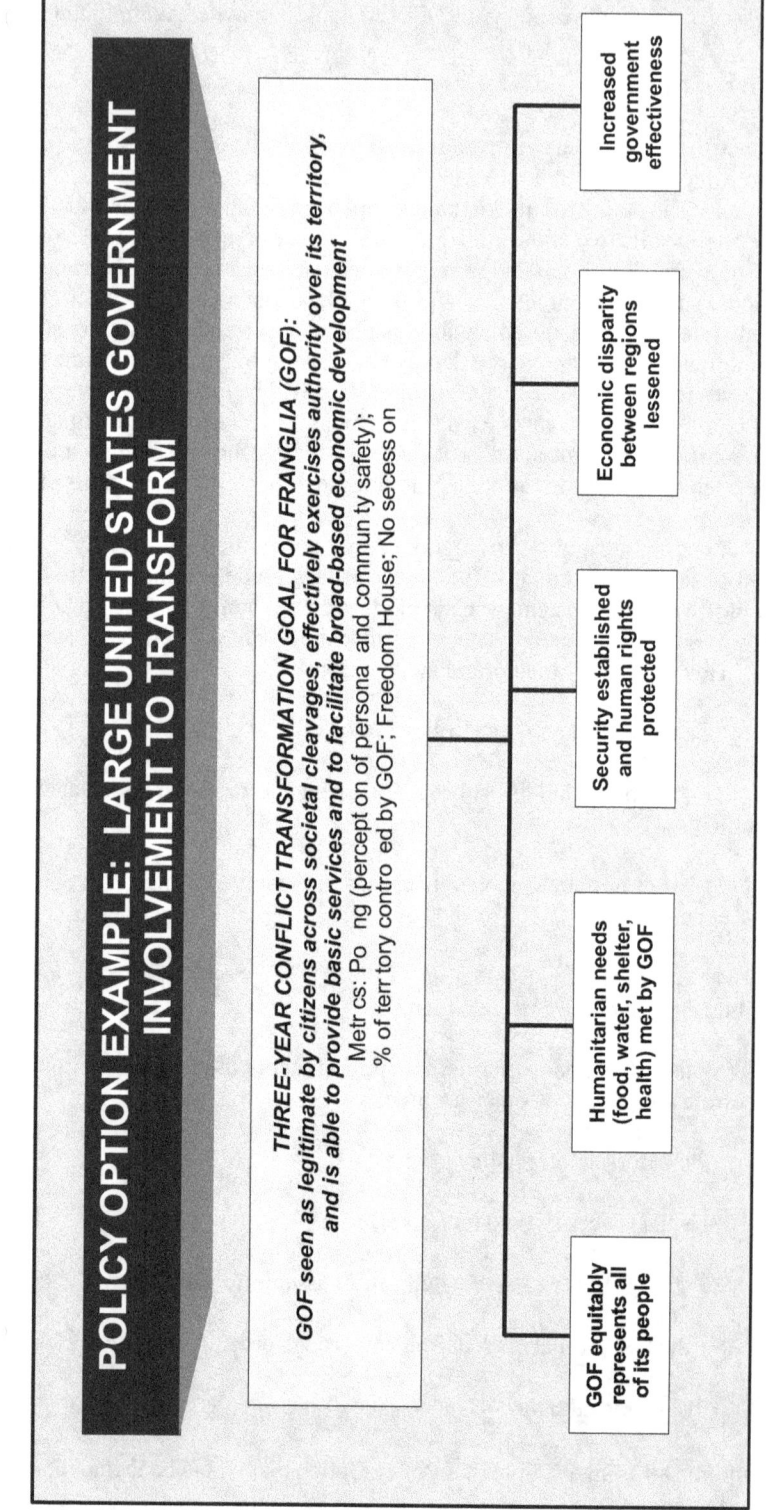

Figure D-1. Policy Option Example: Large USG Involvement to Transform

(1) **Assumptions**

    (a) **USG Resource Assumptions**: $350 million a year for three years (including money for peacekeeping/military force, significant government capacity building, infrastructure projects, and humanitarian assistance for the first two years), provision of 40% of necessary troops.

    (b) **Behavior of Others**: UN will request NATO lead of an international peacekeeping force and provide significant humanitarian aid; coalition of other nations will provide 20% of needed assistance resources and 60% of troops required; external groups will not directly support parties to the conflict.

    (c) **Environment**: Local population will welcome international peacekeeping force; most areas of the country remain permissive for civilians; elected government will have the political will to make necessary changes; performance of government functions by IC not necessary; 50% of infrastructure still functional.

    (d) **Causal**: Insurgency/insurrection is based primarily on economic and political grievances and will be lessoned by increasing economic opportunities and putting into place a representative government; capacity building can increase the effectiveness of the government enough to make a perceptible difference in timeframe.

(2) **Risks**: Insurgency grows despite progress in economics/governance; Other groups do not provide sufficient troops, and their assistance is delayed (missing critical window of opportunity); USG capabilities reduced for other/future conflicts; poor information on current state of economic & infrastructure needs – estimates could be significantly under actual need; extensive USG efforts, if they fail to transform the country, could hurt image longer-term in the region.

(3) **Legislative Constraints**: Military aid restricted to MOD because of prior human rights abuses; budget environment very tight.

d. The policy goal is the overall objective, stated as an outcome, that the USG as a whole plans to achieve in a specified timeframe (two to three years). Figure D-2 lists some examples of policy goals.

e. The PC/DC will respond to the Policy Advisory Memorandum with either a Policy Statement or a request for new options. The Policy Statement with determine the overarching R&S goal by approving one of the policy options, including stipulating the critical planning considerations for the Strategic Plan and providing a preliminary estimate of the USG resources likely to be available.

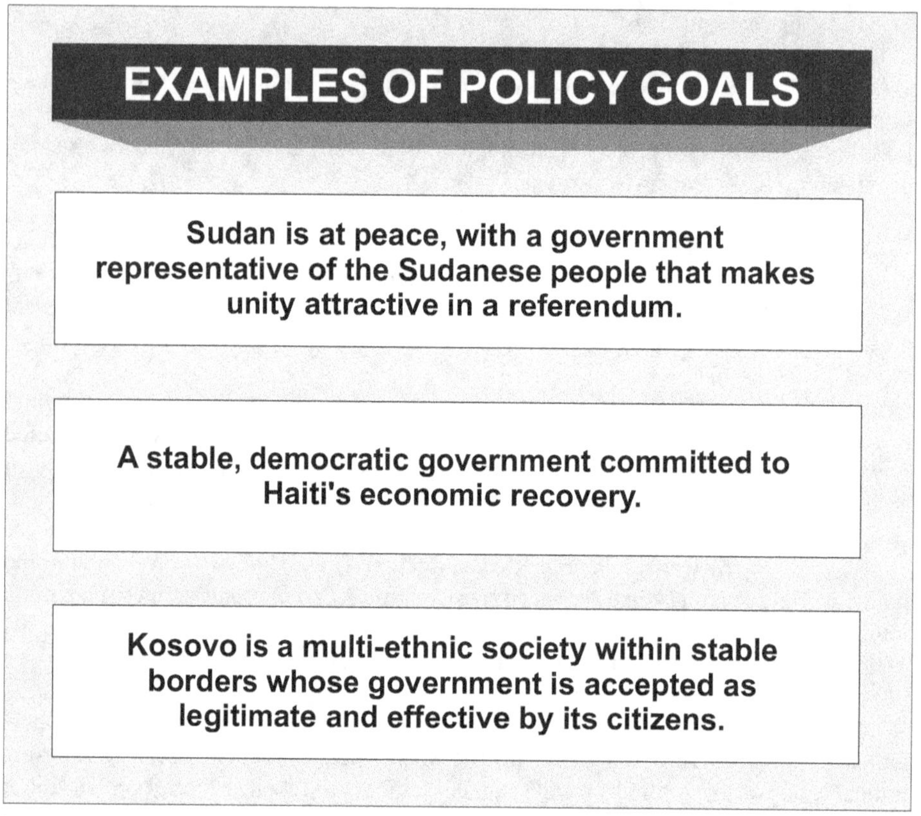

EXAMPLES OF POLICY GOALS

> **Sudan is at peace, with a government representative of the Sudanese people that makes unity attractive in a referendum.**

> **A stable, democratic government committed to Haiti's economic recovery.**

> **Kosovo is a multi-ethnic society within stable borders whose government is accepted as legitimate and effective by its citizens.**

Figure D-2. Examples of Policy Goals

6. Strategy Development

a. The SPT, whether part of the CRSG when the IMS is activated or working with the relevant Interagency Policy Committee when the IMS has not been activated, uses the *Policy Statement* to begin the iterative process of developing the USG R&S Strategic Plan. This plan will determine how the R&S operation will address the prioritization, sequencing and cross-sectoral linkages of USG efforts. The CRSG or relevant Interagency Policy Committee will initiate a budget planning process drawing on interagency members including OMB, Office of the Director of US Foreign Assistance, and implementing agencies in coordination with the SPT and US presence in the field. The SPT is also responsible for synthesizing the constant flow of information from the field into its deliberations on the plan, including, where possible, input from HN authorities. As a guiding principle, HN authorities should be engaged, as early as possible, in strategic planning. In extreme instances, where outside groups have assumed authority, criteria for triggering a transfer of authority to a responsible HN government should be established early and reviewed regularly for continuing relevance to changing situations.

b. The SPT for major engagements will submit the USG R&S Strategic Plan to the CRSG Interagency Policy Committee, or relevant Interagency Policy Committee in cases when the IMS has not been activated, for approval. The USG R&S Strategic Plan includes the following products:

(1) **Plan Overview Template**, a one-page graphic depiction of the plan;

(2) **Strategic Plan Narrative** addressing the situation analysis, the overarching policy goal for R&S, critical planning considerations, MMEs, MME prioritization, sequencing and linkages;

(3) **Comprehensive Resource and Management Strategy** (laying out rough order of magnitude requirements and availabilities for each MME);

(4) MME Concepts;

(5) Relevant technical annexes (e.g., security, personnel, logistics); and

(6) A determination of what decisions remain in Washington (e.g., the decision whether to work with HN armed forces).

c. The locus of planning during the strategy development phase will depend on the nature of the R&S operation, as indicated in the *Policy Statement*.

(1) A major national security engagement requiring the use of the IMS dictates that the strategy development would be centered in Washington with significant participation and input from non-Washington participants, including the GCC, the COM, a USAID Disaster Assistance Response Team (DART), bi-lateral and multi-lateral partners and/or NGOs. In non-presence countries, once US personnel are deployed into the field, their input becomes a critical component of strategy development and may include recommendations for revisions to the overarching USG policy goal.

(2) The Interagency Policy Committee/DC may determine that strategy development should take place primarily in-country, under the direction of the COM in order to take full advantage of on the ground interagency regional, sectoral, and functional expertise, as well as assure buy-in from HN leaders and stakeholders.

d. An R&S operation likely involving significant US military presence creates the need to integrate crisis action planning or contingency planning occurring simultaneously at the geographic combatant command with the planning in Washington, DC, and the field. A team of civilian planners will deploy to the applicable command to ensure this integration occurs. Likewise, a team may deploy to a multinational planning HQ to integrate USG efforts with an international response.

e. With the policy approved, the CRSG will turn to the task of developing the MMEs. The CRSG SPT will establish MME planning teams to produce **MME Concepts** describing the proposed approach for the achievement of each MME. The term Sub-Objective is used to identify the subordinate objectives that are necessary to achieve a particular MME. The **MME Concepts** developed by MME teams will address:

(1) how the MME relates to other MMEs;

(2) rough order of magnitude capability requirements (both foreign assistance and operational) to achieve the MME;

(3) the Sub-Objectives that are necessary and sufficient to achieve the MME, including a discussion of Sub-Objective sequencing and priority decision points;

(4) criteria for success for each MME to ensure that there is a shared understanding of the desired outcomes;

(5) how additional planning considerations not in the *Policy Statement* relate to the MME;

(6) identification of critical information requirements and knowledge gaps;

(7) potential impediments to success; and

(8) potential strategic, regional, and local consequences, positive and negative, of successful achievement of the MME.

f. MMEs are developed for an assessment of the drivers of conflict and instability. Each individual MME describes a different problem set that needs to be resolved in order to decrease conflict and increase stability. The MMEs include not just those problems the USG will solve, but those problems that will need to be solved to meet that goal. Each MME is necessary and together they are sufficient to achieve the goal. The MMEs identify the lead agency or department of the USG that will have overall responsibility for addressing the problem set identified by the MME as well as those agencies and departments that will collaborate with the lead.

g. An example of MMEs for one policy goal is shown in Figure D-3. Note that these MMEs are only of the elements themselves; they do not include the lead agency.

h. Figure D-4 is an example of a more robust policy goal, note that the goal and associated metrics are in the top blue box. The orange boxes identify the MMEs and below them are the lead and supporting agencies as well as estimated funding required for the respective MMEs.

7. Country-Level Planning and Execution

a. The Country Plan is the plan for executing in-country actions to achieve Washington's overarching goals, to include iterative assessment, planning, and performance assessment. This level is also responsible for advising the Washington level on how realities on the ground may require modifications to overarching strategic approach. The intent is for planning to develop an in-country strategy to achieve the policy objectives articulated by the Washington-level, based on allocated resources. This includes both strategic and implementation planning, to ensure synchronization of all in-country USG activities. The execution of the country level plan may include

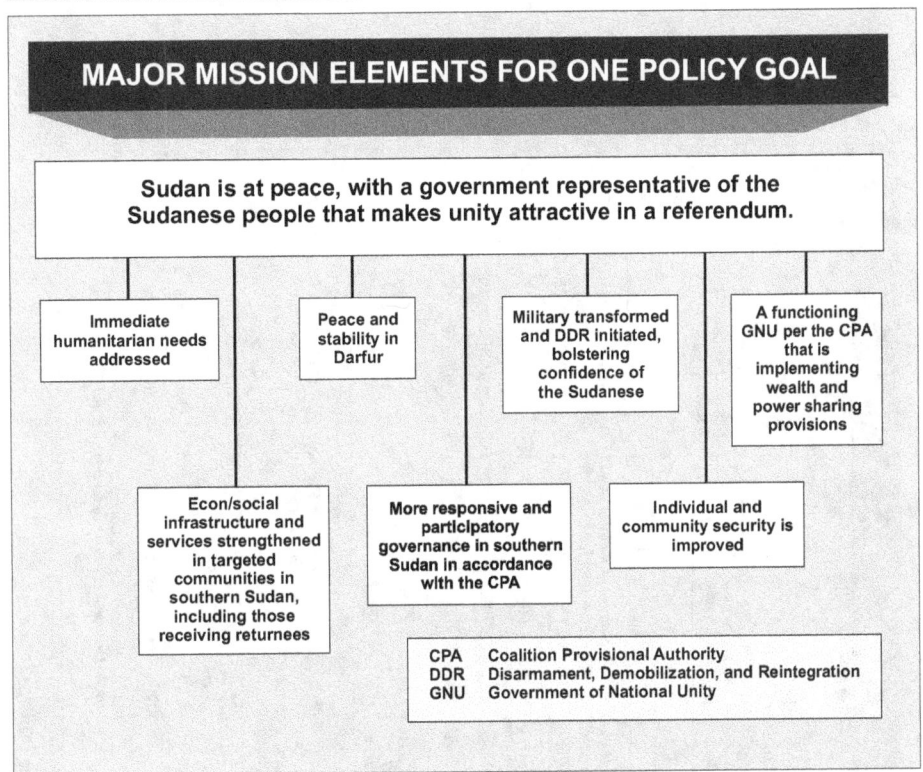

Figure D-3. Major Mission Elements for One Policy Goal

consultation with other internal and external groups. A wide variety of activities may be executed at this level.

b. The planning efforts performed in-country will be a critical determinant of mission success. Country-level planning and execution is complex, dynamic and unique to every whole-of-government operation. What worked in Afghanistan might not work in Liberia. HN relationships in Nepal are very different from those in Lebanon. But in all cases there will be IGO, NGO, and non-US governmental entities that have a stake in what is happening in the HN. Most of the time these entities will have the same objective of stabilizing and reconstructing, but they may go about it in ways much different than the USG does and even in ways that are counter-productive to USG objectives. These entities need to be considered and worked with in one way or the other.

c. Following the approval of the USG R&S Strategic Plan, country-level planning becomes the responsibility of the COM. Country-level planning is an iterative process to synchronize diplomatic, development and defense implementation planning and tasks, towards the goal of executing the USG R&S Strategic Plan. Country-level planning is distinct from agency implementation planning in that the planning effort involves the input and participation of a number of separate agencies.

d. Staffing the development of a large, multi-sectoral, multi-agency planning process is a complex undertaking requiring expert planning, coordination, and facilitation as well

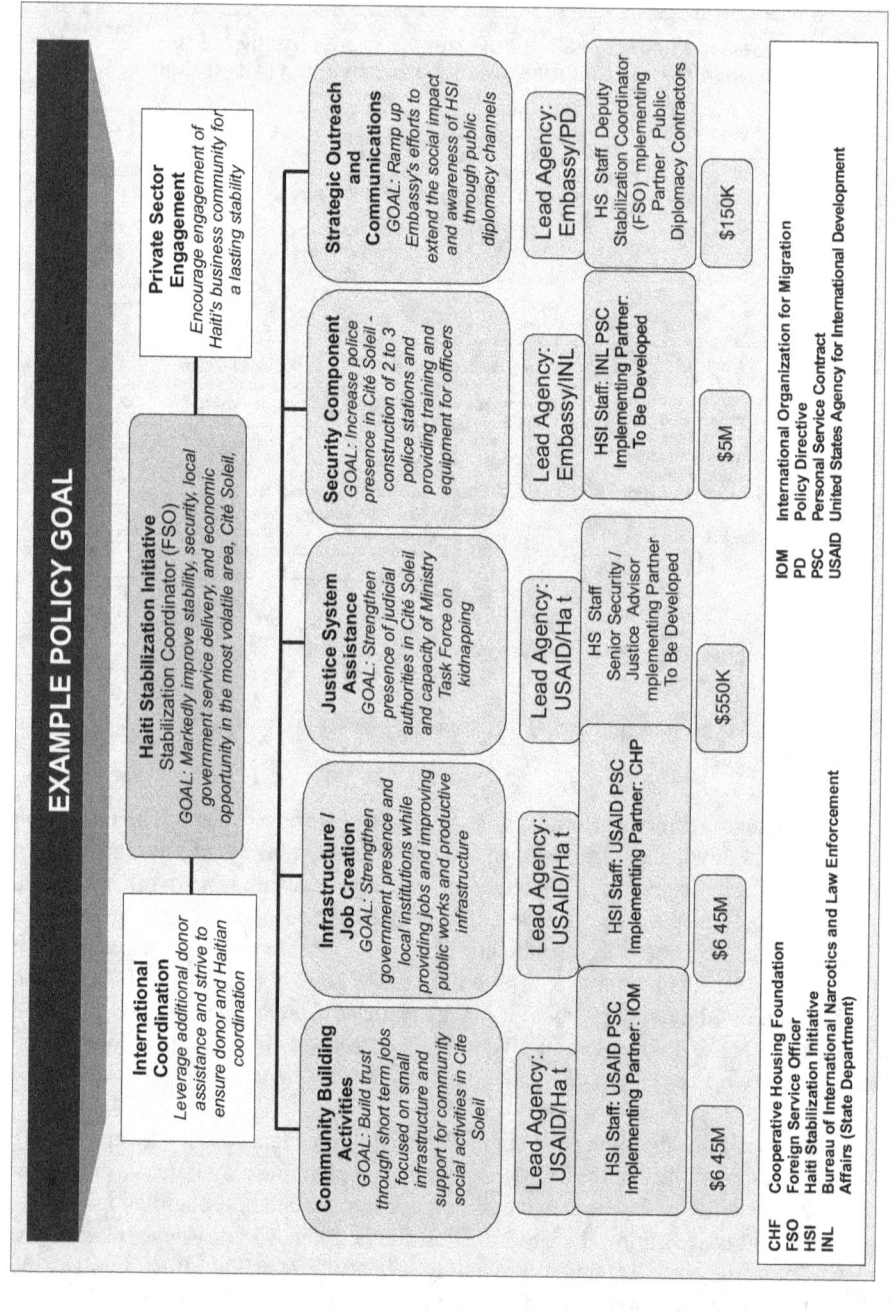

Figure D-4. Example Policy Goal

as technical and operational expertise. If the IMS is not activated and a US Mission exists, the COM informs Washington of additional planning personnel requirements. If the IMS is activated, the CRSG, in consultation with the COM, forms the ACT to support the COM and the development of the Country Plan.

e. The ACT forms an implementation planning team to support the COM. The implementation planning team will consist of the implementing agencies that will be accountable for carrying out the actions and developing the programs that will impact the results for R&S strategic objectives or MMEs. This team will function throughout the life of the plan and will be responsible to the COM for planning, monitoring and achieving the R&S policy goal.

f. To accomplish R&S country-level planning, the implementation planning team will form multi-sectoral sub-objective teams for each MME that will consist of representatives from the various implementing agencies. These sub-objective teams will detail multi-sectoral approaches within MMEs and consolidate sectoral country-level plans across the MMEs. In cases where the implementation of a sub-objective falls within the mandate of one agency, the planning is carried out by that agency with its own planning processes with relevant information informing the country-level planning process. Implementing agencies will provide operation and technical specialists as necessary to support country-level planning. It is critical that planning teams charged with designing and implementing programs have the authority over resources and field expertise to operate in uncertain and changing environments. The implementation planning team will be joined by member(s) of the SPT in order to provide continuity to the USG R&S Strategic Plan.

g. The MMEs that are developed at the CRSG comprise the bulk of the USG R&S Strategic Plan. The MMEs will be diverse, complex and interrelated. From these MMEs and the overarching strategic plan, the Country Team, led by the COM and augmented by the Advanced Civilian Team, will develop the Country Plan. The USG interagency community has identified five common sectors that represent key elements and functions that interact within a society during R&S operations. They are:

(1) security,

(2) governance and participation,

(3) humanitarian assistance and social well-being,

(4) economic stabilization and infrastructure, and

(5) justice and reconciliation.

h. These five sectors enable an ACT to effectively manage the R&S effort. It is important that none of these get ignored and each is seen to have an impact on all the others. Equally as important is to organize MMEs not by sector, but as achievable outcomes. This will ensure the right agencies comprise the interagency teams at the objective and sub-objective levels while negating the tendency to organize around individual agency stove-pipes.

i. In cooperation, the JTF commander and the ACT director, with the approval of the COM will endeavor to start making a positive impact, recognizing that local acceptance and cooperation are vital. They will want to "do something" right away to make their presence felt. They will need to map the rest of the players in the JOA to know who is there and what they "bring to the table." A center, like a CIMIC should be set up for international actors to meet and coordinate. Local leaders need to be identified and a means of working with them established. The strategy for achieving success needs to be developed – quickly. It can be modified over time, but is needed as soon as possible.

j. The IPT will provide the following planning functions:

(1) provide the COM and the CRSG with strategic information and facilitate communications;

(2) design, coordinate, organize, and manage the country-level planning process, including provision of data collection and analytic support;

(3) provide interpretation and guidance on the intent of the senior policy makers and SPT decisions;

(4) facilitate stakeholder input into the planning process;

(5) coordinate the operations and inputs from sub-objective teams;

(6) provide support in the development of indicators, performance monitoring plans, and data collection, analysis, interpretation and reporting; and

(7) serve as the mechanism for communicating feedback, including proposed revisions to the USG R&S Strategic Plan, and additional planning requirements.

k. The implementation planning team will need to validate the strategic planning assumptions, "ground truth" the broad outlines of the USG R&S Strategic Plan, and determine a planning approach that will assure HN ownership, civil society participation, and the strong donor coordination that will be critical to the development and acceptance of the country-level plan.

l. Country-level planning must also balance immediate requirements with long-term transformational requirements to assure progress can be made on both. The implementation planning team is responsible for designing a Country Plan that will:

(1) provide an overview of the operating environment, including critical elements/impediments that may affect implementation of the plan that were not described in the USG R&S Strategic Plan;

(2) map donor and IGO program inputs and determine gaps that the USG approach will address, including tracking negotiations on the use of common approaches and on roles and responsibilities;

(3) refine **MME Concepts** based on **Sub-Objective Concepts** developed by Sub-Objective planning teams that focus on required accomplishments in three-month benchmarks throughout the course of the plan;

(4) determine program approaches at all levels in the Country Plan: short-term/long-term trade-offs, geographic priorities, and targets;

(5) address the multi-sectoral nature of Sub-Objectives for each MME;

(6) determine an approach to strengthening host-government short and long term capacity (e.g., resident advisor vs. technical assistance);

(7) determine what mechanisms will be used to implement the program approach (use of pre-positioned agreements, new procurements); which contractors can stand-up programs rapidly; what requests for assistance might be required from the DOD and how to include civil society partners in the implementation process to avoid creation of parallel systems;

(8) develop a performance monitoring plan with short and long term stability and social indicators, targets and benchmarks, including use of negotiated common indicators with other partners whenever possible;

(9) identify/refine resource and logistics requirements;

(10) employ an interagency information management system for sharing and accessing information; and

(11) at the appropriate time, begin the process of transitioning into out-year normal budgeting processes of participating agencies.

m. One of the most vital planning challenges is to estimate when the R&S operation can be completed in total or in part. While iterative planning is likely to predominate, at all times the senior policy makers must be kept informed of what the likelihood is of meeting the desired end states and the interim milestones. When applicable, planning for the following transfers of authority may be necessary:

(1) a military transfer of authority from "supported" to "supporting" relationship with civilians; or

(2) transfer of authority from non-HN to HN authorities.

n. The Country Plan format has not been approved as yet, but the outline that is being used, and the elements that will be expected in future Country Plans are provided below.

COUNTRY PLAN OUTLINE

1. Interests, problem statement, goal
   1.1. Summary of higher's interests
   1.2. COM's statement of interests
   1.3. Problem statement
   1.4. Overall hypothesis
   1.5. Overall USG goal

2. Situation Analysis
   2.1. Recent developments
   2.2. Country context
   2.3. Critical dynamics
      2.3.1. 1
      2.3.2. 2
      2.3.3. 3…
   2.4. HN authority's interests, political commitment, priorities, most probable course of action
   2.5. External actors (donors)
   2.6. Constraints, restraints, legal and other considerations

3. Assumptions, risks, considerations
   3.1. Risks
   3.2. Opportunity costs of inaction or tradeoffs
   3.3. Assumptions
   3.4. Overview of branch and contingency plans (details in annexes)

4. Concept of operations
   4.1. Critical points of intervention
   4.2. Results framework
   4.3. Critical dynamics
   4.4. Obj 1 overview
      4.4.1. Responsible authority
      4.4.2. Situation
      4.4.3. Hypothesis
      4.4.4. Concept
      4.4.5. Sub-Objectives
   4.5. Obj 2 overview…(repeat steps outlined in 4.4 as necessary)

5. Authorities, command and control, structures

6. Instructions and tasks

7. Resources and budget

8. Monitoring and evaluation

Annexes
A. **Organization chart**
B. **Trip wires for; Branch planning & plan revision**
C. **Branch and contingency plans**

o. The Country Plan, once completed and approved by the COM, and following consultations with the JTF commander, is sent to the CRSG for Washington-level final approval. Once approved the plan is used as the basis for executing the R&S operation in the affected country. The ACT will serve as the oversight element on behalf of the COM for implementation of the USG R&S Strategic Plan. The FACTs will work with HN officials, NGOs, IGOs, and other external entities to accomplish the sub-objectives that will satisfy the MMEs.

p. Military commanders, staff officers, and forces will be integral to this process in all areas. The military will likely lead responsibilities for security MMEs. Military SMEs will work closely with the ACT and the FACTs. Within these relationships the military will be expected to assist the functional teams at the FACTs to establish a USG presence on the ground to supporting R&S operations at the provincial and local level.

8. Monitoring, Evaluation, and the Planning Cycle

a. The planning process must be flexible and enable the communication of developments on the ground to senior policy makers in Washington, DC, in order to add or modify resource support in these highly fluid environments. Similarly, as the COM adapts and refines the plan in order to meet new challenges and seize temporary windows of opportunity, communication with Washington is critical to keep policy and implementation in synchronization.

b. To drive constant analysis and revisions, the Planning Framework establishes metrics at the MME level to monitor strategic progress and critical assumptions as well as at the Sub-Objective level to monitor additional assumptions and enable ongoing synchronization of activities. These analyses "ground-truth" the core elements of the USG R&S Strategic Plan and Country Plan. Confronted problems and identified/anticipated windows of opportunity are channeled into the plan revision. To support this analysis, the USG must undertake appropriate assessments and immediately begin collecting relevant information.

c. The implementation planning team will continually update critical planning considerations and budgetary and financial management factors of the USG R&S Strategic Plan and report them to the SPT, which is responsible for proposing to the COM and CRSG necessary changes to the USG R&S Strategic Plan and monitoring MME and USG policy goal-level metrics at established intervals (typically six months). The implementation planning team also monitors the targets for each Sub-Objective at three-month intervals in order to synchronize activities and benchmarks to signal when transfers of authority should occur (military to civilian, USG to HN). The COM will report progress and proposed changes to the USG R&S Strategic Plan to the CRSG or relevant Interagency Policy Committee in cases when the IMS has not been activated.

Intentionally Blank

APPENDIX E
SECURITY AND FORCE PROTECTION

Military Contribution to Security and Force Protection Planning and Implementation Considerations

1. Introduction

The establishment of security and creating the conditions that allow civilian organizations to become fully engaged in implementing the USG R&S Strategic Plan will likely be a major responsibility tasked to a joint force. In light of this, the JFC's mission to provide security may include the role of providing additional security and force protection measures to USG civilian personnel in uncertain or hostile operating environments. In the event the IMS has been established these personnel and the implementation bodies they are a part of are likely to be operating under COM authority. Due to this coordination measures regarding security and force protection must be established between the joint force operating under GCC authorities and the COM directed implementation bodies of the IMS – the ACT and FACT. These coordination measures must address the role of and how the joint force will work with the DOS's Diplomatic Security Service (DS) and DS contracted security concerning the protection of COM personnel assigned to the US mission. This appendix will describe security and force protection planning supporting both the USG R&S Strategic Plan and the Country Plan. It will further define the military contribution to these plans and will offer considerations for the implementation of security and force protection measures provided by the military to civilian led interagency implementation teams.

2. Security and Force Protection Planning at the Strategic Level

a. Upon formation of CRSG, a security working group (SWG) may be established. The SWG will develop the Security Annex to the USG R&S Strategic Plan and assist with the development of post or mission specific security plans that enable R&S activities. The SWG will coordinate the development of the Security Annex with the COM if present in the affected country. It may also be used as a forum within the CRSG to mediate security and force protection issues not resolved by the ACT.

b. The SWG will be comprised of interagency personnel, to include DOD representation. DOD representatives, including the relevant GCC, should possess security and force protection responsibilities in their current position and have the authority to speak on behalf of DOD or their commander regarding such issues. The SWG is co-chaired by a senior special agent from the DS and a representative appointed by the CRSG. In most cases, particularly when DOD is a sizable component of the operation, DOD will co-chair the SWG.

c. The Security Annex of the USG R&S Strategic Plan represents the interagency security baseline that enables post, ACT, and FACT to conduct mission specific implementation level security planning. It will outline departmental and agency security and force protection roles and responsibilities. In addition to agency roles and responsibilities, the Security Annex will include a current threat and security assessment, identify broad R&S mission requirements, budget and security resources requirements, including personnel and equipment, and significant issues concerning security, resource, legal, and policy that may impact the USG R&S Strategic Plan.

d. In the event new, unforeseen, or additional security and force protection requirements arise that is not addressed in the Security Annex a memorandum of agreement may be drawn up between the relevant agencies. There is recent precedence for this between DOS and DOD concerning security for PRTs. The establishment of an MOA in this context addresses issues that are specific to the crisis and the environment. Therefore it will assist with the Country Plan development by providing a greater degree of clarity for the implementation of security and force protection measures shared by both the COM and the JFC. See Appendix C, "MOU/MOA Between Military and Civilian Components for a Whole-of-government Effort," for an example MOA regarding security.

e. An interagency security assessment team should be deployed to the embassy to assist the SWG, COM, and ACT with the development of the Security Annex and mission specific security plans. Assessing the security requirements for deploying, particularly in hostile environments, is a critical planning requirement. In addition to the SWG and Security Assessment Team, the CRSG and ACT Implementation Planning Teams will determine with the military the requirements for civilian team protection, site protection, and government authority protection. This assessment should be provided to the JFC, the COM, the CRSG, and sub-objective task teams to inform planning.

f. DS will be responsible for coordinating and leading the interagency security assessment due to specific legal authority and responsibility vested in the COM regarding the protection of USG personnel under their authority. Under this scenario the GCC retains the authority for providing for the security and force protection of forces under GCC control. If DOD is given responsibility for securing the protection of all USG personnel, DOD will coordinate and lead interagency security assessment efforts with the assistance of the relevant GCC.

3. Planning for Security and Force Protection Implementation

a. The Country Plan Security Annex is distinct from, yet informed by, the USG R&S Strategic Plan Security Annex. This annex will consist of a collection of separate mission and post specific security and force protection plans. These are designed to address the multiple aspects of a comprehensive security program to include physical security, protective security details, information security, counter-intelligence, and investigations.

b. In addition to mission or post specific security and force protection plans, the Country Plan Security Annex should address the requirements in Figure E-1:

c. Security and force protection plans will be jointly developed in country by the ACT, through the COM, with the assistance of the Security Assessment Team with advice and assistance from the relevant GCC when there is an established USG presence. In the absence of a COM, the ACT will establish an Emergency Action Committee (EAC) to coordinate development of the security plans. This EAC will integrate mission or post security and force protection plans into the Country Plan Security Annex and submit to

ADDITIONAL REQUIREMENTS FOR COUNTRY PLAN SECURITY ANNEX

- Updates to or further detail on the Security Annex as required:

  - Threat assessment
  - Analysis of the security situation
  - A broad list of mission requirements, to include:

    - Number of sites to be secured
    - Number of USG personnel under COM or GCC authority and their agency affiliation at each site
    - Movement/Transportation requirements

- Recommendations on waivers and exceptions for the Secure Embassy Construction and Counterterrorism Act of 1999 and Overseas Security Policy Board standards and policies
- Command and control relationships
- Administration and logistics support
- Common operating procedures and guidelines for USG entities and personnel operating under COM authority
- Pre-deployment training standards and requirements
- A detailed deployment timeline (timing and sequencing) for security forces and resources
- Deadly Force Policy (Rules of Engagement)
- Contractor regulations and legal status

Figure E-1. Additional Requirements for Country Plan Security Annex

the SWG for review. If DOD has been assigned responsibility for providing force protection to deployed civilian personnel, DS will coordinate development of security plans with the relevant GCC through the Joint Staff and OSD representatives on the CRSG. The GCC will ensure integration of all security plans into the Country Plan Security Annex and submit to the SWG for review.

d. The GCC is responsible for all military joint security operations (JSO) conducted in the AOR. The GCC establishes measures, procedures, and policies to preserve combat power of their forces and provide an appropriate level of security and safety for joint forces and civilians who are authorized to accompany the force that are assigned, attached, in-transit, or otherwise physically located within their AOR. In addition, the GCC may be directed to provide security and force protection support for interagency, IGO, and HN elements to enhance and improve security conditions enabling civilian professionals to conduct their vital R&S activities.

e. Subordinate JFCs provide security of all military bases and lines of communication within their JOA and have the authority to organize forces to best accomplish the assigned mission based on their concept of operations. To facilitate JSO, JFCs should establish a joint security element to coordinate JSO. The individual who normally leads a joint security element is referred to as the joint security coordinator (JSC).

f. The COM is responsible for the security of all USG executive branch employees inside the country which they are appointed to represent the President. This authoritative responsibility does not extend to those under the command of a US area military commander, or GCC. The RSO is the COM's senior security officer and is charged with managing and implementing programs to ensure the security of all AMEMBs and consulates in a given country. In some circumstances this responsibility may include adjacent countries. The RSO works closely with the senior defense official in a given country to ensure the security of non-combat DOD elements and personnel whom are under COM authority.

g. The GCC security and force protection responsibilities are authoritative and extend to all DOD elements and personnel in their AOR, except for those for whom security responsibility has been transferred to the COM under a MOA. GCC and COM security related MOAs do not alter command relationships, nor relieve a commander of responsibility for unit security.

h. In cases where DOD has been assigned responsibility for providing force protection to deployed civilian personnel, the GCC and by extension the JSC will have an important role aligning the civilian and military security and force protection plans. Once aligned, this role will include the responsibility of integrating all security plans into the Country Plan Security Annex and submitting them to the SWG at the CRSG for review.

i. CMO assists the JSC in establishing and maintaining positive relationships between joint forces, civil authorities, and the HN population. The conduct of CMO is important to ensure civil authority and understanding of military security measures and compliance thereof. Successful conduct of CMO will alleviate conditions that may result in local interference with military operations. Consideration of the impact JSO can have on the civil populace can be very important, especially in long-term stability operations. CMO personnel and forces can assist in conducting joint and multinational security operations by providing assessments on local civilian capabilities and vulnerabilities.

j. The JSC, with the assistance of joint force CMO elements and the GCC JIACG integrates JSO with the activities of the COM and USG civilian agency personnel and programs on the country team. The JSC also coordinates JSO with IGOs as well as HN forces and activities of various HN agencies conducting security operations in the GCC AOR or subordinate JFC JOA. By understanding the interagency coordination process, the JSC gains an appreciation of how the resources and expertise of USG civilian agencies interact with HN, regional, and IGOs to assist in the development of the overall USG civil-military security posture.

4. Planning Considerations for Implementing Security and Force Protection Measures

a. Additional coordination measures between DOD and DOS to implement security and force protection plans for civil-military teams operating in the field are traditionally arranged through the use of a MOA. Existing MOAs concerning security and force protection for USG civil-military teams conducting field operations utilizing a whole-of-government approach are signed at the deputy secretary level between DOD and DOS. The seniority of these signatures emphasizes the importance security and force protection measures have concerning the ability of the USG to implement and conduct R&S activities. The existence of these MOAs reaffirms the need to provide greater detail specifying the operational requirements, authorities, and responsibilities that are shared between the COM and a JFC. While these MOAs are signed by deputy secretaries in Washington, the roles and responsibilities of the COM and JFC and subordinate commanders detailed in them feature prominently. This is due to the authorities vested in both the JFC and COM concerning the provision of security to protect personnel placed under their respective control.

b. A recent example of a MOA specifying operational requirements, authorities, and responsibilities, including security provisions, shared between a COM and a JTF commander is the MOA regarding PRTs, in Iraq signed on 22 February 2007 by the deputy secretaries of both DOD and DOS. Excerpts of this MOA are included in Appendix C, "MOU/MOA Between Military and Civilian Components for a Whole-of-Government Effort."

c. The FACT is an IMS implementation body that has a critical role in executing R&S tasks to accomplish the objectives outlined in the USG R&S Strategic Plan. They are established outside of the ACT HQ or embassy to establish a presence, provide an on-the-ground assessment of conditions, and support R&S operations conducted at the local level. In this regard, the FACT is built upon the lessons learned from PRTs. As a COM directed entity; the FACT will likely integrate its activities with the joint force to maintain unity of effort. To this extent the lessons learned concerning the security and force protection of PRTs will have direct application to future security measures that may be implemented to protect FACT personnel as they operate in the field.

d. Recent R&S operations have demonstrated the need for the use of private security contractors to provide protective security for bases, facilities, USG, coalition, and HN civilian personnel, and for civilians contracted to conduct specific R&S activities. The requirement for private security contractors is highly unlikely to dissipate in the near future. These contractors have enabled the military to utilize economy of force and focus limited resources while conducting security operations in higher threat level environments requiring the use of military force. However, in the early phases of a joint force deploying to an area embroiled in conflict it is likely that the specific requirements to provide the basis for the use of PSCs will not be immediately known. This is because each conflict will contain certain elements that are unique and situational dependent. As a result, the military may be tasked to provide security initially for functions that may be determined later to be fulfilled by PSCs.

e. If consistent with applicable US, HN, and international laws as well as relevant SOFAs, a defense contractor may be authorized to provide security services for other than uniquely military functions. The supported GCC and subordinate JFC should, however, use caution when contemplating the use of contracted security to protect US forces, facilities, and supplies in any operation where there is a current or expected level II or III threat. In general, threat levels above level I (Negligible) require significant FP measures (e.g., crew served weapons, combined arms response, indirect fire) that may be considered to be an inherently governmental function.

f. The use of contract security to protect military assets is dependent on the situation and requires detailed legal analysis and coordination by the subordinate JFC and staff judge advocate. Variables such as the nature of the threat, the type of conflict, applicable HN laws, and the nature of the activity being protected require case-by-case determinations. The JFC must also ensure that contracts with private security firms and other contractors give the government the flexibility to require the removal of contract personnel whose actions are counterproductive to the USG and joint force mission. Finally, the JFC must ensure that there are adequate jurisdictional arrangements to ensure that contract personnel can be held criminally accountable for offenses conducted during operations. Failure to hold contractor personnel accountable for offenses frequently is unjust; sends resonating messages through the joint force regarding double standards for contract personnel; counters US strategic communication regarding transparency and the rule of law; undermines the joint force and USG legitimacy; and can harm the HN government's credibility. The use of force by contingency contractor personnel is often strictly limited by HN and US laws and not protected by SOFA provisions. Contingency contractor personnel, providing security services which exceed the limits imposed by applicable law, may be subject to prosecution.

g. The GCC, subordinate JFC, and designated subordinate Service or functional component commanders must ensure specific procedures to coordinate contractor provided security and military provided security are developed, promulgated, and enforced within the operational area. This includes incident reporting and investigation. Additionally, the GCC and subordinate JFC must work closely with the contracting officers, the contractors, the HN, and DOS in establishing rules for the use of force (RUF) for contract security companies inside the operational area.

h. Of all of the non-DOD contracting related coordination tasks, none is more important and challenging than coordinating with non-DOD agencies who hire private security firms. These private security firms, sometimes including contracted uniformed foreign military members, are routinely used to provide protection of non-DOD personnel in transit and at work sites in high threat areas – oftentimes exceeding level I. Without proper coordination the risk of an incident involving friendly military forces and contractor employees can be significant. The subordinate JFC and its subordinate commanders must take great care in establishing adequate visibility (location, mission, RUF) of these non-DOD private security related contracts.

i. Some key planning considerations for coordinating with non-DOD contracted security are outlined in Figure E-2.

j. During recent R&S operations, DOD has been given the mission to provide security for USG personnel – in some circumstances including personnel operating under COM authority. Providing this mission has created an inseparable connection between security and transportation for implementation-level civil-military teams. This type of support is likely to continue to be provided for IMS teams, such as the ACT or FACT,

PLANNING CONSIDERATIONS FOR COORDINATING WITH NON-DOD CONTRACT SECURITY

- Does the subordinate JFC have back-up security support requirements to DOS or other non-DOD organizations? If so, are these organizations using private security firms for protection?

- What is the subordinate JFC's authority, if any, in planning and utilization of non-DOD contracted security firms?

- Where are these security firms operating?

- What are the RUF? Did the subordinate JFC have input to the RUF?

- Has the JFC, COM, and other interested parties developed workable and reliable information sharing mechanisms? How will the military forces communicate with these private security firms? Are their systems compatible with the on-hand military systems? Has the communication plan been exercised?

- Are subordinate commanders properly informed of their local requirements? Have they conducted proper coordination with these security firms and/or rehearsed back-up security actions?

Figure E-2. Planning Considerations for Coordinating with non-DOD Contract Security

implementing the USG R&S Strategic Plan; especially during the early phases of a R&S operation or when the operating environment is determined to be uncertain or hostile.

k. In recent operations the commander of the relevant military unit has been responsible for providing ground movement to PRTs that were collocated with US military units. It is widely recognized that readily available ground movement capability has been critical to the success of the PRT mission and will continue to be important to the success of any future ACT or FACT mission. Military commanders should continue to make every effort to accommodate transportation requests from ACT or FACT leaders. In cases when the ACT or FACT is not collocated with the military coordination measures between DOD and DOS concerning transportation need to be arranged. These measures will be implemented by, and become the responsibility of, the relevant JFC and COM as well as their designated staffs.

l. The need for ACT or FACT ground movement capabilities is dependent upon a range of factors (e.g., size of the ACT/FACT, specifics of the mission, geography of the AO). The availability of military ground movement assets is similarly dependent (e.g., combat situation, maintenance considerations). The relevant military commander should make convoys available in accordance with existing agreements, absent compelling reasons not to provide them.

m. During recent R&S operations personnel under COM authority assigned to PRTs or to the embassy have been provided air transportation support utilizing both military fixed wing and rotary wing assets. It is expected that in future operations the military will provide similar support to personnel assigned to the ACT, FACT, or larger US mission. For example, in the past for rotary wing transportation, PRTs would submit air mission requests to the MSC G3 aviation element whose area of operation the PRT resided. These requests were considered a priority. When rotary wing movement requests extended beyond the range of the supporting MSC's AO, the JTF implemented procedures for integrating air movements across the MSCs. Rotary wing support requirements should be prepared and submitted in accordance with established JFC and supporting MSC timelines and procedures.

n. For fixed wing air movement support, PRTs were required to submit airlift support requirements to the AMEMB that went to a military group that was subordinate to the JTF. These requests were considered a priority and the requirements were input into the Intra-Theater Airlift Request System (ITARS). These requirements should be prepared and submitted in accordance with existing timelines and procedures of the Air Force component of the geographic combatant command.

o. The responsibility for the provision of static security at a FACT or ACT is dependent on such factors as the threat conditions in the operating environment and whether or not these teams, under the direction of a COM, will be collocated with military units. The specific arrangement for the provision of static security is likely to be detailed in a MOA/MOU between DOD and DOS.

p. In recent operations, with regards to collocated or embedded PRTs, the military commander of the MSC responsible for providing base security in a given AO was also responsible for providing static security to the PRT. This responsibility extended to the movement of personnel based on security concerns. However, it did not direct members of the PRT as to who they should see, nor deny them the ability to contact interlocutors, based on a judgment of priorities other than security.

q. In the case of stand-alone PRTs, PRT members observed COM directions, rules, policies and procedures – to include COM directed security measures instituted by the RSO. In these cases the COM and RSO were responsible for the provision of static security as well as movement of PRT personnel to the extent applicable given the threat conditions in the operating environment. These provisions were implemented by DS or by private security contractors operating under the management of DS and the RSO.

APPENDIX F
COMMUNICATIONS

**Military Contribution to Shared Communications and Information Management
During Reconstruction and Stabilization Operations**

1. Introduction

a. In R&S operations, utilizing a whole-of-government approach, sharing accurate information that is both timely and actionable facilitates civil-military planning and implementation of related tasks and activities. Integrated and interoperable procedures are important to operating in joint, multinational, and interagency environments. The requirement for these much needed procedures has been demonstrated in recent operations. The value of technology, organization, and a strategy that supports these procedures are diminished in the absence of a well trained, ready, and capable workforce of communication systems professionals. The communications system must be versatile enough to accommodate evolving or emerging support requirements during R&S operations. Additionally, the communications system must integrate new technologies into a robust, standards-based, network enabled environment, to facilitate the delivery of the right information to the right location at the right time in an actionable format.

b. DOD has issued guidance concerning interoperability and supportability of information technology (IT) with National Security Systems (NSS). This guidance includes directives and instructions from DOD and the Chairman, Joint Chiefs of Staff (CJCS). According to JP 6-0, *Joint Communications System*, interoperability is a key principle of military communications systems. Achieving interoperability is a vital component enabling effective communication systems to assist the JFC in its conduct of distributed operations in JOA, which include irregular threats often associated with R&S environments. In addition, DOD has issued an instruction (DODI 8220.02) implementing policy concerning the provision of information and communications technology capabilities in support of R&S, disaster relief, and humanitarian and civic assistance. This instruction stipulates the establishment of information sharing between DOD and non-DOD partners to support an integrated whole-of-government response and to enable a common understanding. DOD or Military Department HQ may resource information and communications technology capabilities in response to combatant command defined and JS validated requirements to support civil-military partners when in the best interest of the mission and not in conflict with host country ordinances.

c. DOD uses the term "information management," as defined in JP 1-02 in lieu of the term "knowledge management (KM)," which is commonly used in interagency forums. However, there are instances where the term "knowledge management" is used in this handbook. The term is used when it applies to a named staff section in the IMS or when the DOS and/or interagency forums specifically use the term.

2. Communications Systems Principles

a. A joint force that is linked and synchronized in time and purpose is considered networked. A networked force has the ability to expand its operational reach by taking advantage of "reach-back" to exploit non-organic capabilities inherent in other organizations. By integrating information from across the breadth of the JOA, the joint force is able to maintain more relevant and complete situational awareness. This integrated picture allows the JFC to better employ the right capabilities, in the right place and at the right time. An effective communications system helps the JFC conduct distributed operations across the operational area. To do this, the communications system must be **interoperable, agile, trusted, and shared** (Figure F-1).

   b. **Interoperability** is a key element to the joint force gaining information superiority in today's network enabled environment. The joint and Service communications system must possess the interoperability necessary to ensure success in joint and multinational operations as well as interactions with USG civilian agencies and NGOs. Interoperability can be achieved through commonality, compatibility, standardization, and liaison. To support joint forces and operational concepts, the communications system must be **agile**. The key dimensions of communications system agility are responsiveness, flexibility, innovation, and adaptation. A **trusted** network must be transparent to its users. The joint force must have confidence in the capabilities of the network and the validity of the information made available by the network. **Sharing** allows for the mutual use of information services or capabilities between military and civilian entities within the joint operational area. This ability may likely cross functional or organizational boundaries in R&S operations.

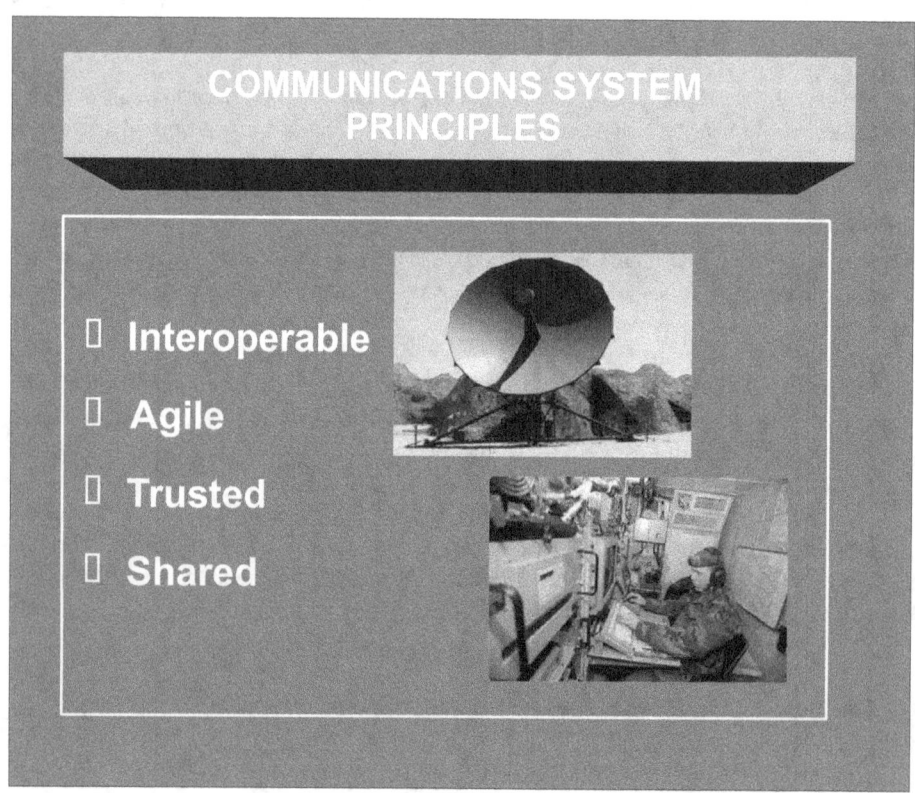

Figure F-1. Communications System Principles

c. Within the Global Information Grid (GIG), GCCs identify communications systems requirements for coordination with USG civilian agencies, IGOs, and NGOs. Any communications support requests should be consistent with US law, regulations, and doctrine. The GIG is the globally interconnected, end-to-end set of information capabilities, associated processes and personnel for collecting, processing, storing, disseminating, and managing information on demand to war-fighters, policy makers, and support personnel. The GIG includes owned and leased communications and computing systems and services, software (including applications), data, security services, other associated services and NSS.

3. Planning Considerations

a. At the direction of the SECSTATE, the S/CRS has significant responsibilities concerning the operation of the IMS. The IMS and its components will impose knowledge management[7] and information technology requirements versus burdens on participating agencies, to include the interface between DOD, DOS, and USAID supported communication systems.[8] Investments in information technology and communication resources required to support IMS teams under a range of deployment responses should be considered in the context of a greater KM and IT strategy.[9]

b. Regardless of the operating environment, CRC members providing the manpower for IMS ACT/FACT implementation teams will rely on networks supported by DOS or DOD. Prior to a crisis the DOS IRM Bureau Enterprise Network Management Directorate (IRM/OPS/ENM), the DOD Defense Information Systems Agency (DISA), and other interagency partners should prepare formal agreements enabling IMS implementation teams communication capabilities across multiple types of operating environments.[10] Additionally, MOAs should be established between DOS and DOD down to the combatant command level to provide IMS ACT/FACT implementation teams access to military communications equipment and networks when deployed alongside the military during R&S operations.[11] Prior to the establishment of an MOA resource requirements for the use of DOD information and communications technology capabilities must be identified, further developed, and validated.

c. Selection of equipment for IMS ACT/FACT teams will be context specific to include the following considerations:

(1) availability of Internet connectivity;

(2) need for ClassNet;

(3) military deployment and access to NIPR/SIPR networks;

(4) military frequency management procedures;

(5) international groups;

(6) existing AMEMB systems;

(7) commercial cell phone availability; and

(8) agreed upon arrangements for connectivity to NGOs.

d. Also, deployments of IMS ACT/FACT teams or other civil-military implementation teams under the direction and authority of the COM must follow the applicable DOS Diplomatic Security (DS) standards and must be DS approved. The size of the implementation teams being deployed, length of deployment, conditions in the operational environment, both military and non-military efforts, and the agencies involved will affect the design of the communications platforms used for the deployment.

4. Interagency Communication Capabilities

a. Currently, capabilities are in place that may be shared between civilian and military elements conducting R&S operations through the use of MOA/MOUs. The requirement to resource these capabilities should be validated prior to establishing a written agreement.

b. A formal MOA will need to be established between DOS and DOD concerning the utilization of DISA NIPR and SIPR networks by S/CRS and its interagency partners participating in the IMS in the event the US military is deployed to support a R&S operation.[12] The provisions of these agreements should include, at a minimum, the purpose, scope and background of the MOA, along with clear roles and responsibilities for DOD/DISA providing worldwide networking capabilities at the unclassified and classified levels.[13] Additionally, the agreement should include a list of key IT network support contacts within DOD/DISA to ensure proper technical support for IMS teams attempting to connect to a DOD network.[14]

c. To ensure IT equipment interoperability and effective communication and coordination among civilian and military personnel participating in the IMS, DOS should establish formal MOAs at the DOD/Pentagon and combatant command levels.[15] The provisions of these agreements should also include the purpose, scope and background of the MOA, along with clear roles and responsibilities for all participating agencies.[16] The agreements should include the process for allowing IMS teams' access to military communications equipment, and detail the specific voice, data and/or radio requirements necessary while operating in an environment alongside the military.[17] These provisions will ensure the necessary pre-planning processes have been established to ensure both civilian and military participants have the ability to effectively communicate without impacting the successful completion of a R&S mission or military operation.[18]

d. Recent precedence has shown that DOD unclassified and classified networks may be shared when the equipment and access are provided to civilians, with the proper security access, who are operating with DOD directly. For example, at PRTs in Afghanistan limited access to unclassified and classified military networks was available to civilians; eventually a DOS V-SAT system was provided to civilians to facilitate communications. In Iraq, for example, the initial non-collocated PRTs established an operations center whereby unclassified (NIPR) and classified (SIPR) networks were stood-up and maintained by the military. Civilian access to this network was limited and mainly facilitated through LNOs in order to give PRT leadership timely information for decision making purposes. All Iraq PRT members, with the proper badge access, were able to utilize the DOS OpenNet or ClassNet systems for most day-to-day activities.

e. DS and IRM Bureaus at DOS established and approved "fly away" Internet packages. They are: Transportable OpenNet Package (TOP); Enhanced Transportable OpenNet Package; and the Small Tactical Package. The TOP provides temporary OpenNet multi user access in a secure environment. This package requires access to the Internet through an Internet Service Provider (ISP). The Enhanced Transportable OpenNet Package is for temporary or semi-permanent multi-user OpenNet access in a secured facility with power, but with no Internet connectivity through an ISP. The Small Tactical Package uses a Broadband Global Area Network (BGAN) to provide rapid, mobile, single user OpenNet access where no power or Internet connectivity exists. This system may be used worldwide.

f. Through IRM Bureau Remote Expeditionary Area Communications Hub (REACH) Program and robust lifecycle support practices and methodologies, IRM possesses the ability to immediately support S/CRS in providing the list of general equipment identified above to support CRC personnel in effectively communicating in the field and with possessing the ability to reach-back to key S/CRS and interagency stakeholders located at the IPC, ACT and CRSG.[19]

g. Through the REACH Program, IRM offers three mobile stand-alone satellite communications packages that will support S/CRS's and its interagency partners' response to R&S missions and provide communications during a failure of the HN's or AMEMB's IT networks. The three communications packages[20] consist of:

(1) Backpack Internet Communications (BIC),

(2) Secure High-speed Area Reach-back Kit (SHARK), and

(3) Mobile Information Program Center (MIPC).

h. Lessons learned regarding PRT communications and information systems capabilities have been applied to inform the development of network solutions for IMS teams. Similarities can be drawn between PRTs and FACTs regarding requirements to facilitate communications between an AMEMB, ACT, and a JTF in a R&S operation. For a PRT, the team leader was required to determine what capabilities were essential to the mission of their PRT, identify requirements for network access, and number of telephones, computers, radios. These requirements were coordinated with the AMEMB and forwarded for action to DOS Information Management Office for non-collocated PRTs or to the JTF chief of information systems for collocated PRTs. The level of fulfillment of requirements was dependent upon asset availability and on-site support. The AMEMB performed the function as the communications center for PRT communications, and established standards and procedures for interoperability.

5. Role of Knowledge Management in Stabilization and Reconstruction Operations[21]

a. KM encompasses the principles, practices, and technologies that can leverage information and knowledge assets to make an organization or community more efficient and effective. Being able to find and use the best information available in a timely and efficient manner is critically important for planning and conducting R&S operation programs and projects.

b. One KM technique for quickly locating and retrieving needed information is to create a knowledge map. A knowledge map should be a dynamic and interactive product available to a community of interest, where content is organized, managed, and updated on a regular basis so that the information and knowledge remains relevant and fresh. Another technique is social network analysis, which uses software to trace and visualize the information sharing relationships among different organizations and individuals. This is particularly useful in mapping the organization that exchange and use each other's information and identifying disconnects and possible linkages between organizations.

c. Most R&S operations involve a variety of organizations and agencies exchanging mutually beneficial information, working together on shared tasks, and coordinating their activities for synergistic benefits. This type of inter-agency collaboration and coordination is constrained by having personnel residing in different locations and often in different time zones, which makes arranging real-time face-to-face meetings or conference calls difficult. Other constraints to inter-agency collaboration can include incompatible systems and software that inhibit the transfer of data files and bureaucratic cultures that reinforce vertical stovepipes and information hoarding.

d. A set of technologies that can help facilitate information sharing and break down bureaucratic and technical stovepipes are collaboration tools, including virtual communities of practice or interest, wikis and blogs. Most communities of practice or interest are web-enabled, invitation-only networks of individuals with a common interest in some subject or problem to share ideas, coordinate activities, and work together on common tasks. There are several commercial-off-the-shelf (COTS) software packages that furnish individual user licenses for participating members of such communities. This collaboration software provides such features as shared calendars and contact lists, asynchronous discussion groups, a content repository, and distributed document drafting and editing.

e. Attaining situational awareness is fundamental for decision makers to understand what is happening, why it is happening, how the situation is changing. Pre- and post-crisis situations involve a complicated set of issues and influence factors, including history, current political dynamics, international relations, economics, population demographics, health conditions, geography and environment. Monitoring the changing situation is critically important for identifying the countries at risk of instability, designing and adjusting assistance strategies, targeting assistance programs, and evaluating R&S projects.

f. KM roles and functions are applied across all levels of the IMS, facilitating policy development and strategic planning in Washington, DC, to reporting, monitoring and evaluating the implementation of R&S programs and projects in the field. Prior to the activation of the IMS, the role of KM support for the CRSG SPT will focus on:

(1) gathering, synthesizing and managing critical information;

(2) identifying and filling knowledge gaps;

(3) liaison with IC, providing relevant intelligence to planning and decision/ policy making bodies (e.g., SPT, Sub-Interagency Policy Committee); and

(4) contribute to Situation Analysis Overview, providing visualized situational awareness;

g. Upon activation of the IMS, the KM role supporting the CRSG Secretariat will focus on:

(1) Supporting decision-making and activities of the CRSG through organizational support (agendas, papers, records, paper preparation, and clearance), NSC PC/DC meeting preparation, management of Sub-Interagency Policy Committees and teams charged with developing the R&S Strategic Plan's MMEs (i.e., strategic objectives), and dissemination of information.

(2) Ensuring widespread situational awareness within the USG of all agencies' activities and of the field perspective, coordinating assessments, and disseminating information (including situation and progress reports) through the Washington, DC community, Congress, and the field.

(3) Supporting mobilization, activities, and policy requirements of USG field elements. Providing support for these teams in information management, incorporating best practices, policy review and guidance, and logistical support.

(4) Facilitating international relationships, information sharing and partner coordination.

(5) Establishing and tracking strategic-level metrics, assumptions, and other trend indicators to assess progress.

(6) Managing and supporting IT and KM tools.

h. In the field, the role of KM support to the ACT and FACTs will focus on:

(1) Consolidating and transmitting regular ACT/FACT reporting, including planning and programming recommendations, to the AMEMB, combatant command/JTF, IPC, and CRSG.

(2) Maintaining and disseminating a COP of R&S activities throughout the lifespan of the ACT/FACT.

(3) Conducting monitoring and evaluation and recommending program adjustments as necessary to support implementation of the USG R&S Strategic Plan.

(4) Managing and supporting information technology and KM tools.

i. One of the fundamental principles of KM is the value of leveraging knowledge in the form of lessons learned and best practices for use in other applications and experiences. Two KM methods or strategies for leveraging existing knowledge are codification and personalization. Codification refers to the techniques and technologies that enable knowledge to be collected, stored, indexed and retrieved when needed. Personalization is a more human-focused strategy, emphasizing training, networking and team collaboration as a method of leveraging knowledge.

j. R&S operations can take place in many different countries around the world, under a myriad of different circumstances. There are lessons from past operations that add to our understanding and knowledge. Personnel participating in R&S activities can benefit from using existing knowledge that is derived from past experiences, recognized expertise and training events. Frequent staff turnover in R&S focused organizations necessitates that this knowledge be captured, transferred through training, and made available as widely as possible amongst the community of interest. Information standards and guidelines, best practices and collaborative technologies should be integrated into the work processes and management structures of civil-military R&S organizations. The more efficiently an organization can collect, manage and utilize information, the more effectively the organization can plan, implement and coordinate its operations.

APPENDIX G
INTERAGENCY MANAGEMENT SYSTEM RECONSTRUCTION AND STABILIZATION REFERENCES

In the past several years there has been a proliferation of materials, books, publications, and news articles; all related to the IMS and a whole-of-government approach to R&S operations. These pieces originate all over the world and not all of the best come from US sources. The list of references offered here is not intended to be either exhaustive or comprehensive. The following list captures those publications and products that can best serve professionals interested in advancing their understanding of the whole-of-government approach and supplement what they can extract from this handbook.

a. African Union and New Partnership for Africa's Development. "African Post-Conflict Reconstruction Policy Framework." 2005.

b. Bush, Kenneth. "A Measure of Peace: Peace and Conflict Impact Assessment (PCIA) of Development Projects in Conflict Zones." *Peacebuilding and Reconstruction Program Initiative and Evaluation Unit Working* Paper, no 1 (1998): 1-42.

c. Challenges Project. "Challenges of Peace Operations: Into the 21st Century. Concluding Report, 1997-2002." 2002.

d. Challenges Project. "Meeting the Challenges of Peace Operations: Cooperation and Coordination. Challenges Project Phase II Concluding Report, 2003-2006." 2005.

e. Collaborative Learning Projects. "The Do No Harm Handbook (The Framework for Analyzing the Impact of Assistance on Conflict)." 2004.

f. Collier, Paul, ed. *Breaking the Conflict Trap: Civil War and Development Policy.* Washington. DC: The International Bank for Reconstruction and Development and The World Bank, 2003.

g. Country Support Team (CST) Project Technical Team. "Strengthening the Capacity of Local Administration." 2008.

h. Covey, Jock, Michael J. Dziedzic, and Leonard R. Hawley. eds. *The Quest for Viable Peace: International Intervention and Strategies for Conflict Transformation.* Washington DC: United States Institute of Peace Press, 2005.

i. Defense Science Board. "Study on Transition to and from Hostilities." 2004.

j. Dobbins, James, Seth G. Jones, Keith Crane, and Beth Cole DeGrasse. *The Beginner's Guide to Nation Building.* Santa Monica, CA: RAND Corporation, 2007.

k. France, Interministerial Committee on International Cooperation and Development. "Fragile States and Situations of Fragility: France's Policy Paper." 2007.

l. Ghani, Ashraf, Clare Lockhart, and Michael Carnahan. "An Agenda for State-Building in the Twenty-First Century." *The Fletcher Forum of World Affairs* 30, no 1 (2006): 101-123.

m. Ghani, Ashraf and Clare Lockhart. *Fixing Failed States: A Framework for Rebuilding a Fractured World.* Oxford, United Kingdom: Oxford University Press, 2008.

n. Gordon, Maj. Gen. Robert DS (Ret). "DRAFT: A Comparative Study on Doctrine And Principles for Multinational Peace Operations: A Case for Harmonization and Enhanced Interoperability." International Forum for the Challenges of Peace Operations. 2007.

o. Guttieri, Karen and Jessica Piombo, eds. *Interim Governments: Institutional Bridges to Peace and Democracy?* Washington. DC: United States Institute of Peace Press, 2007.

p. Human Rights Web. "A Summary of United Nations Agreements on Human Rights." Available from: http://www.hrweb.org/legal/undocs.html. Internet; accessed September 9, 2008.

q. International Monetary Fund. "The Fund's Engagement in Fragile States and Post-Conflict Countries - A Review of Experience – Issues and Options." Policy Development and Review Department. 2008.

r. Jakobsen, Peter Viggo. "European Union Civilian Rapid Reaction – trouble ahead!" *Danish Institute for International Studies Brief* (2006): 1-10.

s. Japan International Cooperation Agency. "Handbook for Transition Assistance." 2006.

t. McFate, Sean. "Securing the Future. A Primer on Security Sector Reform in Conflict Countries." *United States Institute of Peace Special Report* 209 (2008): 1-20.

u. Natsios, Andrew. "The Nine Principles of Reconstruction and Development." *Parameters* Autumn (2005): 4-20.

v. Organisation for Economic Co-operation and Development. "Fragile States: Policy Commitment and Principles for Good International Engagement in Fragile States and Situations." Development Co-operation Directorate and Development Assistance Committee. 2007.

w. Organisation for Economic Co-operation and Development. "Whole-of-government Approaches to Fragile States." Development Assistance Committee. 2006.

x. Perito, Robert, ed. "Guide for Participants in Peace, Stability, and Relief Operations: Guidelines for Relations Between US Armed Forces and Non-Governmental Humanitarian Organizations in Hostile or Potentially Hostile Environments." Available from https://

wwwdev.usip.org/training/tg/guidelines-brochure.html. Internet; accessed September 9, 2008.

y. United Kingdom Stabilisation Unit. "Helping Countries Recover From Violent Conflict." 2008.

z. United Kingdom Stabilisation Unit. "DRAFT: The United Kingdom Approach to Stabilisation - A Stabilisation Unit Guidance Note." 2008.

aa. United Nations. "Civil-Military Guidelines & Reference for Complex Emergencies." 2008

bb. United Nations. "Civil-Military Coordination – Officer Field Handbook." 2007

cc. United Nations. "Convention on the Elimination of All Forms of Discrimination against Women." Available from http://www.hrweb.org/legal/cdw.html; Internet; accessed September 17, 2008.

dd. United Nations. "Handbook on United Nations Multidimensional Peacekeeping Operations." 2003.

ee. United Nations. "Integrated Mission Planning Process (IMPP)." 2006.

ff. United Nations. "DRAFT 3: Peacekeeping Operations Principles and Guidelines Capstone Doctrine." 2007.

gg. United Nations. "United Nations Security Council Resolution 1325." Available from http://www.unfpa.org/women/1325.htm; Internet; accessed September 17, 2008.

hh. United Nations Department of Peacekeeping Operations and Department of Field Support. *United Nations Peacekeeping Operations. Principles and Guidelines.* New York, NY: United Nations, 2008.

ii. United Nations Development Group and Executive Committee for Humanitarian Affairs. "Interagency Framework for Conflict Analysis in Transition Situations." 2004.

jj. United Nations Development Group and World Bank. "WORKING DRAFT FOR CIRCULATION: Joint Guidance Note on Integrated Recovery Planning Using Post Conflict Needs Assessments and Transitional Results Frameworks." 2007.

kk. United Nations Development Programme and United States Agency for International Development. "First Steps in Post-Conflict State-Building: a UNDP-USAID Study. Draft Final Report." 2007.

ll. United Nations Office of the High Commissioner for Human Rights. "Frequently Asked Questions on a Human Rights-Based Approach to Development Cooperation." 2006.

mm. United States Agency for International Development. "Conducting a Conflict Assessment: A Framework for Strategy and Program Development." Conflict Management and Mitigation Office. 2005.

nn. United States Agency for International Development. "DRAFT: A Guide to Economic Growth Program Planning in Rebuilding Countries." 2007.

oo. United States Agency for International Development. "Economic Governance in War Torn Economies: Lessons Learned from the Marshall Plan to the Reconstruction of Iraq." 2004.

pp. United States Agency for International Development. "Fragile States Strategy." 2005.

qq. United States Agency for International Development. "Livelihoods and Conflict. A Toolkit for Intervention. Key Issues, Lessons Learned, Program Options, Resources." 2005.

rr. United States Army. "Field Manual 3-07: Stability Operations and Peace Operations." 2008.

ss. United States Department of Defense. "Joint Publication 3-29: Foreign Humanitarian Assistance." 17 March 2009

tt. United States Department of State. "WORKING DRAFT: Counterinsurgency: A Guide for Policy-Makers – Second Draft." 2008.

uu. United States Department of State, Office of the Coordinator for Reconstruction and Stabilization. "Information Paper: Advance Civilian Teams (ACT) Deployed with US or Coalition Military." (SENSITIVE BUT UNCLASSIFIED - FOR OFFICIAL USE ONLY).

vv. United States Department of State, Office of the Coordinator for Reconstruction and Stabilization. "Information Paper - Country Reconstruction and Stabilization Group (CRSG). (SENSITIVE BUT UNCLASSIFIED - FOR OFFICIAL USE ONLY).

ww. United States Department of State, Office of the Coordinator for Reconstruction and Stabilization. Information Paper - Humanitarian Reconstruction and Stabilization Team (HRST). (SENSITIVE BUT UNCLASSIFIED - FOR OFFICIAL USE ONLY).

xx. United States Department of State, Office of the Coordinator for Reconstruction and Stabilization. "Principles of the USG Planning Framework for Reconstruction, Stabilization and Conflict Transformation." 2008

yy. United States Department of State. "United States Government Draft Planning Framework for Reconstruction. Stabilization and Conflict Transformation. *Practitioner's Guide*" 2008.

zz. United States Government. "DRAFT: Principles of the Interagency Conflict Assessment." 2008.

aaa. United States Government. "Counterinsurgency Guide." 2009.

bbb. United States Office of the Secretary of Defense. "Adaptive Planning Roadmap II." 2008.

ccc. United States Institute of Peace. "Building a USG Civilian Response Capability to Support Stabilization and Reconstruction Operations." PowerPoint presentation. 2008.

ddd. United States Institute of Peace. "Framework for Success: Fragile States and Societies Emerging from Conflict." 2007.

eee. United States National Security Presidential Directive 44. "Management of Interagency Efforts Concerning Reconstruction and Stabilization." Available from http://www.crs.state.gov. Internet; accessed September 12, 2008. "Managing Complex Contingency Operations." Available from http://fas.org/irp/offdocs/pdd56.htm. Internet; accessed September 12, 2008.

fff. United States Presidential Decision Directive 56: "Managing Complex Contingency Operations."

Intentionally Blank

APPENDIX H
ENDNOTES

[1] "Steady State" is a term used in the interagency community (particularly the Department of State and USAID) to refer to the level of USG operations, planning, and other activities that existed (mainly at the country level) prior to the initiation of a whole of government response to a R&S situation. From a planning and budgeting standpoint this term refers to established procedures exercised through: DOD contingency planning and campaign planning; Department of State Mission Strategic Planning and Bureau Strategic Planning; Department of State and USAID Foreign Assistance Planning; and the President's budget request and Congressional budget cycle.

[2] Boot, Max, *The Savage Wars of Peace*, Basic Books, 2002.

[3] A complex overseas contingency is different from an overseas contingency in the interagency community. A complex overseas contingency is a crisis which warrants a full USG military, diplomatic, and humanitarian response and where indigenous institutions have collapsed or are in danger of collapse, posing a threat to USG interests. This is different from an overseas contingency which is a more circumscribed situation such as a natural disaster where established procedures exist.

[4] The use of the term "knowledge management" denotes a named staff section. DOD uses the doctrinal accepted term "information management", however in cases throughout this handbook the term "knowledge management" is used only when Department of State or documents approved by the NSC specifically use the term.

[5] The remaining two chapters are informed by the *USG Planning Framework for Reconstruction, Stabilization, and Conflict Transformation* rather than the *draft IMS Guide*. The former concentrates on whole of government planning while the latter focuses on the form and structure of the bureaucratic management system.

[6] Boot, Max, *The Savage Wars of Peace*, Basic Books, 2002.

[7] DOD uses the doctrinal accepted term "information management", however in cases throughout this handbook the term "knowledge management" is used only when Department of State or documents approved by the NSC specifically use the term.

[8] *Department of State Office of the Coordinator for Reconstruction and Stabilization Knowledge Management and Information Technology (KM/IT) Business Plan,* (© 2009 Deloitte, LLP (Unpublished) All rights reserved.), 1.

[9] *Id.*

[10] *Department of State Office of the Coordinator for Reconstruction and Stabilization Knowledge Management and Information Technology (KM/IT) Business Plan,* (© 2009 Deloitte, LLP (Unpublished) All rights reserved.), 3.

[11] *Id.*

[12] *Department of State Office of the Coordinator for Reconstruction and Stabilization Knowledge Management and Information Technology (KM/IT) Business Plan,* (© 2009 Deloitte, LLP (Unpublished) All rights reserved.), 24.

[13] *Id.*

[14] *Id.*

[15] *Department of State Office of the Coordinator for Reconstruction and Stabilization Knowledge Management and Information Technology (KM/IT) Business Plan,* (© 2009 Deloitte, LLP (Unpublished) All rights reserved.), 34.

[16] *Id.*

[17] *Id.*

[18] *Id.*

[19] *Department of State Office of the Coordinator for Reconstruction and Stabilization Knowledge Management and Information Technology (KM/IT) Business Plan,* (© 2009 Deloitte, LLP (Unpublished) All rights reserved.), 28.

[20] *Id.*

[21] Dennis King, Draft White Paper on Knowledge Management for Reconstruction and Stabilization Planning and Operations, DOS/INR/HIU, (2007).

GLOSSARY
PART I—ABBREVIATIONS AND ACRONYMS

ACT	Advance Civilian Team
CCDR	combatant commander
COM	chief of mission
COP	common operational picture
CRC	Civilian Response Corps
CRP	crisis response planning
CRSG	Country Reconstruction and Stabilization Group
D&F	determination and finding
DC	Deputies Committee
DOD	Department of Defense
DOS	Department of State
FACT	Field Advance Civilian Team
FIG	field integration group
GCC	geographic combatant commander
HN	host nation
HQ	headquarters
ICAF	Interagency Conflict Assessment Framework
IGO	intergovernmental organization
IMS	Interagency Management System
IPC	Integration Planning Cell
JFC	joint force commander
JP	joint publication
JS	Joint Staff
JTF	joint task force
MME	major mission element
MNFC	multinational force commander
MSC	major subordinate command
MSP	mission strategic plan
NATO	North Atlantic Treaty Organization
NDAA	National Defense Authorization Act
NGO	nongovernmental organization
NSC	National Security Council
NSPD	National Security Presidential Directive
OMB	Office of Management and Budget
OPCON	operational control
OSD	Office of the Secretary of Defense

PC	Principals Committee
PRT	provincial reconstruction team
R&S	reconstruction and stabilization
S/CRS	The Office of the Coordinator for Reconstruction and Stabilization
SOFA	status of forces agreement
TACON	tactical control
UCMJ	Uniform Code of Military Justice
USG	United States Government
UN	United Nations
USAID	United States Agency for International Development

GLOSSARY
PART II—TERMS AND DEFINITIONS

(These terms and their definitions are applicable in DOD only within this publication and cannot be referenced in other DOD publications)

Advance Civilian Team (ACT). An interagency team that deploys to the USG field HQ, typically the Embassy, in support of the Chief of Mission.

Comprehensive Management and Resource Strategy. A baseline picture of current funding, personnel, facilities, and other resources being applied towards the country and a rough order of magnitude of the existing gap between those resources and the level necessary to achieve the overarching policy goal. It would outline a proposal for acquiring the necessary resources to eliminate the resources gap.

conflict transformation. The two-pronged approach of seeking to diminish the factors that cause violent conflict and instability while building the capacity of local institutions so they can take the lead role in national governance, economic development, and enforcing the rule of law. The goal of this process is to shift the responsibility for providing peace and stability from the international community to local actors, who can sustain their roles with minimal support from external actors.

Country Plan. The compilation of information that provides an overarching picture of interagency planning (and status of plan delivery once implementation has begun) for achievement of a United States Government Strategic Plan for Reconstruction & Stabilization.

Country Reconstruction and Stabilization Group (CRSG). The main interagency coordination body for comprehensive USG engagement in a post-conflict or complex contingency, consisting of a PCC and a Secretariat.

crisis response planning. The civilian version of DOD's Crisis Action Planning, for a crisis expected to emerge within the next six months.

driver of conflict. An internal or external source of instability pushing parties within an R&S environment towards open conflict.

Field Advance Civilian Team (FACTs). An interagency team that deploys outside of USG field headquarters.

Integration Planning Cell (IPC). The IPC is an interagency team that deploys to the Geographic Combatant Command or to a non-US military headquarters for a multilateral military operation.

Interagency Management System (IMS). An institutionalized system of interagency bodies (Country Reconstruction and Stabilization Group (CRSG), Integration Planning Cell (IPC), Advance Civilian Team (ACT), and Field Advance Civilian Team (FACT)) that manage the whole-of-government stabilization and reconstruction planning and operations.

local institutional capacity. The ability of legitimate local institutions (both governmental and non governmental) to effectively manage resources and deliver tangible results that benefit the population.

locally-led nascent peace. The stage in a conflict transformation process at which the motivations and means for destructive forms of conflict are sufficiently diminished and local institutional capacity is sufficiently developed to allow international actors to pass the lead to local actors, usually with continued international assistance, without the country falling back into conflict.

major mission element. The elements of the plan that are necessary and sufficient to achieve the overarching policy goal. MMEs should be cross-sectoral, stated as outcomes, and based on an analysis of the conflict.

major mission element concept. An overview of how a specific MME links to the overarching policy goal and other MMEs, outlines the measures of success and potential impediments to that success. It also covers the key assumptions behind the MME concept and a comprehensive list of the Sub-Objectives necessary and sufficient to achieve the MME.

major mission element resource strategy and spreadsheet. Creates rough orders of magnitude figures top feed into the Comprehensive Resource and Management Strategy. Determines both the USG resources available and what (if any) outside actor resources will be available. It highlights potential resource gaps and prioritizes filling them based on the MME concept.

operational resources. The funding, personnel, facilities and equipment necessary for the USG to safely and effectively get to the country and deliver assistance to the population.

overarching policy/conflict transformation goal. The overall objective, stated as an outcome, that the US Government (as a whole) would like to achieve and is capable of achieving with the resources available and in a short-term (2-3 year) timeframe.

Policy Advisory Memorandum. A memorandum informed by the situation analysis that outlines several policy options for the DC or PC based on differing assumptions on USG resource availability, the environment within the country, and the anticipated roles and resource commitments of other actors.

policy option. A potential course of action presented to the DC or PC that has an overarching goal and a description of what success would look like. It is based a defined set of critical planning assumptions and outlines specific MMEs to reach success.

reconstruction. The process of rebuilding degraded, damaged, or destroyed political, socio-economic, and physical infrastructure of a country or territory to create the foundation for longer-term development.

reconstruction and stabilization contingency planning. Planning focused on addressing alternative, but feasible assumptions about the trajectory of conflict in a country or region in a timeframe of up to three years.

resources. The funding, personnel, facilities and equipment that can be utilized in the pursuit of an objective.

Situation Analysis Overview Memorandum. An approximately 10 page summary consisting of strategic level conflict analysis, legal considerations, critical planning gaps, US interests at stake, a summary of existing USG and other actors' plans, assumptions, possible contingencies, anticipated USG and other actor resource availability, the dynamics of the regional and international context, critical knowledge gaps and intelligence requirements.

stabilization. The process by which underlying tensions that might lead to resurgence in violence and a break-down in law and order are managed and reduced, while efforts are made to support preconditions for successful longer-term development.

steady-state planning. Ongoing planning (e.g., Mission Strategic Plans, theater security cooperation plans, foreign assistance Operational Plans) that occurs on a regular basis regardless of whether a country is in crisis.

Sub-Objective. A process or activity that is an essential component of a Major Mission Element. When possible, Sub-Objectives should be stated as outcomes.

Sub-Objective Strategy. A narrative of indicating assumptions, priorities, resource requirements, an overall timeline, risks and potential impediments to success, cross-Sub-Objective and MME linkages and dependencies and any contingency planning. It identifies a lead agency and outlines specific tasks/activities within 3 month targets and benchmarks.

task. A specific process or activity, stated as an outcome when possible, that is one part of a Sub-Objective.

USG R&S Strategic Plan. Term used to identify the overarching whole-of-government planning process, including policy formulation, strategy development, and interagency implementation planning. R&S planning is undertaken in support of achieving transformation in the specified country or region undergoing violent conflict or civil strife. The goal of this approach, referred to as "conflict transformation," is to reach the point where the country or region is on a **sustainable positive trajectory**, where it is able to address on its own the dynamics causing civil strife and/or violent conflict.

USG Strategic Plan Overview Graphic (Also called the USG Strategic Planning Template). A one page diagram produced by the CRSG Secretariat that enables planners and policymakers to visualize the interrelationship among constituent elements of the plan. It shows at the top in blue the overarching policy goal, directly below in orange the MMEs and their metrics, and finally the green Sub-Objective Areas. This color scheme has been accepted and approved by the NSC Deputies Committee. This one-page diagram should also include the critical contextual and causal assumptions, as appropriate, and any overarching guidance for implementation.

USG Strategic Plan Narrative and Briefing. A fuller description of the US Strategic Plan that explains how Sub-Objective areas feed into MMEs and ultimately the overarching policy goal. It outlines the critical planning assumptions, the metrics necessary to gauge progress towards the policy goal and provides overarching guidance for implementation.